Caffeine Night



# The Films of Danny Dyer

James Mullinger

&

Jonathan Sothcott

GREAT BRITISH BOOKS
GREAT BRITISH AUTHORS

Published by Caffeine Nights Publishing 2013



Printed in Great Britain by Clays Ltd, St Ives plc

Published in Great Britain by Caffeine Nights Publishing
www.caffeine-nights.com

British Library Cataloguing in Publication Data.

A CIP catalogue record for this book is available from the British Library
ISBN: 978-1-907565-66-3

Cover design by
David Laird from DGL Creative
Artworked by
Mark (Wills) Williams

Everything else by
Default, Luck and Accident

# Acknowledgements

Some of Danny's colleagues and friends were gracious enough to recall their experiences working with him for us, and we would particularly like to thank JK Amalou, Phillip Barron, Robert Cavanah, Craig Fairbrass, Frank Harper, Vicki Michelle, Christopher Fosh, Neill Gorton, Gavin Claxton, Lucy V Hay, Bart Ruspoli, Stephen Reynolds, Millie Sloan, Jake West, John Luton, Simon Fellows and Raoul Girard.

Special thanks as always to Danny himself, as well as Jo and the family. Also to his management team Denee and Becky, both of whom were always extremely accommodating and supportive. Also, Harry Grindrod and Matt Glasby for their expertise and research.

James Mullinger would like to thank Pam, Hunter, and River for their patience. And his parents Joss and Margaret for nurturing his love of movies from a very young age.

Jonathan Sothcott would like to thank Martin and Shirlie Kemp, Nick Aldrich, Kugan Cassius, Dougie Brimson, Darren Laws, Joel Kennedy, Rod Smith, Colin Lomax, Richard Thompson, Adele Silva, Nick Nevern, Sean Gascoine, Mum & Dad and Nick Hamdy and his staff at The Soho Hotel.

For Pam, for putting up with me. – JM

For Charlie, because, as Danny put it,
"I've rung the bell there." – JS

# Introduction by James Mullinger

If you stopped the average man over the age of forty in the street and asked them who their favourite British actor of all time is, most would probably reply Michael Caine.

No surprise there.

But if you ask any working-class male under the age of forty the same question, he will almost certainly answer Danny Dyer – and so would many of the females in that age bracket.

Dyer is the most bankable British film star we have in the independent sector. A man adored by both sexes. Admired by luminaries such as the late, great Harold Pinter. And he worked his way to the top. The hard way. No favours. No family connections. No help from friends.

But you rarely read about him in the mainstream press in a positive light, even though his films fly off the shelves in supermarkets and DVD shops and fans flock to his personal appearances in nightclubs. He's a talented, decent, hard-working lad done good. So why the snobbery?

A case in point: On 21 February this year, a low-budget British film was released in a handful of cinemas for even fewer screenings. The distributor never intended it for a wide release. And it brought in a not unexpected £602 in ticket sales.

A non-news story, I think you would agree. But instead, it was given a full-page splash on almost every newspaper, the film's supposed failure greeted with glee.

Why? Because Run *For Your Wife* starred this inexplicably divisive, yet hugely prolific actor, Danny Dyer.

You would rarely read a news story reporting the millions of DVD sales he has generated, and that he is one of the most bankable actors in British film.

*Run For Your Wife* is indeed bad. Dyer himself would be the first to admit it is not on a par with his work with Pinter. But it's not as bad as you've heard – and I personally preferred it to Paul Thomas Anderson's *The Master*. I went to see *The Master* on the day of release in Birmingham. There were just three of us in the cinema. Fewer than the lowest audience figures for Dyer's film.

*The Master* put me to sleep with its delusions of grandeur, mounds of pretension, overlong running time and non-existent plot. *Run For Your Wife* made me chuckle as Denise Van Outen chased Dyer around, shouting insults at him.

Hollywood makes tripe movies every single day. Yet they rarely get panned like a Dyer film. It seems the press can't stand that a real working-class boy has taught himself this craft and done well. Dyer didn't go to a posh school. He taught himself, impressed everyone from Helen Mirren to Harold Pinter, and now makes a good living for his beautiful family.

Sure, he's made some bad films – but who hasn't? And Dyer admits when he makes mistakes.

Unlike any other actor you can name, he admits to his fans when he has made a bad film. Take these recent Tweet exchanges:

**Fan:** When I see a film with @MyDyer in it, I don't even bother reading what it's about because I know it's gonna be gooood. #7lives tonight
**Danny's response:** Hate to do this to ya Grace. I'll be the first to admit I've made some shit films but 7 lives is fucking awful. #sorry

**Fan:** just downloaded just for the record on my ipad. What am I going to expect danny?? Love your films. #legend
**Danny's response:** Bruv. I ain't gonna lie. It is the biggest pile of shit I have ever done and that's saying something.

But here's the thing. He's a genuinely great actor. He appeared in two of Pinter's plays at the behest of the late, great writer – and it's generally agreed that Harold Pinter knows thing or two about visual arts. Dyer's breakout role as Moff in 1999's *Human Traffic* still stands up today as one of the great characters of that decade. In Andrea Arnold's short film *Wasp*, Dyer turns in a magnetic performance in the lead with Nathalie Press, which led to the film winning an Oscar for Best Short Film in 2003.

In my opinion, *The Football Factory* is one of the most underrated British films of all time. I genuinely think it to be as good as *Trainspotting* and far more entertaining. Why isn't it recognised as such? Because heroin is chic and affects all classes, while hooliganism is not, even though it stems from the same social ills.

I find Dyer to be charismatic and eminently watchable. I love the fact that YouTube is full of clips of him at nightclubs completely off his face. His guard is always down. He doesn't try and hide who he is. But he always gets up and goes to work in the morning. He likes a drink, but Lohan he ain't.

Speak to anyone who has worked with him and they will say the same thing: he is a total pro. And much more than that. The fridge on the set has run out of milk? "Don't worry," pipes up Danny. "I'll go." And before the runners have a chance to stop him, he runs off down the road to get it.

And, tellingly, his fans adore him. There will be those who say a book on Dyer's films should not exist but I laugh in their faces. A man of his considerable talent, with such prolific output, deserves to have his life's work critiqued. But like Dyer himself, we will not be pulling any punches here. When he has made a bad film, we will be saying so. But equally we will not be following the lead of broadsheet critics and Mark Kermode by slating underrated masterpieces like *The Business*.

Dyer is often accused of being an alpha male. A hard man. Sure, compared to me he is tough – but then so is Christopher Biggins. I have observed Dyer on a film set and I just see a charming, hard-working family man, a gentleman to all women, a great father to his daughters, and a loving husband to his wife. It is testament to his acting prowess that people still believe him to be a hard man, which presumably stems from his magnetic performance in *The Football Factory*.

He has never pretended to a tough guy. His Bravo series meeting *Britain's Hardest Men* invariably consisted of him cowering in their presence.

In his latest film he does play a genuine hard man however, and I can assert it is one of his best performances yet. In the frankly awesome *Vendetta*, Dyer plays a former SAS man out for revenge after his parents are murdered. Imagine *Death Wish* if Charles Bronson has been trained in the art of inventive ways of torturing people. Sounds utterly magnificent, right? Sure, it's not going to be for everyone, but when my wife's away, my son is tucked up in bed and I crack open a four pack, I can assure you that *Vendetta* will be top of my list to watch for the tenth time.

And as proven by recent appearances on *8 Out Of 10 Cats* and *Celebrity Juice,* Danny is genuinely funny. The bookers for both shows clearly thought they could book him and make him a laughing stock. Dyer proved them wrong. Sean Lock rarely laughs but he had tears in his eyes after Dyer's since endlessly quoted line about *Postman Pat*. Recently he appeared in ITV2 sitcom *Plebs* as a gladiator. Described as *The Inbetweeners* meets Ancient Rome, it featured many top young comedy actors – yet Dyer stole the show.

Before this decade is over, I predict he will have won a BAFTA or some other honour. But in the meantime we will have to sit and watch as *Vendetta* shifts hundreds of thousands of units – and the press choose to ignore it.

You may love Dyer, or you may hate him – but you can't ignore his work ethic, or the performances he has put in. So sit back, and enjoy the inside story of his films – those you know and love, those you know and hate... and those you won't have heard of but may now want to seek out.

And raise a glass for the best of British, Danny Dyer.

James Mullinger. London. 2013.

# The real Danny Dyer by Jonathan Sothcott

I gave up film journalism to become a film producer and this book has finally brought me full circle. In his introduction, James has given a far better overview of Danny's career than I ever could, so I wanted to write something more personal – as not only is Danny is the subject of this book, he's also one of my close friends, after working on many films together.

I first met Danny back in 2007 in London nightclub the Embassy. I was a very green would-be filmmaker who'd met Dyer's frequent co-star and friend Tamer Hassan a few weeks earlier. Ever the gentleman, Tamer had invited me for a night out with him and Dyer and although I didn't really know who either of them were it didn't seem like a bad idea. If I was expecting a gangster in a long coat, the truth could not have been more different – my first impression of Dyer was that he was very polite, a little bit shy and taller than I had expected (he's comfortably six feet tall in his socks). Fast forward a year, and I've been roped into helping produce a promo for an action film called *The Rapture*, starring Danny. By then I had realised that he was a seriously big deal in the independent film arena and working with him was a fantastic opportunity. As you'd expect, he didn't remember me (I was probably the 300$^{th}$ person he met that night) but I liked him immediately – he was funny, charming, and personable. You can read more about the disastrous collapse of *The Rapture* later on, but during those few weeks I learned something else about Danny – he is incredibly charismatic – and I am talking real, old-fashioned Hollywood star charisma. One night, we were filming at a racecourse during a live race – and when Danny walked out, 3,000 people turned and stared.

We stayed in touch over the next few months – there was talk of a low-budget gangster film called *The Manor*, but it never came to anything, I visited the set of *Jack Said*, where I found him looking depressed enough to jump in the Thames, and I saw him at the premiere of *City Rats* early in 2009. That summer, I approached him about making a cameo in the ill-fated comedy *Just For The Record* playing a smarmy producer. "I'll play it like you, son," he said, leaving me filled with a mixture of pride and concern. The result was a film-stealing comedic performance that, had it been in another film, would have silenced many of his critics. By this point we were starting to become friends – there was the odd bit of lunch here, a few drinks there. Premieres for *Doghouse* and *Malice In Wonderland*. One particularly memorable night during this period saw me go to the opening of a new restaurant in Knightsbridge – there was no alcohol and with a couple of pals, including Craig Fairbrass, I beat a hasty retreat. As we were coming out, Danny and his girlfriend Joanne were coming in. I warned him that there were only banana milkshakes on the menu and Danny and Jo joined us in The Arts Club for a long, boozy night. Throughout 2009 I saw more of them – there was a glitzy Leicester Square premiere for *Call Of Duty* – and he kindly did a day on a terrible vampire film I made, called *Dead Cert*. Then came an offer from my friend Joel Kennedy at Revolver – would Danny be interested in doing a football DVD? I put it to him, he loved the idea and the DVD sold bucket loads of copies upon release in 2009. At this point, people started coming to me with other offers for Danny – I remember politely but firmly turning down a sequel to *Jack Said* on his behalf – and of course we made the zombie film *Devil's Playground* together, one freezing December at Elstree Studios.

Over these years I learned two things about Danny – he puts on the 'cor blimey' Cockney act because he thinks it is what people expect – and he's a very sensitive, caring guy who is absolutely devoted to his family.

One day in 2010 I had a call from actor Billy Murray. Could I get hold of Danny? There was a teenage lad in Essex who was very sick with cancer and his biggest wish was to meet Danny Dyer. He said yes immediately and asked me to get a bundle of DVDs together. We met this lad and his family in Café Rouge in Loughton – and within two minutes Danny was like a new member of that family. We stayed for a good hour, he posed for pictures and signed every DVD. I remember saying to Billy that I wish more people could see this side of him. But Danny isn't a man to chase cheap publicity. We were chased that day though – walking down the high street a cry went up "look there's that geezer off *The Bill*" followed two seconds later by "and DANNY FUCKIN' DYER!!!" with which about 30 teenage girls actually chased us down the road (and we were running).

I sat with Danny in The Soho Hotel the night of the *Basement* premiere as we tried to drink ourselves into going (we didn't). I did interviews about him on the BBC. We went through a lot together – good times, bad times, fun times. I knew him at his peak, when his name above a title greenlit a movie. I saw his fall from grace as bad decisions caught up with him. My career, such as it is, owes a great deal to Danny – the fact that he did a couple of pictures for me gave me a bit of clout within the industry: it moved me up to the next level. But his innate niceness lead to bad decisions – when I asked him to do *Dead Cert* and *Just For The Record*, he should have said no. But he didn't, because he's a good man and a good friend.

By the time the *Deviation* premiere rolled around, I decided not to go – Revolver, the distributor which had done so much to destroy Dyer's credibility, was on its last legs and there was a smell of death around the film, even though it wasn't at all bad.

We started talking about making another film together late in 2011. I had lost interest in the film business, I was making terrible straight-to-video films with people I didn't like, and I'd had enough. Danny was at a low ebb too – the phone wasn't ringing and he only had bad films in the pipeline. We both needed to get our hunger back. I financed *Vendetta* privately and we made it on a shoestring but with care and passion (and were blessed with a terrific director). By the time you read this, the film will have been released and you can make up your own minds as to whether or not it's the return to form for Danny it was conceived as. I'm fiercely proud of it and I think it showcases the best performance of his career.

So why a book about Danny Dyer's films? Highbrow critics will mock us, of course, but there is no other UK actor of his/my generation with a body of work worth analysing and celebrating. Dyer has been remarkably prolific and his hit rate might not be the best, but in a short space of time he has built himself a film career that – warts and all – is the envy of his peers. He is the best known, most popular independent film star in the UK, and has made enough films with legitimate cult followings to be worth a book.

In the spring of 2013, after meeting Danny on the set of *Vendetta*, *GQ* contributing editor James Mullinger wrote an article about him on the magazine's website. James's feelings about Danny echoed my own, that he was an underrated and unfairly maligned film star and that it was time to address this imbalance. Half in jest, I suggested to James that we should write a book about Danny's film career. He loved the idea and we quickly found a sympathetic publisher. What you now hold in your hand is the product of months of research, sitting through some incredibly bad and spectacularly good films, and hours of taped interviews with Dyer himself.

From the beginning, it was our intention to be as honest and candid about the films as we could – this is not a glossy, copy-approved love letter to my best mate, it's a serious (well, sometimes) review of his work. We've warned you which of the films are the stinkers – and I have to hold my hands up and admit that I've been responsible for quite a few of them! In some chapters you'll find that I've referred to myself in the third person or that James has interviewed me – this isn't some grand conceit on my part, it just seemed to be the least confusing way of dropping my contributions into the text.

We've also tried to put the films in the context of the film industry of their day – you'll see the rise of the 'mis-sell' DVD cover (*Borstal Boy, City Rats, Just For The Record* etc) pioneered by distributor Revolver, which effectively destroyed Dyer's credibility for a while, both within the industry and with his audience. You'll also see how, in the wake of this, practically every major distributor snapped up Dyer's back catalogue and attempted the same thing, often with less than impressive results (*Malice In Wonderland, Devil's Playground*). But the critics never helped – they understood that token theatrical releases for direct-to-video films were merely platforms to get traction with Video-On-Demand platforms and national press reviews, yet still triumphantly jumped on the minimal box office takes as though the films had failed. In the case of *Pimp* in particular, this was laughable – it was a DVD film and it sold incredibly well on DVD, on a level many Hollywood blockbusters could never achieve. But that's Danny, the Marmite movie star – you love him or you hate him. As we go to print, Danny's about to find a whole new audience when he takes over the Queen Vic in *EastEnders* on Christmas Day. Joining one of the biggest TV shows in the country will raise his profile dramatically and introduce a whole new legion of fans to his back catalogue. We hope that this book will serve as a useful companion to new and old fans alike and that we've done justice to this country's most controversial film actor – my mate, Danny Dyer.

Jonathan Sothcott. London. 2013

**Authors note:** Films appear throughout the book in the order that they were filmed, as opposed to when they were released.

*Human Traffic (1999)*
*The Trench (1999)*
*Borstal Boy (2000)*
*Greenfingers (2000)*
*Goodbye Charlie Bright (2001)*
*High Heels & Low Lives (2001)*
*Mean Machine (2001)*
*The Football Factory (2004)*
*Tabloid (2004)*
*The Great Ecstasy Of Robert Carmichael (2005)*
*The Business (2005)*
*Severance (2006)*
*The Other Half (2006)*
*Outlaw (2007)*
*Straightheads (2007)*
*The All Together (2007)*
*Adulthood (2008)*
*City Rats (2009)*
*Dead Man Running (2009)*
*Jack Said (2009)*
*Doghouse (2009)*
*Malice In Wonderland (2009)*
*Just For The Record (2010)*
*Pimp (2010)*
*The Last Seven (2010)*
*Basement (2010)*
*Dead Cert (2010)*
*Devil's Playground (2010)*
*7 Lives (2011)*
*Age of Heroes (2011)*
*Freerunner (2011)*
*Deviation (2012)*
*Run For Your Wife (2012)*
*In A Heartbeat (2013)*
*Vendetta (2013)*

# HUMAN TRAFFIC (1999)

WIDE SCREEN
"The last great film of the nineties"
The Guardian
Human Traffic
the weekend has landed
DVD
VIDEO

**"Do you take drugs?' And I was totally honest and said, 'Yeah, I love drugs'"**

**Director** Justin Kerrigan **Producer** Emer McCourt, Allan Niblo **Writer** Justin Kerrigan **Production Designer** David Buckingham **Costume Designer** Claire Anderson **Music** Mathew Herbert, Rob Mello **Cinematography** Dave Bennett

**John Simm** Jip **Lorraine Pilkington** Lulu **Shaun Parkes** Koop **Nicola Reynolds** Nina **Danny Dyer** Moff **Dean Davies** Lee

*Human Traffic documents the lives of five protagonists and takes place over a single weekend. The characters party together as a means of escape from the drudgery of their everyday lives. Jip suffers from sexual anxiety after being unable to perform on several occasions; Jip's best friend Koop suffers from jealousy over his confident and popular girlfriend Nina; Nina is stuck in a job she hates, having failed a college interview, and feels forced to accept her boss's sexual harassment; Jip's friend Lulu has recently split with the latest in a line of dishonest and unfaithful boyfriends; Moff, the most recent addition to the group, makes his way as a small-time drug dealer at the behest of his high-ranking police officer father. Through a serious of intoxicating events the five experience a weekend together, working through their respective issues against a nineties club-culture backdrop.*

Dyer's first motion picture is possibly one of the most talked about big-screen debuts of all time. Moff: the loveable pill head. His legendary scene in the back of the cab asking a taxi driver if he relates to Travis Bickle while speeding his tits off is quoted more in nightclub chill out rooms than Cheech and Chong. *Human Traffic* was embraced by young people everywhere because it was the first film not to demonise drug takers. Millions of clubbers were taking drugs every weekend, yet every film that had addressed it did so negatively. Even BBC2's 1995 drama *Loved Up* featuring Dyer in a small yet memorable part, which had the confidence to show people initially having fun on ecstasy, ultimately depicted it as paving the path to ruin.

For its understanding of drug culture and rave culture, there has never been another film like *Human Traffic*, before or since. Never matched, never surpassed. While it sounds like a cliché, the youth felt like this was a film that finally spoke to them and understood them. Writer and director Justin Kerrigan was just 25 when he made the film with the help of producer and his film school mentor Allan Niblo and he fought to make the film he wanted to make about people like himself. Normal, fun-loving twenty something's. The *Daily Mail* considered them drug barons. The rest of us called them the nation's children.

Anyone who remembers seeing *Human Traffic* in a packed cinema will remember marvelling at how the filmmakers had attracted an audience so previously neglected by film and TV. Ravers didn't go to the cinema. They raved. But they went to see this again and again. The unique perspective the film offered is primarily what attracted Dyer to the role. "*Trainspotting* had been out, and I remember being fascinated by that film and just how raw it was," he remembers. "But when I got the script for *Human Traffic*, I loved that it was more my world of partying. Of course the idea of smack and the dark, underground, weird world that these smackheads live in was fascinating, but I'm not part of that, so *Human Traffic* was the other side: the partying, the joy and the ecstasy, which was basically the world that I was living in at the time. So to read something so honest, so brutally honest, with no moral ending. It is just about a group of people going out getting fucked up. They've got shit jobs, getting off their nut, bit of a comedown, roll credits. I just thought that was so great, I'd never read anything like it. It was my first film audition, so it was like, 'Wow!'. The idea of making a movie, especially a movie that would be really close to my heart, and when I knew it would be really controversial, was really exciting to me. The only thing that I was a bit worried about was the fact that my character was Welsh, and I couldn't do the Welsh thing. I just couldn't do it; I'm not very good at accents. Because it was Justin Kerrigan and every character was part of him, and Moff was his most hedonistic side, I remember the first question when you walked into the audition room by Justin was, 'Do you take drugs?' And I was totally honest and said, 'Yeah, I love drugs.' There was other big actors that went in and who do take drugs – I won't name names – but they said, 'No I don't take drugs,' so he'd shake their hand and go, 'See ya later'. You can't really be part of this film unless you've experienced drugs and you know that world. So I just said, 'Look, I can't do the Welsh accent. Can I just be me?' And I blew him away on the first audition. It was the speech in the taxi, that was the audition scene, the taxi driver scene, so I remember just going for it. Then we did the opening scene and I'm sending smoke signals, and it was all played at the camera. That excited me as well, the idea of playing to the camera, because obviously as an actor it's a rare thing to be able to do that – you're told to never look at the camera. I was quite young – not naïve, I'd done quite a lot of work – but to do a film, and to do a film like this, it was the dream."

There was no doubt that the film was controversial, especially given the tabloid scaremongering in the early Nineties coupled with some high-profile tragedies. "It was certainly a good way of telling my parents that I take drugs," laughs Dyer. "And it helped them understand what it was all about. But it's important to remember that it was off the back of Leah Betts' tragic death, which the tabloids exploited, so it was very controversial. *Human Traffic* was not condoning drugs, it was just stating the fact that millions of people take drugs, and they take drugs because they want to, and the majority of people have a fucking good time. And I think it left a bit of a bitter taste in people's mouths."

Mark Morris covered the film when writing for *The Guardian* in May 1999 and interviewed the cast. Clearly some cast members were nervous about being seen as drug takers even though the film was just that. A film. "All the actors are careful to point out that their clubbing days are over," wrote Morris. "'It's galaxies away from my life,' says actress Lorraine Pilkington. 'I'm very clean living. I haven't touched a drop since 1 January. But there was a time when I used to club a lot.' Nicola Reynolds, the Welsh member of the quintet, thought that acting 'wasted' was the biggest challenge. 'You're thinking, "Am I looking like a complete twat?" When you're really out of it, you don't care what anybody thinks.' Not that the cast is shying away from the film. Danny Dyer – a motormouthed Cockney who comes close to stealing the film from Simm – is ready to come out fighting if a tabloid backlash comes. 'A lot of people ain't going to like it. If they want to do live debate programmes on it, I'm prepared to go on. This film shows the way it is, every weekend. If people don't like it, bollocks to 'em. It'll only be good for the film.' 'It's every parent's nightmare!' Kerrigan jokes. 'It's educational!' Aly counters. 'If the film's controversial,' Kerrigan says, 'that means that life's controversial.' In fact, the film is so amiable it seems unlikely anyone will object. If it makes taking drugs seem like an everyday activity, that's because for hundreds of thousands, possibly millions, of people in Britain, it is. 'We're talking about a massive mainstream youth culture,' Kerrigan says. 'It's the biggest youth culture in the history of Britain. We don't have any filmic representation of it.' And although the film treats taking drugs as natural, it doesn't ignore the downsides – commonplace problems such as paranoia, painful comedowns or just the way that drugs encourage people to be very boring."

Dyer knew *Human Traffic* was something special, a fact that anyone who has watched the film late at night with a group of friends can attest. "When I watched it back I was so proud of it," remembers Dyer. "I was proud of my performance. I really felt I stood out. And it was great to work with people like John Simm – he's really talented and a different style to me, completely, so it was a step up for me as an actor, I felt. I'd never really been around them sort of people that I really buzzed off working with to that extent. I wanted to play the game and I wanted to go, 'Come on then, I'll show you what I'm about.' And the great thing was then I was the underdog then – no one knew who I was – so people started to take notice and go, 'Fuck me, who is he?' I had the best part and I knew that, and I knew that when I got it, so I just knew that I had to work hard."

He did work hard. But he also played hard. Too hard. And this meant spending everything he was making on partying during the production. "In all honesty, I owed them money by the end of the job," admits Dyer "I'd spunked all my wages – I think I was on 500 quid a week for that job. It was a tight budget. I remember on the back of the call sheet every day there'd be another ten scenes that had been cut because the producers were quite ruthless about it, but my scenes never got cut. I was always the one that got the call sheet, had a look on the back, and thought, 'Fuck fuck fuck…' except they kept all my stuff in. So I thought, well, it's time to express myself, and show people what I can do."

The popularity of the film meant Dyer started to get recognised for the first time in his career. "It's weird because that's when I first started to experience fame, and I experienced it on a weird level," he says. "It was like, I was this nutty cunt, fucking Moff – cane head. So I'd walk into a club and it would be like, 'Fucking hell, look who it is!' And people are off their nut – I'd see them rushing out of their head, and they'd see me, and it would send their fucking nut to another level. And people would just be giving me drugs all the time, and you get wrapped up in that world. So it did fuck my head up for a while. Moff really was me at that time, and I was playing myself to be fair. The by-product of the fame thing can really confuse you. You feel that people have a perception of you and you have to play up to it a little bit I suppose, and I think that still happens today. But because that was just one film they just wanted to see Moff. Now I've played other roles, and I've got the hippy-type people that love *Human Traffic* and love Moff, but then I've also got the idea of *The Football Factory*-type people: the little fuckers with the scars and the Burberry caps that wanna see Tommy Johnson. So you're constantly trying to keep everyone happy, which is no way to live your life really. But that's just what fame is I suppose, keeping a grip on that."

The film took two years to come out as Kerrigan and Niblo battled to finance the final cut. *The Guardian* reported at the time: "Executive producer Renata Aly assembled the money from venture capital and by selling the television rights, by-passing film companies. Even so, financially, it was a struggle to make. There were no big stars to pay – the most famous people in the film are retired drug smuggler Howard Marks and Andrew 'Egg from *This Life*' Lincoln – but the club scenes pushed up the costs. It was important not to have the oddly empty dancefloors that feature so often in Hollywood films. And without a strict structure to work to, they found themselves with a sprawling film. 'The first cut was two hours 50 minutes,' Niblo admits. 'We knew we had to lose an hour. We took 56 weeks to edit it. We only booked 16. We couldn't afford that.' Kerrigan was worried. 'This time last year, we were convinced we had a turkey on our hands. Everyone was getting paranoid and depressed.' "

"It was a weird thing because it took two years to come out," says Dyer. "I remember when Madonna was attached to it on the production company. She loved it but she wanted to try and change it, so that someone needed to die at the end, or there needed to be more of a love story with John: there needed to be something to wrap it up instead of all of us going, 'Fucking hell I feel like shit,' roll credits. But she pulled out. I remember we shot it in 1997 and it didn't come out until 1999. So we didn't know if it was actually going to come out, just because of the controversy, and the fact that Justin stuck his heels in and said, 'Look, this is the movie that I want to make. This is how it has to be: there is no moral ending; people don't necessarily because they've taken drugs think they can fly and jump off roofs.' The other clever thing that I loved about it is that there's no obligatory shots of anyone taking an E. You never see that thing like most clubbing films with the E on the tongue in the girl's mouth – a load of bullshit – in fact in the scene with John and Shaun when they're cutting the coke up they never sniffed a line. We never fetishised it. *Trainspotting* had the big shots of the syringes and the needles going into the arm. I think he learned from that, and just wanted the audience to assume that they've taken drugs; were not actually going to see it happening. You don't see anybody take any drugs whatsoever, other than the spliff that's passed around with the spliff politics, which needed to be there, because of the clever thing with getting Howard Marks involved. It's just genius."

Renowned *Guardian* film critic Peter Bradshaw loved the film (the headline even stating he was "mad for it") and admired the honesty in the depiction of drug taking: "The unphotogenic business of buying, selling and ingesting drugs, the actual human traffic, is kept mostly out of shot. But in style, it feels very derivative, with lots of cheeky pieces to camera from its characters, freeze-frames, and twangily ironic voiceovers. *Human Traffic*, in its insouciant way, is a pro-drugs film. No one gets to climb out of a lavatory; there are no crisis scenes, no scenes in which four of them panickingly jog alongside the fifth on a trolley in a hospital corridor, with the doctor sternly asking if they are the patient's 'friends'. There is no Leah Betts hysteria in this film. They do drugs; they have a fantastic time; that's it. This is refreshingly honest. But it also makes for a strangely depthless film. *Human Traffic* is all surface. There is no real human drama or emotion, no sense in which the characters are importantly or interestingly changed by what they experience."

A combination of the drug consumption and lack of budget, however, meant that not everything was smooth on set. "I remember that I had to do a lot of ADR (Additional Dialogue Recording)," says Dyer. "We had this camera that was fucked basically, it was whirring and we had to shoot it. The whole last scene when I'm in the pub and I'm sitting they're going, 'I can't do it any more,' and they're going, 'What would you like to drink?' And I go, 'Pint of vodka and a packet of Maltesers.' That was all ADR, so that's how I cut my teeth really because I had the most to do and it was fucking hard. So I was only seeing clips of it during the ADR but I really had to learn my trade with the ADR then, because I was stuttering constantly, it flowed out of my mouth on the day, but to go back fucking eight months later and recreate that was really frustrating. You have to guess as well, they can only give you beeps to start the dialogue, but when you're stuttering as I'm speaking now was fucking really hard. Because I'm quite a perfectionist I just wanted to get it right, and I did. If you watch it again you might see a couple of slip-ups on that last scene, but I got it bang on."

It was Dyer's first film, and one of the films he is most proud of. He's still overjoyed to this day to have been involved. "I was just proud to be in it, because I knew that if this movie had come out and I hadn't been in it, it would have been a film I'd love to have seen," he says. "That's always a beautiful thing. I've done that a few times: been in movies that I'd love to have seen if I wasn't in it. Just to be in a fucking movie and watching yourself on the big screen, there's no better feeling, with something like that and all which was really funny as well, and to have all the funny lines as well. It's great to go a premiere when you're in a funny film and people are laughing instead of stuff that's more serious and dark. People were pissing themselves. There's no better feeling."

Everyone who watched the film of course wondered how they recreated the effects of ecstasy so successfully when every other filmmaker before and since has failed so miserably. The answer is simple. "We were all off our fucking nut," states Dyer. "Justin won't mind me saying this, but he'd turn up for work on half an E. There were crew there and everyone was skidded up, it was real liberal and hippy. All his mates were on the crew as well; no one really got paid on that job. It was just about the love and the fact that we was making a film about clubbing and the late nineties – and it's changed now, but everyone just loved clubbing and club culture. We were getting changed in pub toilets; there was no trailer or nothing like that. There was a dining bus I think, but it was everyone just getting up and just generally getting off their fucking head. The hard thing was trying to time your E – for when the cameras started to roll – so you had to time it to be off your nut at the right time. But what other job are you going to be able to do that? To be encouraged to do that? Never going to happen. From the first audition when he said do you take drugs, that was the start of it. We knew it was going to be like that, but obviously you needed to have some professionalism about you as well. But in general it was encouraged to fucking get off your head. The only character who didn't take drugs was the young brother who has his first E and stuff, and he didn't want to take the drugs so he stayed away from it and he was young. But all us lot, we was fucking bang on it, loving every second of it to be honest. It was the worst comedown of my life after that job though. I had just had a baby as well so I was up in Cardiff, and it was a cool place at the time. And it was over, and that was my first experience really of being part of something and really falling in love with a film. Every actor I loved on that job and all of a sudden the full stop was put on it and it stopped and I had to go back to reality. And it was a real kick up the bollocks. Usually you finish your job and you've got some money to go back to but I was in debt, and I knew that I'd made something beautiful, and I knew that it was gonna be a powerful thing. But it was now just sitting back and waiting for it to come out."

Despite rave reviews for the film, a BAFTA nomination, an impressive £2,271,369 at the UK box office (not to mention 182,732 DVD sales to date) and exceptional praise for the 25-year-old, Justin Kerrigan has not made another film since. He fell out with producer Allan Niblo, who he claimed betrayed him by forcing him to sign over all rights to the film. Niblo subsequently released a "director's cut" of the film featuring a new soundtrack in 2002, which angered a lot of people, most notably John Simm.

"I think that a lot of people have forgotten about *Human Traffic*, because of maybe some of the movies that I've made since," says Dyer. "It still has got its cult following, but if you think about it it's nearly fifteen years ago. There's a whole new generation of people. I always love it when people do come up and talk about *Human Traffic* but it is a rare thing. I don't think it did typecast me, I think it made people stand up and pay attention to me, but I was so young in it. I was young, and I watch it and I'm just like a baby. It was the start of my journey, so it's always going to be close to my heart."

# THE TRENCH (1999)

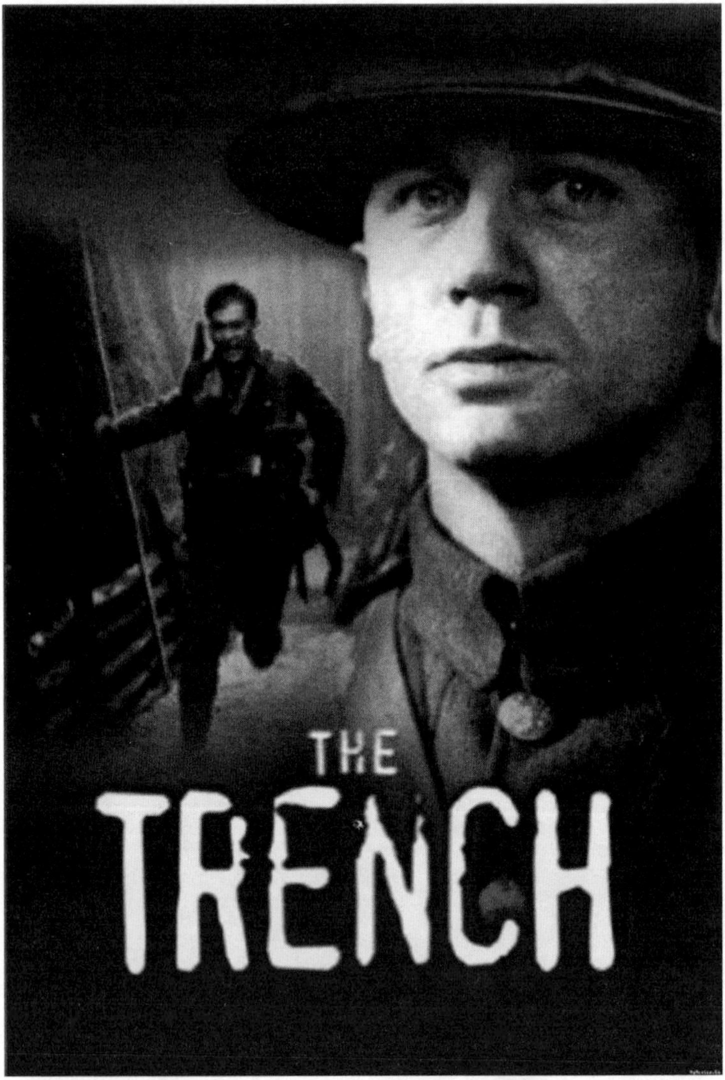


"Daniel Craig just reeked of acting talent; it just came off him constantly"

**Director** William Boyd **Producer** Steve Clark-Hall **Writer** William Boyd **Production Designer** Jim Clay **Costume Designer** David Crossman, Lindy Hemming **Music** Evelyn Glennie, Greg Malcangi **Cinematography** Tony Pierce-Roberts

**Paul Nicholls** Pte. Billy MacFarlane **Daniel Craig** Sgt. Telford Winter **Julian Rhind-Tutt** 2nd Lt. Ellis Harte **Danny Dyer** Lance Cpl. Victor Deli **James D'Arcy** Pte. Colin Daventry **Tam Williams** Pte. Eddie MacFarlane **Ciaran McMenamin** Pte. Charlie Ambrose **Cillian Murphy** Rag Rookwood **Ben Wishaw** Pte. James Deamis **Danny Nutt** Pte. Dieter Zimmermann

*Having volunteered for service, seventeen-year-old Billy MacFarlane, his brother Eddie, and a platoon of fellow teenagers rely on the unsentimental Sergeant Winter and Lieutenant Hart for their survival in the depths of the First World War trenches. The boys soon receive news that they will be joining the first wave of attacks against the enemy. They are blissfully unaware that they will be fighting in a battle remembered as the most tragic day in the history of the British Army.*

Written and directed by the renowned novelist William Boyd, *The Trench* has a theatrical feel in the vein of R.C Sherriff's classic play *Journey's End*. Only the most ignorant viewer could be unaware of how the story ends, but like all great works about known events, it plays on the tragic outcome as a dramatic device as we get to know this group of likeable yet realistic young lads over the two days leading up to the ill-fated battle of the Somme in 1916. Refusing to patronise real soldiers and paint them as empty heroes, they are drawn out and multi-layered as vivid and real people.

Boasting one hell of a line-up of young, hot acting talent (Dyer, Paul Nicholls, Cillian Murphy, James D'Arcy, as well as Daniel Craig and Ben Whishaw who were reunited as Bond and Q respectively in *Skyfall*), there is a real sense of these ambitious thespians on a real life mission to out-act each other. The result is hugely impressive, and each actor absolutely nails every nuance in every scene. The strong performances were picked up on by almost every critic. *Time Out* stated: "The claustrophobia contributes to an effective build-up of tension, and the film is actually very engrossing, partly due to the clarity, wit and assurance of Boyd's writing, partly to an excellent cast. Not original, then, but in its own old-fashioned, unpretentious way, impressive and affecting."

American movie bible *Variety*, was equally impressed with the film: "Novelist William Boyd's first film as director, *The Trench*, is a slow-burning, emotionally powerful account of the two-day build-up to the battle of the Somme in 1916, which remains the bloodiest massacre in British Army history. Boyd has dealt with the First World War in some of his novels. His original script here rather bravely chooses to concentrate entirely on a period that serves as a mere prelude to action in most war films. Set in the deep frontline trenches of the Somme Valley in Northern France, the film is concerned with exploring the psychological and physical effects on the soldiers of battle – or more precisely, the anticipation of battle – portraying sustained action only in its final five minutes."

Dyer was aware of, and friends with, many of the cast, but was not as familiar with Boyd's literary work. "I didn't have a fucking clue who he was," Dyer admits. "Mary Sellway (the BAFTA-winning casting agent) was so lovely to me. She's dead now, she was a wonderful woman. I remember auditioning for her and I really wanted the part. I loved it because it was a war film as well, and I loved the idea of doing a period war film as well. It was really interesting to me, and I loved the role – the Cockney-swagger-but-he's-actually-a-coward. A fascinating character to get my teeth in to. This was the first time I'd met Paul Nicholls of *EastEnders* fame. A good-looking boy and he was really hot at that time. And I hadn't met Daniel Craig before but I had always been a fan of his work. Obviously he wasn't where he is now but I would just remember thinking, 'Wow, I fucking love this guy from *Our Friends In The North*', and even then I thought of him as this seriously powerful actor. I remember I had to audition like three times for it though to get the part – it certainly wasn't a given for me. I had to fight for it."

Despite this, it was now a point in Dyer's career where he was a known entity. His work in *Human Traffic* and *Borstal Boy* had led to a certain expectation and this was only too clear to him. "People had started to know who I was now, so you walk on set and people would be talking about my work," Dyer remembers. "Whereas before I had just done television and nothing really that anyone had taken notice of, this time a film had just come out – a controversial film that was doing really well commercially and critically – so I had a bit of a reputation now. I can't deny that it was nice to walk on a set with people expecting something and being able to show off. I met William Boyd and he was a lovely man, very intelligent. It was the first time I had had to do research for a role (other than for *Human Traffic* with pills obviously). He gave me these books of poetry by Wilfred Owen. So I was really starting to get a bit more professional, a bit more into it, and a bit more, 'Wow, okay, yeah, I'm really getting into this shit'. I was reading dozens of books about the First World War and the battle of the Somme at the same time. It was originally going to be called *Somme*, just *Somme* – but he changed his mind because people would read it wrong; 'Sommey' and all this stuff. I think for me it was the first time I'd done a studio film all in one set, all lads together, and it was a hard job. It was fucking hard because it was really cramped and the costumes were really heavy and you had to put that on every day. Although I think our teeth were a bit too clean and stuff, I think it was a little bit too glossy for me. I think unfortunately, as much as it's a great piece of work, do people rush out to watch a film about the First World War? Not necessarily, and though I think everyone was really strong in it, it's not nothing new. It was more about the desperation of these kids who had no idea about what they were going to do. They weren't really soldiers, they were just sitting in a fucking trench. They wasn't really trained, and all of a sudden the whistle blows and they've got to run over the top because they've been lied to and told that the Germans were all dead, and we lost 160,000 soldiers. Just mowed down. Quite a tragic sad film really because it's true. But it didn't do any business."

The film was indeed a commercial failure (£86,012 at the UK box office on 54 screens), perhaps being a touch too depressing for mainstream audiences. *Variety* magazine stated that: "The very confined setting and claustrophobic nature of the material make this a commercially difficult proposal, but careful positioning and critical support may help it find an appreciative audience in select markets."

Of course, things would have been different had Daniel Craig been Daniel 'Bond' Craig then. He was still a jobbing actor at this point and not able to open a film under his name despite being incredibly respected in the industry.

"Despite his inexperience in dealing with actors, Boyd has drawn strong performances from the little-known cast," said *Variety*. "Nicholls' openness and fresh-faced looks make him a moving conduit for the script's observations; James D'Arcy registers strongly as a smart, cynical soldier more willing to face reality than his comrades; and Craig, following his impressive work in *Love Is The Devil*, brings complexity and hints of sadness to his character, a tough, rigorous and honourable man."

"Daniel Craig's quiet, very quiet," Dyer recalls. "He kept himself to himself, just a real presence, you know. We all knew how brilliant he fucking was, he knew how brilliant he was, we didn't really have to talk about it. But it was the first time that I'd come across an actor where I just watched everything he fucking did from afar. I've had a few of them throughout my career, but not many – and there's some people you just watch and go, 'Wow, fucking hell, I never would have thought to have said a line like that.' Everything he seems to do is interesting, whether he's sparking a cigarette, or he's lifting up his little tin cup, or he's eating the strawberry jam out of the jar. And he's there eating, and there's this moment where he eats it and he gets overwhelmed because it reminds him of home because his wife grows these strawberries, and there's no dialogue, and I just think that as an actor to be able to do that, to be able to portray that, just eating and the taste and the sensations… You can just taste it with him… It just blew me away. And I couldn't wait to do our scenes together because obviously I fuck up to go get the rum and obviously I drink it. I get drunk and then a bomb goes off and I break the rum, and he finds me and he just holds my head into a puddle. He's going to kill me because he knows I'm a bit of a coward. But I loved working with him; it was just the best part of the job for me."

Despite Dyer not wishing to go too method on the role, Boyd was keen for his leads to have some idea of what it was like in the trenches, given the entire film is set in one. "William Boyd's really into this research thing," Dyer says. "So he basically said we had to pack a bag. We didn't know what we were doing, we thought we were just going to do a bit of rehearsals and stay in a hotel. Anyway we got this coach and pull up near Southend actually, we get marched off the coach by these weird geezers who like to re-enact the war, and they'd built these trenches in Southend. You know, proper trenches with these little underground beds that we had to sleep in. We were marched off, we were in our roles now – we had to play the fucking characters. We had to bring the rations onto the trip, and they were letting off all fireworks and bangers, and I was thinking, fucking hell. We sort of played along and we had to eat gruel. We were all just looking around and getting shouted at. Then we went to stay on watch for an hour at Southend just in case the Germans come over, and it started to get cold, and it started to get a bit irritating and we started to get a bit fucked off. I remember Julian Rhind-Tutt who played the officer, he had lovely digs: he had a nice bed and stuff, and we had to sleep on the floors and that. And he fucked off. He left a note, he said, 'Sorry, I've gone back to Blighty.' So me and Paul thought, 'Do you know what, fuck this!' We were meant to do it all night, so we basically fucked off, in full get up – World War One stuff: bayonets and everything – found the train station, jumped on a train, and we bunked the fare when we got off the train at the other end at his house in Kilburn. I got over the barriers; he didn't make it and got fucking nicked, and it came out in the newspaper. William was very upset with us. Well, we fucked off, couldn't help it, it was just too much, just couldn't do it at six o clock in the morning. It's just ridiculous, getting shouted at by these podgy fucking geezers all dressed up in their uniforms, which are 10 times too small for them. It's not really method in my eyes because we were in Southend and there's nothing at stake really. He wanted us to get a sense of how it was to live like that, but I think you can do that through books. And at least tell us, warn us. But we were wrong, we were young and that. But listen, as an actor, you're always lucky to get a role, and you should never take that for granted. Having had the periods where I haven't had any acting jobs… It's like, you look back on them roles and think, 'Fucking hell man, you think you're invincible! How dare we do that, fuck off and leave everybody?' "

Being young and foolish is one thing, but Dyer was also oozing confidence at this point. "I knew I was going to nail it," he states. "I knew what I was going to do. It was just you can't really get any sense of what it was really like, you just can't. Being 17 and young and on the trenches and being petrified and not really knowing how to clean your gun, just sitting around doing fuck all and watching people get killed… How can you really get a sense of that? I just knew what my character was about, I knew what he had to do, that he was all bravado and giving it all the fucking big 'un – but when it came to the crunch he was fucking petrified. And he was sobbing his heart out before he went over the top, my character, I'm the only one crying his eyes out, drunk, and I just get thrown over the top. And I'm basically the first one to get shot. There are actors that are just naturally born to act I suppose, and they just have a presence. And there are actors who think about it. I didn't ask Daniel Craig questions because I just felt embarrassed to, but there are actors who analyse it so much that they would even analyse everything, and how their character would do each and every thing. Daniel Craig just reeked of acting talent; it just came off him constantly. Like I said though, he's quiet, he's very quiet, he's not a very confident person, and he still isn't today, even though he's playing James Bond, the most charismatic, confident man ever written. We became quite good friends after, and I haven't seen him for years, but I would have thought that it was a big decision for him to take on James Bond, because he knew what he was taking on, as much as it is a great part and that you don't really turn that down as an actor. Also, once it's over, you are now a national treasure: you can't go anywhere in the fucking world without there being some sort of circus around you. I always feel it when it's right, and it's like music to me, dialogue as well: you just hear – and especially when you're in sync with another actor – then you just hear a dong if you've missed the beat. And that goes with lifting things up or just generally doing things, or a look, or a ponder: it just comes naturally. And I think I'm lucky for that, and I always feel it when it's right and we move on. Sometimes you can't get it and you don't know why, and that's why you need a good director to tweak you, and that's why it's really frustrating if you work with someone who's a shit director, because they don't know how to work it. That's what the directors there for, just to give you that little slight tweak. There are some directors that I've got so much out of that, and others that are just a nonentity. And despite it being his first time, William Boyd was just great."

# BORSTAL BOY (2000)

"ENGAGING...WARM-HEARTED"
-Stephen Holden, THE NEW YORK TIMES
Strand Releasing presents a film by Peter Sheridan
BORSTAL
BOY
In the tradition of MAURICE and ANOTHER COUNTRY


**"I got the script and I read it and I go, 'Fuck me, I'm gay!'"**

**Director** Peter Sheridan **Producer** Nye Heron, Arthur Lappin, Pat Moylan **Writer** Brendan Behan, Nye Heron, Peter Sheridan **Production Designer** Crispian Sallis **Costume Designer** Marie Tierney **Music** Stephen McKeon **Cinematography** Ciaran Tanham

**Shawn Hatosy** Brendan Behan **Eamon Glancy** Manning **Ian McElhinney** Verreker **Danny Dyer** Charlie Milwall **Michael York** Joyce **Lee Ingleby** Dale **Eva Birthistle** Liz Joyce **Mark Huberman** Mac

*In the midst of the Second World War, teenage IRA volunteer Brendan Behan (Shawn Hatosy) embarks on a terrifying mission from Ireland to Liverpool with one intent: set off a bomb to further his cause. His mission is never realised. Caught red-handed, he is imprisoned in borstal, a British reform institution for young offenders. Here, Brendan is confronted by his 'enemy', and comes to find his deeply held beliefs are strongly questioned. Not least when he becomes the object of affection for a young, charming gay sailor named Charlie Milwall (Danny Dyer).*

*Borstal Boy* is the only feature film directed by the hugely respected Irish playwright and novelist Peter Sheridan (brother of *In The Name Of The Father* director Jim Sheridan). Based on the 1958 memoir of the same name by Irish nationalist Brendan Behan, it had previously been a stage play in 1967. Adapted by Frank McMahon for the Abbey Theatre in Dublin, the play was a critical and commercial success in both Ireland and America, with McMahon scooping a Tony Award (Antoinette Perry Award for Excellence in Theatre) in 1970.

The book was known for its authentic dialogue, with the book cover stating: "His years of indiscretion, error and rip-roaring life painted – without a single regret – in the bold and brimming language of Ireland's own boy-o." A review from *Time Magazine* was also quoted on the jacket: "He has Gabriel's own gift of the gab, a cold eye for himself, a warm eye for others, and the narrative speed of a tinker..." Meanwhile the *Glasgow Herald* called it: "a prison masterpiece". Despite the undeniable literary ambitions of the work, the authentic dialogue was too much for many and the book was initially banned in Ireland for its obscenity.

The film was released on 8 December 2000 and is considered to be one of Dyer's best performances – but at the time he was unsure of taking the part. "*Borstal Boy* was a strange one, because I remember I came home from being out for dinner and I had a message from Peter Sheridan on my answer phone," says Dyer. "I was obviously aware of who Peter Sheridan was. It was really Irish; he sounded a bit pissed really. There was this mad message about how he was a massive fan of mine and he'd seen *Human Traffic* and he really wants me to do this movie called *Borstal Boy,* so I immediately was like, 'Fuck, it's going to be like *Scum.'* I could see it, I knew what it was going to be. It was going to be me running around, snooker balls in socks like a fucking borstal, fucking... you know... being a right little cunt. But then of course I get the script and I read it and I go, 'Fuck me, I'm gay!' So I was in two minds because I thought the idea that he wants me to play this gay role... I was really proud because I'd never been seen in that light, but at that point in my career it's the last thing you'd think that I'd be known for, or do well, so I was in two minds about whether I could do it and I was thinking, 'How do I approach this? I'm a gay sailor.' I mean for fuck's sake, clichés and all that. I thought, 'What do I do here?' I mean, am I going to do this camp? Or do I just play it, you know, 'Fuck me I like cock,' but it doesn't change my demeanour or anything like that?" And it really did excite me. I was very intrigued to find out who was going to play the Brendan Behan part because that was the key for me, of gelling with that person. It was going to be Jonathan Rhys Meyers. He pulled out. I can't understand why he wouldn't want to play being Irish, an Irish legend. Well, he looks gay, so it'd be a bit weird. I'd be the gay one that looks straight, and he'd be the straight one that looks gay. So they got a guy called Shaun Hatosy, an American guy who wasn't really up my street to be honest; a good actor, a fucking good actor, big task, very American. Lee Ingleby – a great actor – was in it too. I love working with Lee but I felt a bit lost on the job to be honest with you. I just didn't know whether people were going to buy it – believe it – and for me to all of a sudden be so in love with this man just went against everything in my nature as a human being. It was really strange. It was, if you like, my first acting role, because I really had to get into a different mind-set. You go and think about *The Trench* and all the war stuff and all that, but it's a completely different thing to being totally and madly in love with another man, and just wanting his affection, which is all I want throughout the film. And I try and convince him that he's gay as well. It was really weird, strange. It stretched me, it was the first time I'd really been stretched and every day was a struggle. I'm really proud of it as a piece of work and, you know, me dressing up and doing the whole tranny thing. I really embraced it because every job you have to embrace it. I thought it would have done better. I know it did quite well in Ireland but I really thought people would stand up and take notice, and go, 'Wow, I see what you're trying to do there.'"

Reviewing *Borstal Boy*, renowned critic Stephen Holden of the *New York Times* said that: "the movie puts a glowing romantic spin on Brendan's attraction to his best friend, Charlie Milwall (Danny Dyer), a sailor who, although openly gay, is not seriously harassed. When the two exchange a kiss, it is a liberating moment unencumbered by guilt or shame. Nor does that kiss have any effect on Brendan's deepening passion for Joyce's daughter, Liz (Eva Birthistle), who returns his affection. (Behan eventually married another woman in 1955.) An engaging nostalgia piece. The ensemble acting has a relaxed confidence typical of British movies nowadays, and the literate screenplay by Mr. Sheridan and Nye Heron flows without a hitch. Except for one bad egg, a skinny knife-wielding sociopath, Brendan's fellow prisoners are a surprisingly easygoing bunch of likable ruffians, and Mr. Hatosy's Brendan and Mr. Dyer's Charlie exude a beguiling mixture of charm and naivety. As Brendan's attachment to Charlie overrides his initial homophobia, their bond becomes touchingly palpable."

Critically acclaimed both in the UK and Stateside, it has become something of a classic in the gay community and Dyer was determined not to do them a disservice. "I didn't want to patronise the gay community and I wanted to get it right, so that's why I just felt like, if you're gay, all it means is that you just like cock instead of cunt – if you put it in language terms that is it – so I didn't have to change my physicality," Dyers says. "When I was dressed up as a woman I did, but I didn't really feel that I needed to do that. It's just looking into the man's eyes and really selling that, especially as I didn't really like him off screen. The kissing stuff was a really strange feeling. I can still feel the sensation now of his ginger stubble and all that on my lips, because the build up to that kiss is a massive thing for me. I definitely became a different actor after that, because I put myself in a situation where I was very uncomfortable, and I just felt a bit strange and a bit odd and I thought people were going to laugh at me – just coming from a very working class, homophobic background, really."

Dyer admits that his old mates were not exactly understanding about him playing a gay character. "The reaction back home, honestly, it was horrendous," he says sagely. "As an actor, and an actor coming from where I come from, it's not about art and about creativity or expressing yourself, it's about the fact that you're kissing a geezer. So I did get a lot of fucking shit for it, but I was proud of it as a piece of work and it stood up and I think it definitely opened a few doors for me, especially with the gay community and people like that who probably assumed that I was homophobic, racist, a misogynist, whatever. And I still get loads on Twitter – loads of gay guys who say it's their favourite film of all time and stuff like that."
Theatrically it did not do badly (it grossed £89,012 at the box office), but on DVD has sold 353,872 copies to date. Unfortunately this was all due to misleading packaging

suggesting the film was some sort of vicious *Scum* remake. It took eight years for it to reach DVD after its cinema release – and when it did, Revolver mis-sold it and it shifted 353,872 copies. Not a bad seller. But a lot of disappointed fans were expecting a Dyer-in-the-nick flick.

Now, Dyer is enormously proud of his work on *Borstal Boy,* not least because it proved he is not a one trick pony. It also highlights the absurdity of those critics who say he only plays gangsters. "A lot of people labelled me a gangster because I did three gangster movies in a year, but it's lazy, it's lazy journalism isn't it, at the end of the day," says Dyer. "If you think about *Human Traffic* to *The Trench* to *Borstal Boy*, okay, I've got the same accent but look at American actors, look at Tom Cruise. He's a movie star and he does the same accent; he tried to do an Irish accent in *Far and Away* and it didn't work. But I think, as an American, if their natural dialect is just American, and they don't need to change their accent, they don't do it – they don't have to, they play the same roles with the same accent. With mine, I think, because it's a Cockney accent, it's more distinct. That's what makes you typecast, like I'm playing the same role all the time. I'm not. It's just snobbery that will never go away. But I feel proud that in *Borstal Boy* I proved them wrong. "

# GREENFINGERS (2000)

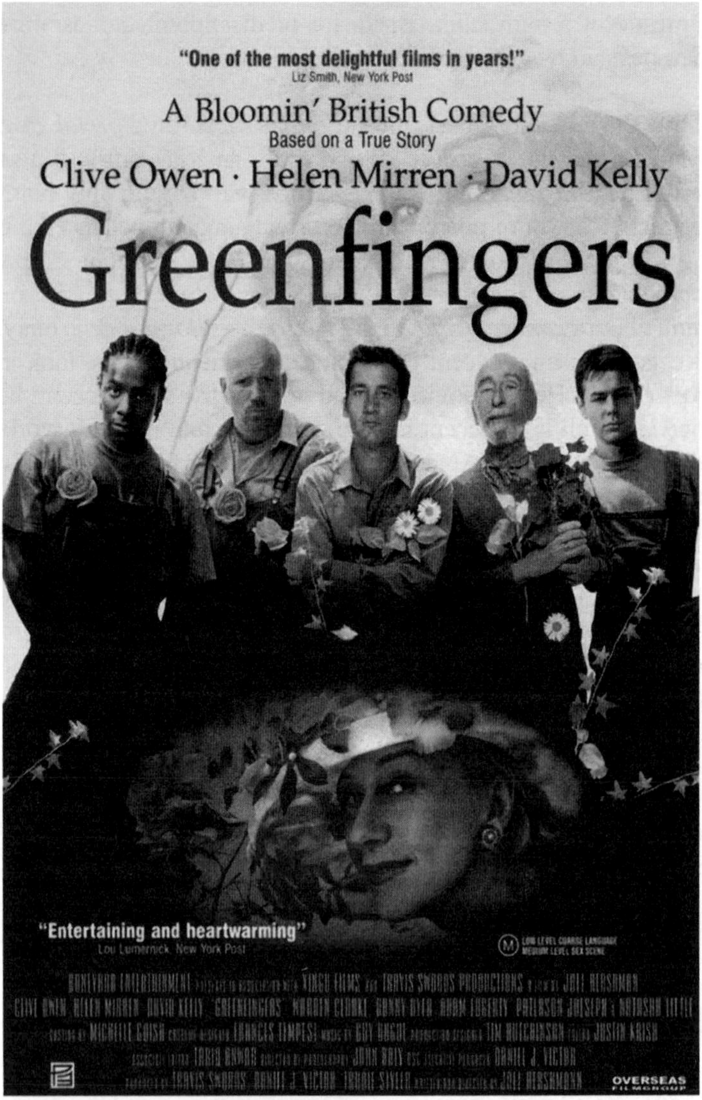


**"These are at the top of their game; I could stand toe to toe with this lot."**

**Director** Joel Hershman **Producer** Trudie Styler, Travis Swords, Daniel J. Victor **Writer** Joel Hershman **Production Designer** Tim Hutchinson **Costume Designer** Frances Tempest **Music** Guy Dagul **Cinematography** John Daly

**Clive Owen** Colin Briggs **Helen Mirren** Georgina Woodhouse **Natasha Little** Primrose Woodhouse **David Kelly** Fergus Wilks **Warren Clarke** Gov. Hodge **Danny Dyer** Tony **Adam Fogerty** Raw **Paterson Joseph** Jimmy **Lucy Punch** Holly

*Convict Colin Briggs (Clive Owen) is allowed to begin a reform programme that provides training for those nearing release in an open prison. When introduced to the art of gardening and flower arranging, Colin discovers a talent and passion for the art form. Well-known gardener Georgina Woodhouse (Helen Mirren) hears of his exploits and facilitates his entry to compete in a national gardening competition. And Georgina's daughter Primrose gives him an extra something to fight for.*

A British comedy starring Clive Owen, Helen Mirren and Warren Clarke was undeniably a very tempting proposition commercially. Devised to emulate the success of 1997's *The Full Monty*, it was produced by Trudie Styler (AKA Sting's wife), hot off the heels from *Lock, Stock And Two Smoking Barrels,* so there were high hopes for *Greenfingers* – but it was a little too quaint to reach a wide audience. Dyer's part was not a big one, playing a prisoner in the open prison with Clive Owen's character, but he was now in the enviable position of not having to audition for roles which, as he points out is, "almost unheard of for an actor of my age".

"I just couldn't believe it," he admits now. "You know it's like you've got to go in and prove yourself and sit and wait by the phone. You know, 'Fucking hell, am I going to get this part?' All of a sudden I'm getting parts offered to me. Not big roles. This was at the time just before Clive Owen became really hot, but the most intriguing thing for me was the presence of Helen Mirren, because I'd worked with her on my first ever job, *Prime Suspect 3*. That was my first ever piece of work into acting and it was with her. That really was one of those moments when I thought: 'Wow this person's unbelievable, just sit back and watch. Learn. Soak it up.' She was one of those perfect people. She made me feel really at ease and I loved showing off in front of her. And I remember she said to me on *Prime Suspect*, 'Wow, you're really good!' and that was it, she sort of walked away from me and I was just thinking, 'Fucking hell, you are seriously sexy!' She is just the most amazing woman that I've ever met. My dad came on the job because I was 14 at the time. My dad was chaperoning me on the job which was really nice. I was getting fifty pounds a day. I was a kid but I was giving my parents money and that, and giving them stays in hotels in Manchester. I remember Helen Mirren being really lovely to my dad and sitting on his lap in the bar, and my old man with these fucking old tattoos – she was just pointing at his tattoos. I was thinking, 'Fucking hell.' He was with my mum at the time, and I wouldn't have minded him having a little slippery chat with her, you know. He was just like, 'Wow boy, what's happening here?' So she always was a big part, and I remember thinking, 'I wonder if I'm ever going to see her again?' So *Greenfingers* came along and I was chuffed to bits she was in it. It was a bigger moment for me obviously than it was for her, but she fucking remembered me. She came up to me and said, 'Where's my Danny?' And oh my God, I ran into her arms like a little boy I did, trying to nestle myself into her beautiful breasts, and I was just so overwhelmed by the fact that she remembered me. I tried to play it down but I remember going back to my little rabbit hutch trailer sort of dancing around and being so happy. A weird film really, a weird idea. But true."

Dyer may not have had to audition but he was not best pleased at the size of the role. "I read the script and in a way I wanted my part to be bigger," he says. "I wanted to have more stuff with Helen, and unfortunately that wasn't the case. I suppose it was a sweet little story really. It's a nice little Sunday afternoon film. And it's true – that's what really gives it an edge I think. The fact that these rapists and murderers all got really into gardening, entered the Hampton Court Flower Show and came third. I mean it's amazing. It was quite a touching relationship between Clive and Natasha Little, but I could do it standing on my head. It wasn't a challenge for me. A few little funny lines and stuff; it was a breeze really, that job.

"It was produced by Trudie Styler and I remember we premiered in New York, and she's got a house in there so I went to her house and she really loved me. She was really nice to me and it was just cool being wrapped around Sting I suppose, for a little while, and getting a taste of that side of it. But as a piece of work for me it just sort of came and went. I didn't learn much from it. I think the film had quite a big budget on it as well but I just wanted to have more scenes with Helen. Clive seemed like a nice guy but I would never have thought he'd have gone on to do what he did, because I think he was really struggling at the time. I feel they just missed the boat with him as well because obviously if they'd have made it when Clive was Clive it would have probably done really well, but he was just the bloke off *Chancer* then. And Helen was Helen obviously, but she wasn't yet Dame Helen. You think about a film opening now with the two of them in it – it would be a huge hit."

It didn't get a cinema release in the UK and has only sold 23,689 DVDs to date. It did, however, gross a not unrespectable $1,143,067 at the US box office on just 39 screens.

The BBC's Danny Graydon summed up the film well when he wrote: "Content to ply its simplistic morality and plucky courage message, *Greenfingers* is by no means a poor film, mainly frustratingly pleasant, with any depth that could be applied to the redemption of a murderer cast aside to well-worn and all too familiar genre staples. You are never in any doubt of how the story will turn out. While Owen's trademark detached cynicism and cool is wasted here, Mirren's posh gardener is enjoyably hammy and David Kelly's ailing jailbird is poignantly dignified. Lacking the crowd-pleasing verve or power of Brit-hit *The Full Monty,* it's unlikely that *Greenfingers* will set the big screen on fire, but it's certainly likely to bring a warm glow to a lazy afternoon's TV viewing."

Styler was always in the unique position of being able to pick projects she believes in, as opposed to what is simply a commercial prospect. "It was definitely close to her heart and she liked the fact that it was quite sweet," Dyer says. "I don't think that was ever going to do really big business, and they did spend a lot of money on it. It just didn't do what it should have done. But at this point in my career I was just going along really nicely, stress free, getting offered parts, working with major talent, on the back of *Human Traffic*. Acting with the likes of Daniel Craig, Helen Mirren thinking, 'Wow, this is where I'm supposed to be, I could do it with these people. These are at the top of their game, I could stand toe to toe with this lot.' I never ever had fear or felt I was out of place, I always felt blessed and lucky that I'm there. But I also knew that I was there on merit. No favours, no family leg-ups. And I'm in movies. As an actor you never really devise or plan what your career is going to be. You can't just go, 'Oh I'm just gonna do this,' or 'Oh I'm gonna do that.' All you can do is what is put in front of you and shine in it, and you never know what's coming next. All of a sudden I'm thinking, 'Whoa okay, fucking hell, I'm making films, this is the path I'm taking.' So it was an exciting time. Even if the film itself wasn't."

# GOODBYE CHARLIE BRIGHT (2001)

**"There was a lot of money round at the time. It was ridiculous the budget on this."**

**Director** Nick Love **Producer** Lisa Bryer, Charles Steel **Writers** Nick Love, Dominic Eames **Production Designer** Eve Stewart **Costume Designer** Ffion Elinor **Music** Ivor Guest **Cinematography** Tony Imi

**Paul Nicholls** Charlie **Roland Manookian** Justin **Danny Dyer** Francis **Phil Daniels** Eddie **Jamie Foreman** Tony Immaculate **Frank Harper** Tommy's dad **Dani Behr** Blondie **Brian Jordan** Duke **Nicola Stapleton** Julie **Richard Driscoll** Hector

*Charlie has known nothing but a life of parties, casual sex, drugs, and petty crime. Though he aspires to better himself, a constant stream of events, symptomatic of his circumstances, not only prevent him from being able to move on, but land him in more trouble than he could ever previously have imagined.*

Nick Love's debut was heaped with critical praise upon its cinema release in the summer of 2001. Alexander Walker of the *Evening Standard* gushed that: "*Goodbye Charlie Bright* shares with *Billy Elliot* a feeling for the absolute compulsion to escape from the ghetto of environmental pressures or tribal entropy that stifle the best and the brightest. A small film, yes; but unexpectedly a very good one." Twice in his review, he made reference to the "excellent" acting.

Those aware of the snobbery Love has faced since this magnificent debut will be surprised to hear of the plaudits this received. *The Sun* described it as: "Hilarious, terrifying, tender, an awesome rollercoaster ride you won't want to get off." Sure it is subtler than his subsequent works, but it is no less uncompromising in its depiction of youth and the temptations that face young men in 21$^{st}$-century Britain. As Alexander Walker stated in his review: "It is basically about friendships sealed and broken, about gang loyalties and gender bonding."

Nick Love had previously made an impressive short film titled *Love Story* in 1999 starring his girlfriend at the time Patsy

Palmer, but this was his first full-length feature. Many fans of *The Football Factory* hunted *Goodbye Charlie Bright* down after seeing the former, hoping for more of the same. Not least because the film shares much of the same cast, but while Love had worked with Jamie Foreman on *Love Story,* this was the first time he had worked with Dyer. This was the beginning of the professional relationship that – depending who you speak to – is one of the best or worst things to happen to British cinema. What is indisputable is that they made an impact. A splash.

Six years later, Love would say of Dyer: "He's easy to work with. He may say 'cunt' a lot, but he's very down to earth, generous and an easy-going person. He's easy to identify with if you're a working-class man aged between 18 and 30 – the kind who have traditionally gone to see our films. People can relate to him." And this role as Francis, the emotional and tragic friend of Charlie Bright, is undoubtedly one of the most relatable.

Dyer remembers his first meeting with Love. "I met Nick with Paul Nicholls," he says. "It was Paul Nicholls who I'd stayed friends with from *The Trench,* and Paul said, 'Listen, there's this guy, you've got to meet him.' Paul had done his short film with David Thewlis, and Patsy Palmer who was big at the time. So I went up to the meeting, and we just fucking clicked straight away. It was a bit like Paul was the gooseberry in the room even though he was friends with him. It was a bit weird because we didn't stop rabbiting, and he just said to me, 'Listen, I'm doing this film, I'm doing this movie, you've got to be in it, I'll put you in it.' He sent me the script and I ain't gonna lie, I wanted the lead. I wanted that Paul Nicholls role because I knew I'd be brilliant at it, and the character is a Cockney and Paul's having to fake the Cockney thing so I sort of rung Nick up and said, 'Look listen, I don't want to tread on no one's toes here but…' And he said, 'Listen Dan, I ain't gonna deny it, you would probably be the better man for the job but I've got to be loyal to Paul. Paul's a great actor; I think he can do it, so I want you to play this smaller role, Franny.' And I was like, 'Fuck it, I'll do it, I'll work with you, all over it.' Phil Daniels was in it and I'd always wanted to work with him again. Massive budget on that, over two million. There was a lot of money round at the time. It was ridiculous the budget on this, it had epic trailers and we shot it all in South London on a council estate, I mean it was a lavish fucking production, it really was.

Although the film has many themes, it is ultimately about one thing, Dyer believes. "It's about two young boys who are in love," he says. "That's what Nick likes to do. It's about man-love; it's what every movie he's ever done is about. *The Business*, *Football Factory*, it's the same thing really. It's about how men communicate with each other: they love each other; not in a way that they want to fuck each other but in a way that we just don't express ourselves enough, and I think that love story between Paul's character and Roland's character is so sweet because they're little fucking cunts but at the same time they adore each other. They're like a married couple. So that was the crux of the story, and I loved the way he used the colours and stuff. It was the first time I sort of got a real sense of film-making because usually you're just an actor and you come on, but all of a sudden I was looking at what he'd done with the grade and things like that, and noticing that he'd really brought out the pinks and the yellows, because it's such a drab council estate and he wanted to bring out these colours, and when you see a colour you really go, 'Wow!'."

For all the joys of working with Nick Love on a quality film with a decent budget, Dyer was aware that he wasn't stretching himself. "For me, again, I could do it standing on my head," he admits. "I was a fan of Nicola Stapleton and she plays my girlfriend in it. I think the big scene for me was the one at the end, the one where she breaks my heart and I have the big showdown in the car, because the rest of it was just little bits. I flit in and out of the movie. Paul Nicholls was hard work on that film, because he was constantly doubting himself. He was insecure and he kept telling me that I should be playing this part. In the end I was like, 'Fuck off man, you've got to stop this,' which put me in good stead with Nick really, because Nick was so fucked off with it. Nick had enough on his plate. It was his first big movie; the last thing he needed was a whiny actor who was just so insecure, who was just going, 'Was that all right? Was that all right? Was that all right?' I'm not saying he was necessarily fishing for compliments but he was generally an insecure person. I mean if I had to do a movie full of northerners and I had to play a northerner in the lead, I'd have been fucking petrified. You've got to think he's got to pull that accent off with me, Roland, Frank Harper... That's daunting for a little boy. He just should have embraced it a bit more. It put me in good stead for *The Football Factory* because Nick was fucking sick of whiny actors. To be fair, Nick kept to his promise – he said, 'Don't worry about the next road, I've got some ideas and you're going to be the lead.' And I obviously in my wildest dreams couldn't have imagined what it was going to be."

Love is famously something of an autocrat on his film sets. But Dyer admired this. "It was aggressive but he did it in the way that he was a leader, you want to follow him, because a compliment from him is a massive thing," he says. "You trusted him, his vision, he knew what he wanted, he didn't fuck around, he said 'cunt' every other sentence, which I loved. He was just a lad really, a general lad who had the power to be a director, and most directors I didn't have much in common with. Justin obviously from the drug thing we sort of bonded, but he didn't come from my area, he didn't talk like me, he didn't have the same sort of outlook on life. Nick gave up smack when he was sixteen. That's what *Love Story* was about, his smack days. A drop of alcohol hasn't passed his lips in twenty fucking years. That didn't stop the rest of us though! I think he was still intrigued and fascinated by that. Of course as long as it doesn't affect the work then he's fine with it. If you turn up off your head then you fucking know about it; I've learnt that the hard way with him. On that, he was young and it was his first film and he was nervous and he just wanted to make the movie he wanted to make. I think he had to make a few exceptions and people like Dani Behr in it – I wasn't sure he actually wanted Dani Behr – I think he wanted someone else and he couldn't get them so he went with Dani Behr, who at the time wasn't known as an actress but she was in the public eye, and she was quite sexy as well. But I didn't believe her in the movie, I didn't think she was strong enough. I didn't believe their relationship, Paul's and hers. There was no truth in it. She's just saying lies, he was petrified and being a bit paranoid and a bit like, 'Oh god I'm shit, I'm shit, I'm shit.' She didn't really feed off that. To be fair I was rooting for him because I liked him a lot, he was a very good friend of mine and I didn't like to see him beating himself up, but in the back of my fucking mind I was like, 'Why am I fucking doing this, I shouldn't be doing this', and I was young and hungry. But the way it panned out it was the right thing."

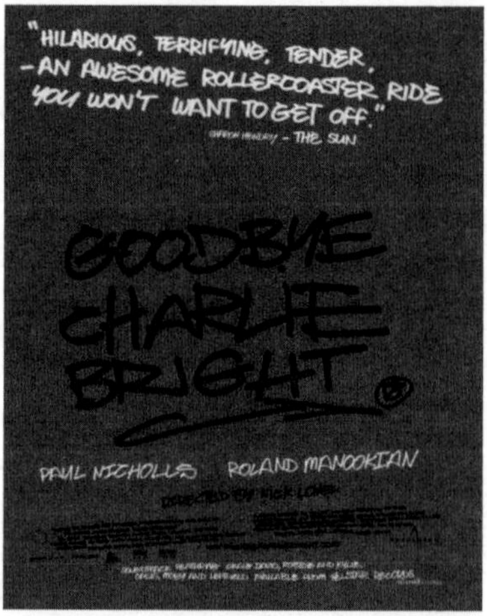


Interestingly, *Empire* magazine's Jo Berry did not mind Dani Behr's performance in their review which praised the film as a nice change from US teen movies such as *American Pie*: "As a debut effort, this is great stuff. The kids' performances shine, and support from the likes of Phil Daniels and David Thewlis always helps. It certainly makes a refreshing change from jizz in a cup. Nicely played – even Dani Behr as the 'new bird' isn't bad – this has some genuinely funny moments and provides an enjoyable addition to the CVs of the talented young cast."

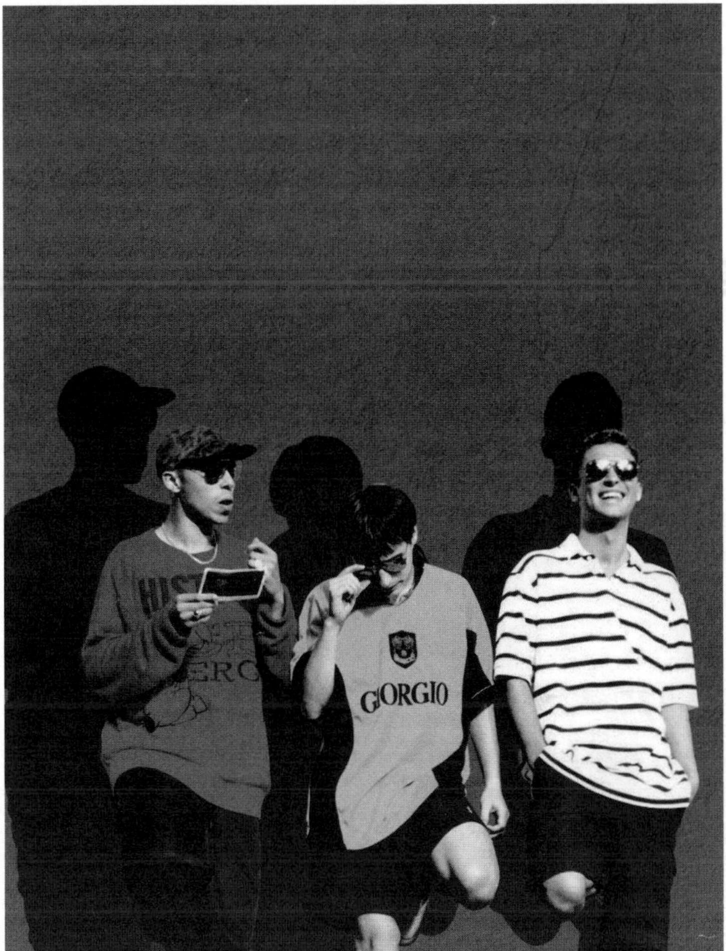


The UK box office was not great, but above average considering it was only on 51 screens, with a total haul of £82,665. It has sold 159,400 DVD copies to date and remains something of a British noughties classic – and the film that critics believe to be Love's best. The fans favourite would arrive three years later.

# HIGH HEELS AND LOW LIFES (2001)

**"It was like in them days my feet just didn't touch the floor."**

**Director** Mel Smith **Producer** Uri Fruchtmann, Barnaby Thompson **Writers** Kim Fuller, Georgia Pritchett **Production Designer** Michael Pickwoad **Costume Designer** Jany Temime **Music** Charlie Mole **Cinematography** Steven Chivers

**Minnie Driver** Shannon **Mary McCormack** Frances **Kevin McNally** Mason **Mark Williams** Tremaine **Len Collin** Barry **Danny Dyer** Danny **Darren Boyd** Ray **Michael Gambon** Kerrigan **Kevin Eldon** McGill

*A fast-paced story of drama and deception in which two women become fugitives. A nurse and her actress friend (Minnie Driver and Mary McCormack respectively) listen in on a mobile phone conversation that details the planning of a bank heist. When police are uninterested in their information, the girls concoct a plan to blackmail the robbers to get a share of the proceeds. The criminals, led by the hard-as-nails Mason, counteract with their own scheme, and the caper begins to go wildly out of control.*

There were high hopes for this one. With the late British comedy legend Mel Smith at the helm, and a script written in homage of the Ealing comedy style, it hoped to match the success of *The Full Monty*. It was not to be. Another British film with an almost identical plot named *Beautiful Creatures* was released around the same time, which harmed *High Heels*' box-office potential. It ended with a haul of £1,630,090 – very good for a film in Britain, but its budget was almost five times that. Contrary to popular belief, however, this is not such a disaster as it recouped the rest through DVDs and other international sales.

Reviews were not terrible, but not positive either. Jo Berry of *Empire* magazine stated that: "*Thelma And Louise* meets *Lock, Stock* – or so the makers of this Brit-flick would probably have you believe. But for this to be an enjoyable, fast-paced, chick comedy, it would first have to be a lot brisker than it is, and secondly, a lot funnier." Berry did, however, rate the performances. "The cast are terrific – Gambon is a hoot – and Driver (who should do more comedy) and McCormack, given snappier material, could have given Susan Sarandon and Geena Davis a run for their money in the sassy girls-against-the-world department."

The film does stand up today as an enjoyably far-fetched romp – and its lack of success was disappointing for Dyer but doesn't change his joyous memories. "It was a magical time," he says. "I was on this roll now of being offered parts and I got invited to go and meet Mel Smith. I thought, 'Fuck, wow.' It was like in them days my feet just didn't touch the floor. This is why I suppose later on in my career in the dark periods when people all of a sudden think I'm a laughing stock – just the idea of me being an actor is laughable to someone like Mark Kermode. In them days it was just like everyone thinks I'm fucking brilliant, and I love it so much, and I'm passionate about it and it comes so easy and naturally to me and they're paying me for it and I'm meeting amazing people and I'm getting out of the fucking East London fucking homophobic, racist mentality, I'm feeling a bit cultured and like, wow, you know, I'm going to dinner parties and I'm meeting amazing people and I just feel like I'm really fucking spreading my wings a bit. And I'd done it all on my own, obviously, I had nobody to ask, 'Oh fuck me, what do I wear, how do I do this?' So then I get invited by Mel Smith to a pub, just a boozer. I can't remember where it was now – in North London somewhere. I hadn't even read the script, he just met me and said, 'Listen, I think you're a good actor, I've got a little part in this thing if you want to do it.' He was sitting there with his cigar and we partied a bit. We had a drink and we got on really well, and I said, 'Listen, I'd fucking love to do it, I'm with you'. He said, 'I'll get the script over to you.' I read it, and I thought it would be a lot of fun – and I was right. I mean, come on; Minnie Driver, Mary McCormack. Both incredibly talented, both incredibly sexy. It was a dream working with them every day."

This was Danny's first role as a gangster, but the typecasting had not yet begun. "A role like this, it was a piece of piss. It was again a gangster thing, but I'm not really a gangster in it. It's comedy. You see, what I've really done with my career is play gangsters who are quite endearing. Yeah it's comical; he's a young kid, he thinks he's the bollocks but he's not, he gets everything fucking wrong, makes so many bad decisions it ends up with him being killed but, you know, it was great. Minnie knew who I was – she actually knew who I was – so again, the fame thing was coming on and people were recognising me and calling me Dan before I'd introduced myself. It was all weird and all very intoxicating. I did it on my own, and I did it because I deserved to be there. I wasn't born with a silver spoon in my mouth, I didn't do the drama school thing, it wasn't like my dad got me in it or whatever. I did it on my own, I was just really proud of myself. I had a child at the time and I was being a dad. Really good times in my life then. It seemed like I was just doing quality stuff as well. It was like I was just going quality to quality to quality, and I just thought, 'Wow, this is never going to end.' "

It was not to be. "Again, again, it didn't do well. Massive lavish budget again, and for some reason it wasn't very well received. It was a good idea, I thought the idea of these two woman taking on this little criminal empire and winning was really sweet and cute and nice and it was a harmless movie, I felt. And Minnie Driver was really hot at the time, and it just goes to fucking show that you never know, you just never know. Mel was a great director, I loved being around him, man he was just a fucking joy, and I was devastated to hear about his death, but proud of the fact that I got to spend a good six weeks with him. He just wanted to have a beer with me and stuff, party a bit. I enjoyed it, I got paid handsomely and again just came out of it thinking, 'Wow, what's next?' I think I got fifty grand for that, for about three weeks. Probably about fifteen grand a week, for doing something I love to do. I had my own trailer and completely treated like a fucking king, to be fair. It was a beautiful thing."

MINNIE DRIVER
MARY McCORMACK
Crime
has never
been so
attractive.
HIGH HEELS
AND LOW LIFES
IN CINEMAS JULY 20TH

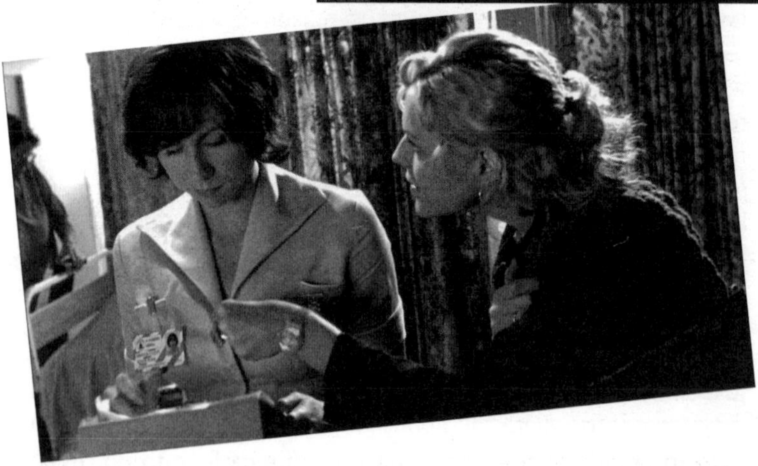

# MEAN MACHINE (2001)

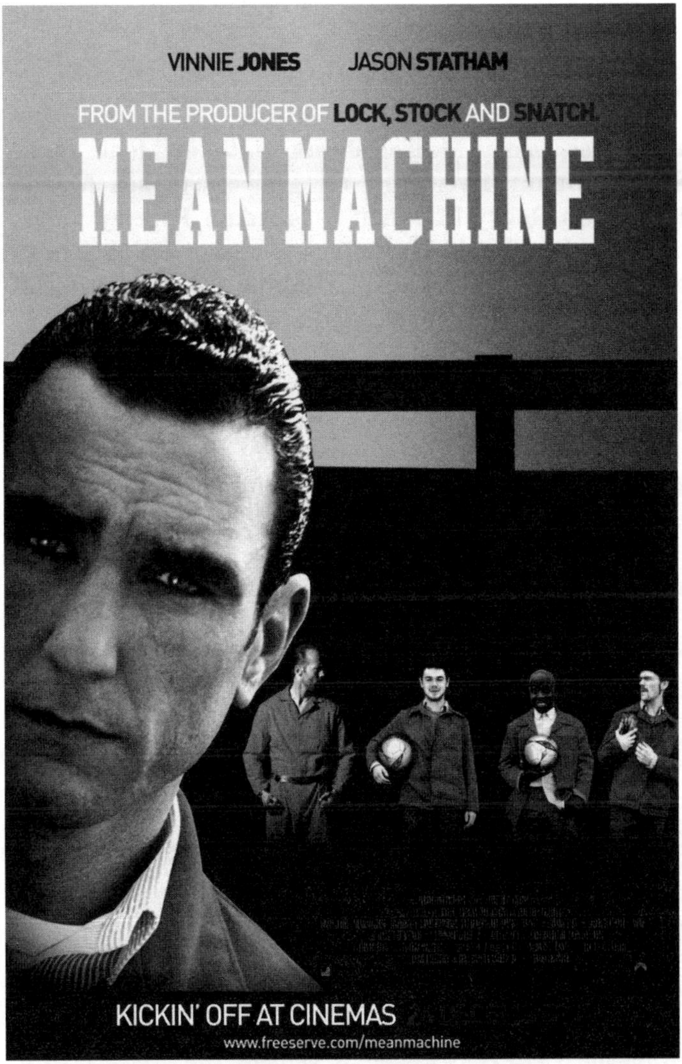


**"I was really chuffed because we filmed two endings – one with Vinnie Jones getting the woman, and one with me scoring the winning goal, and I never thought they was going to use my one but they did."**

**Director** Barry Skolnick **Producer** Matthew Vaughn **Writers** Tracy Keenan Wynn, Charlie Fletcher, Chris Baker, Andrew Day **Production Designer** Russell De Rozario **Costume Designer** Stephanie Collie **Music** Marilyn Manson John Murphy **Cinematography** Alex Barber

**Vinnie Jones** Danny Meehan **Jason Statham** Monk **Jamie Sives** Chiv **Danny Dyer** Billy the Limpet **Stephen Martin Walters** Nitro **Rocky Marshall** Cigs **Adam Fogerty** Mouse **David Kelly** Doc **David Hemmings** Governor **Ralph Brown** Burton **Vas Blackwood** Massive **Robbie Gee** Trojan **Geoff Bell** Ratchett **John Forgeham** Charlie Sykes

*After allegedly fixing a match between England and Germany, England manager Danny Meehan (Vinnie Jones) is sacked and subsequently imprisoned for the assault of two police officers. Outnumbered by a horde of aggressive inmates and violent guards, and angry that England lost in a crucial World Cup game, he suffers daily abuse. Life eventually starts to look up as he has the opportunity to redeem himself by guiding the prisoners in a legendary football match against the prison guards. But the corrupt governor (David Hemmings) has other ideas.*

After the unprecedented, unexpected, but deserved success of *Lock, Stock And Two Smoking Barrels*, producer Matthew Vaughn was so hot that he could have had a *Catwoman* sequel greenlit. *Mean Machine* was his third film as producer and it's a far cry from his current status as Hollywood director du jour (after the blistering box office success of the magnificent *Kick Ass*). His *Lock, Stock* colleague Guy Ritchie took on the role of executive producer.

Based on the 1974 Burt Reynolds vehicle *The Longest Yard*, it's an uneasy mix of slapstick comedy, brutal prison socio-realism and sports drama. It's a combo that isn't entirely successful, but is entertaining enough to make for a sporadically enjoyable romp thanks to director Barry Skolnick's ability to pull off a rare feat: shooting football convincingly on celluloid. He captures the thrill and buzz of a football match with impressive skill, presumably with Jones's help. It's a pity the former couldn't help the latter more with his acting.

That said, *Empire* magazine were impressed by both: "After his truly awful turn in *Swordfish*, it seemed that whatever acting talent the lovable lug possessed had well and truly evaporated. Not so. In this enjoyable remake of the 1974 Robert Aldrich American football movie, Jones may be no Burt Reynolds (it's all his own hair, for one thing), but in giving the film a likeable, commanding central presence, he's banged in a 30-yard, extra-time winner. It's admittedly not saying much, but the climactic 30-minute showdown between guards and cons could be the greatest celluloid soccer game ever – tough, realistic and hilarious. And if *Mean Machine* can't quite match Aldrich's acerbic ferocity, this should be entertaining enough, even if you don't know shit from Ginola."

The film opens with a spoof advert for Umbro featuring Jones' character Danny 'Mean Machine' Mears with the tagline: Danny 'Mean Machine' Mears is licensed to score. The oh-so bitter irony is that it is no less laughable than Vinnie Jones' real life acting career. And herein lies the problem with *Mean Machine*. *Lock, Stock* is undeniably brilliant and gloriously unexpected. That was part of its charm. *Snatch* was a cash-in but still had plenty to enjoy. Unfortunately, someone decided that Vinnie Jones could lead a movie. Sure, he works in *Lock, Stock* as a hardman (based on Lenny 'The Guvnor' McLean) who says little – but carry a movie? It hasn't ever worked, despite many believing it would in the early noughties. But that didn't stop it grossing £4,470,078 at the UK box office and selling almost a million DVDs to date.

*Total Film* stated in their review of *Mean Machine*: "Let's get one thing straight: Vinnie Jones is one film short of being a very big star. He's got the screen presence, he's got the attitude and he's got a CV full of scene-stealing support roles (*Lock, Stock..., Gone In 60 Seconds, Swordfish...*). All he needs is one starring role in one hit movie. Sadly, *Mean Machine* isn't that movie."

The film has dated badly, mainly due to the fact that even in 2001 it – perhaps deliberately – looked like something out of the eighties. It ticks off every prison cliché in its first half as Jones' Meehan meets his fellow lags and corrupt governor. But such is the impressive array of top British talent on display – David Hemmings, Ralph Brown, Sarah Alexander, Geoff Bell, Jason Flemyng, Vas Blackwood, David Kelly – it is undeniably watchable. It is also notable for being Jason Statham's first role as an action man of sorts (well, murderer), which had led to a highly successful and lucrative Hollywood career. It was this gathering of top British talent that attracted Dyer to the part – but was also his undoing on the set.

Dyer appears twenty minutes in as 'Billy the Limpet', Meehan's biggest fan in the prison, and it's a nice performance in a charming role. He also has the honour if having his balls crunched in the film in a manner not dissimilar to Jones' infamous Gazza moment.

"I remember reading the script and thinking, 'Fucking hell, it's a small part for me.' And I wasn't a massive fan of Vinnie Jones. It's not that I didn't like him; I just didn't really rate him as an actor. He wasn't very humble, and he was just a bit arrogant about the whole thing. But I remember reading it, and in the original script my character Billy was meant to be quite aggressive and a bit thick and the reason they let me in the team is because they're scared of me. I said, 'Why don't we put a different spin on it, and let me be really endearing, so the other characters and the audience feel sorry for me?' So they changed the script, which was great. A huge honour. I was really chuffed that they would do that for me because it was clear they really wanted me in it. Matthew was a big fan of mine. I remember on that job he gave me the book to *Layer Cake,* because obviously he was thinking about me playing the lead role (trivia fans note: the novelist JJ Connolly, who wrote *Layer Cake*, appears in *Mean Machine* as Barry The Bookie). So we had a real bond up."

Reviews for the film were surprisingly positive. The renowned Stateside film critic Roger Ebert stated: "Guy Ritchie, who started out as such an innovator in *Lock, Stock,* etc., seems to have headed directly for reliable generic conventions as a producer. But they are reliable, and have become conventions for a reason: they work. *Mean Machine* is what it is, and very nicely, too."

Predictably, many American critics were determined to compare it to the 1974 original, with the *Los Angeles Times* stating: "*Mean Machine* may not have the resonance to linger in the memory affectionately as *The Longest Yard* does, but it plays well, with a fast pace and plenty of punch."

Likewise, *The New York Times*: "Somewhere, audiences must be clamouring for remakes of violent mid-1970s American sports movies. How else to explain the nearly simultaneous appearances of the new *Rollerball* and *Mean Machine,* a British update of *The Longest Yard*, Robert Aldrich's 1974 prison football picture? At least *Mean Machine* refreshes the original by moving the action across the Atlantic, where football is actually played with the feet. The other cultural differences are easy enough to assimilate: instead of a warden, the British penitentiary has a governor. Some of the slang is thick enough to require subtitles. (None are provided.) Reviewing *The Longest Yard* in *The New York Times* 28 years ago, Nora Sayre objected to its clumsiness and violence, but admitted to being entertained by the football sequences. Watching this remake, I had the opposite response: the story was moderately engaging and moved swiftly, but the long soccer match at the end bored me silly. Perhaps this is just American chauvinism, or perhaps that kind of football is inherently less cinematic than ours. It's certainly no less brutal."

Dyer himself fell into the same trap. "I thought the original was a great movie," he states. "I love Burt Reynolds. It was a big ask for Vinnie Jones to be able to step into Burt Reynolds' shoes. I thought the film was a really good idea though; I loved the football – I think they way they shot the football stuff as well, the way it was set up, was really good, it was really interesting. And I had no idea that *The Football Factory* was in the pipeline. I was just cracking on with another job. David

Kelly, an old boy I worked with on *Greenfingers*, he was in it as well, so I was just sort of sitting with him at lunch. Sitting with a ninety-year-old in the corner. But again, as an actor I knew I could proudly stand out in it, but actually as an experience, with the camaraderie and being pals – it wasn't that sort of job."

When Jones agrees the deal with David Hemmings' corrupt governor, he insists that, "What goes on the pitch, stays on the pitch." Thankfully, Danny doesn't feel the same way about the film set, admitting "it was a strange experience. It wasn't really one that I enjoyed too much. Very cliquey – obviously it was all the *Lock, Stock* mob in it and they didn't really know me – the knew *of* me, but they'd be playing cards at lunchtime and stuff, and I wasn't really invited into their little circle of Statham and Vinnie and Vas. I wasn't too fucking bothered, to be honest with you. That's when I first met Geoff Bell, who later I became really good friends with, but this was my proper opportunity to get really into doing comedy – to really milk it. As much as *Greenfingers* was a bit of a comedy, and *Human Traffic* was a comedy in a sense, this was really playing a character – a caricature. I couldn't wait to get in front of Vinnie, I was quite excited about that. Just to show him how it's done, really. As a man he's alright, to be fair. I've got no reason to not like him, I just thought that it was a bit frustrating that after every take he wanted to watch the monitor to see if it was any good. He pulled all the strings on the job; at the time he was greenlighting projects, there's no two ways about that – if he wasn't in them, they wouldn't have got made. He knew that – everybody knew that – but I think he took it to extremes. But he was respectful to me. It was nice, but it *was* the Vinnie Jones show, so I just got a bit bored of that and kept myself to myself on that job."

Feeling alienated by the other cast members was one thing. But really Dyer was feeling frustrated with being lumbered with bit parts. He felt he deserved better. He felt he could do better. "By this point I was ready to carry a film," he states. "I love being there on set every day, but it was the annoying bittiness of having small roles. And to be honest, I think my ego was getting in the way a bit. It was just frustrating coming in for half a day to do two scenes and then fucking off and not coming back for a week. Because I am just sporadically put in the film. I was really chuffed because we filmed two endings – one with Vinnie Jones getting the woman, and one with me scoring the winning goal, and I never thought they was going to use my one but they did."

When Dyer's character scores the winning goal, it is a real goosebump moment, and he ends the film the hero who saves the day. Regrettably the film shoot did not end quite so victoriously. "I said a few things about Guy Ritchie that I probably shouldn't have said, which upset him," says Dyer. "I just didn't like him. He turned up on set with three minders and I was told not to make eye contact with him as he approaches. He was with Madonna at the time, at the height of their marriage. I understand – it's Madonna, and that's a massive fucking thing, but I did an interview with a men's magazine, and said I thought he was a bit of

cunt, which I shouldn't have said. It did me no favours at the premiere and I had to have photos with him. I really wanted to meet Madonna and I didn't get that opportunity because of my mouth. I was a bit embarrassed."

# THE FOOTBALL FACTORY (2004)

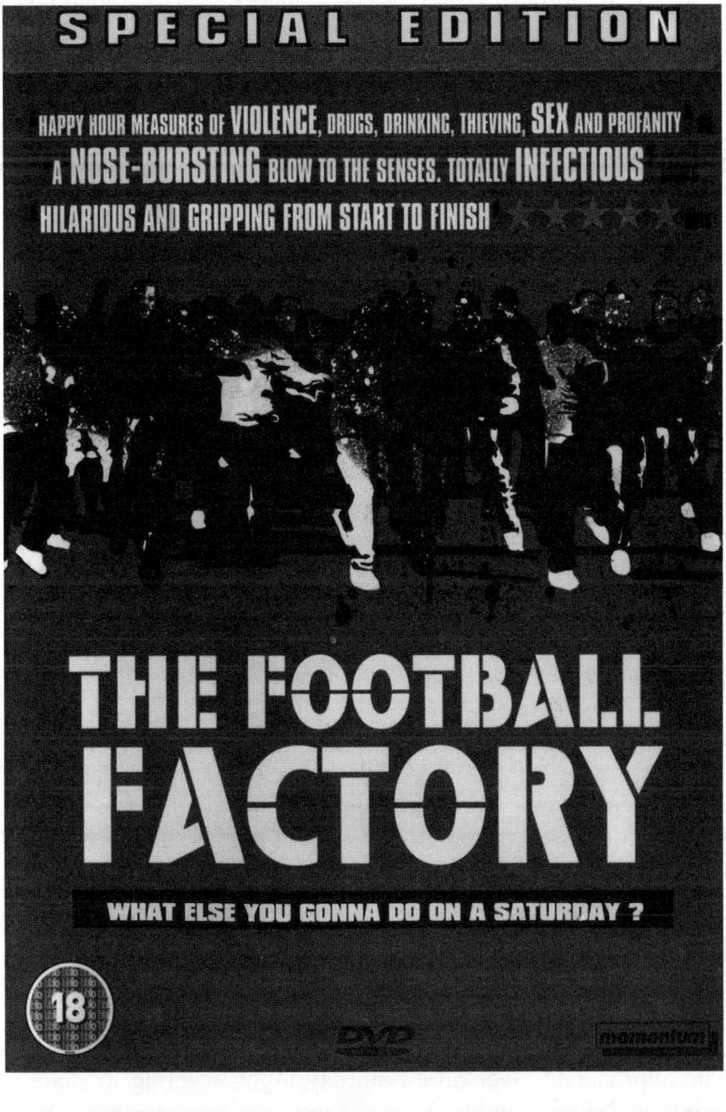


**"I was rolling out of the cab with a bottle of vodka in my hand and stuff; it just wasn't a good look."**

**Director** Nick Love **Producer** Allan Niblo, James Richardson **Writer** John King, Nick Love **Production Designer** Paul Burns **Costume Designer** Jayne Gregory **Music** Ivor Guest **Cinematography** Damian Bromley

**Danny Dyer** Tommy Johnson **Frank Harper** Billy Bright **Neil Maskell** Rod **Roland Manookian** Zeberdee **Tamer Hassan** Milwall Fred **Dudley Sutton** Bill Farrell **John Junkin** Albert Moss

*Tommy Johnson (Dyer), a dissatisfied twenty-something, finds meaning in his life with a group of football hooligans and their violent clashes with rival 'firms'. Tommy and his friends (Frank Harper and Neil Maskell) spend their days drinking, using drugs, womanising and kicking people's heads in, much to the dismay of Tommy's grandfather (Dudley Sutton), a pensioner who plans to leave England for good with his best friend. During a fight with the Tottenham firm, Tommy begins to have second thoughts about his life choices after being arrested for assaulting two Stoke City fans while travelling to an away match. But this is the least of Tommy's problems: the brother of a girl Tommy picked up is on the hunt for him, and just happens to be the leader of the Millwall firm and an arch-rival of Tommy's firm.*

This is the film that made Danny Dyer, simple as that. The majority of Dyer's fans adore him because of this film. It had been three years since his last appearance on the big screen and while that time had been taken up with worthy short films (see Appendix) and voice work on *Grand Theft Auto: Vice City*, he was ready for a challenge. The first high-profile football hooligan film since Gary Oldman's *The Firm*, it is one of the best British films of all time. Prior to *The Football Factory* it had been the peace-loving, pill-popping fans of *Human Traffic* that approached Dyer on a Saturday night, wanting to share a drink (and the rest) with the real Moff. But now it was a whole new breed. The football casual. The hooligan. Or mindless, vicious thugs, as the tabloids call them.

When *The Football Factory* burst onto UK cinema screens on 14 May 2004, there was already a huge stir around the film. Lads in pubs and clubs were raving about it, thanks to a leaked bootleg copy. An early rough cut of the film, it contains many noticeable differences. As the BBC website stated at the time: "Thanks to a rough pirate copy doing the rounds, the film is already causing a buzz before it is even released."

Subsequently, a statement was released by Vertigo Films, the film's production and distribution company, stating:

"We are aware of a pirate copy of *The Football Factory* currently on sale. Please do not buy/borrow/rent this, as it has nothing to do with the actual film. This is not the director's cut but a very early version, put together by an assistant editor. *The Football Factory* which is at the cinemas from May 14 is a far superior version and we want you to enjoy the film as intended."

Rumour has it that the copy was deliberately leaked by the filmmakers to generate interest. This has been furiously denied by everyone involved with the film, from producer Allan Niblo to director Nick Love. Everyone in fact, except Dyer.

"They released this other version of it six months before – stuck a pirate out," he admits. "It has Oasis tunes on it, a totally different version. They used the scenes that were cut in our version. The opening scene in the pirate version is me chinning a reporter who's standing outside the ground making a report about hooligans, and I just come out and smack her in the mouth, and then it freezes, and then I started my speech about how I always wanted to be a hooligan. Totally different feel to it. But yeah, I remember people saying they'd seen it before it came out. They'd go, 'I bought a copy off someone.' It must have been deliberate – we're not talking one or two copies; it must have been about 300,000 copies. It was all over fucking Britain. A completely different version of it. Anyone who likes the film should try and get a copy of it, because it's interesting to watch. I spoke to Nick about all this though and he denied the lot."

Either way, the film was a huge hit (£677,031 at the UK box office and 143,842 DVD sales in the first month alone) and remains every bit as powerful, exhilarating and, like it or not, hilarious as it was then. Like many great movies about friendship (*Dazed And Confused*, *Human Traffic*, *The Warriors*) it is about men and how they bond. It is not simply about hooliganism. It's about relationships, fitting in, and is – to an extent – a love story between the male leads.

Based on the iconic book by John King, the film does not identify itself with a time and place. In 2001, hooliganism was no longer such a huge part of society as it was when King's book was published in 1996. The book was a cult hit and literary success, while the film became the biggest independent DVD of all time in the UK. It changed everything for Dyer. But he almost wasn't in it.

"My reputation was damaged. I was getting a bit of a 'wild man' image. I had done a couple of jobs including a TV movie called *Second Generation* with Parminda Nagra where I was going through a weird stage where I was just constantly off my head," Dyer admits. "I was rolling out of the cab with a bottle of vodka in my hand and stuff; it just wasn't a good look. Nick Love had heard about this; he wanted to offer *The Football Factory* to me but he just couldn't, and he bollocked me big time. He took me out to the Groucho Club to give me the script. He threw it at me and said, 'Fucking read that. I can't offer it you now because you've become a bit of a cunt and you're unreliable, and the producers don't think you're going to be turning up every day.' And I was absolutely just in shock. I was like, 'Fucking hell, I didn't expect this.' I was on the train reading it, and on the verge of tears at how brilliant the script was and how great the part was, but I'd almost got to the part where I'd fucked that up, and I was a bit lost. It turned out that it was between me and Tom Hardy. It was all down to me and Tom Hardy. We were going to the final audition, and I was really down on myself. And then I got the call. He said, 'You're in son. Don't let me down.' And I just thought, this is it. This is it now. I've got to really get my fucking knuckle down and concentrate and prove to him that I do it.'"

Dyer remembers the rigorous audition process vividly. "The first audition was the waking up scene with Rod, where he can't remember anything – and that was just perfect because I know that feeling very well," Dyer says. "I also think he wanted to hear my voice doing some of the monologues, you know, 'What else are you going to do on a Saturday, sitting and wanking off to Pop Idol…' That sort of stuff. He wanted to hear the tone in my voice. So yeah, I was really pleased that I beat Tom Hardy to it. I think the reason I beat Tom Hardy, and he is a fucking great actor, there's no doubt about that, but he is middle class, and he tried to play the working-class thing and it didn't work. It didn't ring true. So I had the edge over him through that, completely."

This was the project Dyer had been waiting for. "I loved every second of it," he says. "It was good being able to work with Nick every day, and I loved that fact that he trusted me, and I was going to be the complete opposite to his last experience with lead actor Paul Nicholls on *Goodbye Charlie Bright* where he had to give him a pat on the arse every two minutes – I was determined he wouldn't have to do that with me. His notes to me were 'Stop acting!', which I'd never heard before, and which really brought a stillness to me that he embedded in me, and I just remember thinking that I don't have to do much really; I just say the line, and not think about 'acting'. It was tough with Frank Harper. I had a lot of respect for Frank, and it was really lads all in. All the cast on that, all the extras, were real hooligans, so there were some on tag and stuff. I'd turn up and there'd be six hooligans in my little dressing room smoking weed. I had to be one of the lads and be the main actor at the same time. I had to keep them on side, but at the same time be able to do six or seven scenes a day, which you couldn't possibly do if you were stoned out of your brain. And obviously Nick doesn't agree with that as well. It was a mad time in my life as well because I'd just split up from a high-profile relationship and I was living back on my Nan's settee at the time. I didn't have any money, I sort of fucked up a little bit. So this was a massive thing for me in every respect to get my life back in order, and concentrate on what I love more than anything, which, other than my children, is acting. This was my opportunity to fucking do it."

Frank Harper loved working with Dyer because, contrary to popular opinion, they weren't actually on screen together in *Goodbye Charlie Bright*. "We had known each other a long while even though we never performed together before, so there was always a mutual respect and understanding between the two of us, and there was a feeling amongst all the cast of that film because we knew each other for a long time, so we just hit the ground running," remembers Harper. "We both have a similar sense of humour so the job was a lot of fun, involving a lot of wind ups and taking the piss out of each other. My personal favourite is when I persuaded him to wear a Millwall shirt for charity. After 30 or 40 photos had been taken of him wearing it the deal was I would then wear a West Ham shirt. When he said to me, 'Put it on then!' I told him to, 'Fuck off, not in a million years, the day I put that on the Queen will have no soldiers!' Done him like a kipper."

This was the point in Dyer's life when he had been living at Supernova Heights (Noel Gallagher and Meg Matthews' former mansion) and partying with the Primrose Hill set. The non-stop party lifestyle of these independently wealthy privileged types was not good for him. "There no way I could have got the part if I was caning it every night," he states. "Absolutely not. It was because of that period of my life that Nick had heard rumours and got pissed off with me. I was doing a play on Broadway and fucked up a lot. I was off my head. I was working with Harold Pinter at the same time, and just lost the plot a little bit. I was in a world I didn't belong in – the world of Kate Moss and all that, the Primrose Hill mob. It started to affect my judgement, and acting all of a sudden started to become a sort of hobby, whereas before it was my whole being. Nick really was my saviour. If I hadn't got that part, who knows? I certainly wouldn't be sitting here talking to you today."

Needless to say, the controversial subject matter was an attraction to Dyer rather than a concern. "It was going to be a controversial thing, of course it was," he states. "Again, like

*Human Traffic,* it was going, wow we're going to upset some people, this is so going to upset people because there is no bollocks about this. Cunt every other sentence. Just the dialogue in it, the violence. It took the next level. The broadsheets wanted to ask whether the film should be made, and what we were trying to prove. Well, we're not trying to prove anything; we're just making a movie. It's entertainment. It's a slice of life, that's what it is. It's about male love. Mine and Rob's relationship's really interesting. He's torn between me and that world, and he meets a girl and he sort of falls in love with her, and of course he fucks her off in the most brilliant fucking way. That scene's just fucking amazing. But it is, I mean it's about male tribalism, lost souls coming together, fighting for a cause that really doesn't mean anything. It's about the look, and the culture of it, and the music, and just the idea of standing up for something you believe in. It just happens to be football on a Saturday afternoon. It's brutally honest: that's why it was always going to upset people. What was clever was that he put me in a role where I'm doubting it. In the film I think I'm a bit psychic and I have the weird dreams and I want to be part of it but it doesn't suit me, but once you're in you can't get out. It was layered; it wasn't two-dimensional."

Predictably, some critics loathed the film. Many loved it. *Empire* magazine's Scott Russon was one of the few who truly understood what the film was about and, as such, blessed it with a four-star review:

"The script's pace is well judged throughout, as the story flows from moments of dark comedy to scenes of disaster with little forewarning. The cast is mostly impressive; Dyer comfortably portrays Tommy with a befitting laddish swagger, while Neil Maskell delivers a subtle performance as his best mate, Rod. Importantly, Love has managed to craft a film that is fond of its characters, yet withdrawn enough to never condone their exploits. An impressive 90-minute performance from all involved. With the story of misguided males bonding around their love for football and fighting, the film is like a mixture of *Trainspotting* and *Fight Club* – with Burberry caps."

Many commentators, however, and to a certain extent people involved with the film, were worried that it may cause a rise in popularity of hooliganism again. Nick Love had defended his film saying: "If someone watches a film for 90 minutes and then wants to go out and batter someone, then I think they probably wanted to batter someone anyway. I wanted to make the film because it's about a largely unreported subculture. No one has had a stab at making a film about the working-class and lower middle-class men who make up 70% of the population."

But *The Guardian*'s Richard Williams disagreed: "As a piece of cinematic art, *The Football Factory* makes *Lock, Stock And Two Smoking Barrels* look like *Wild Strawberries*. The only people likely to enjoy it are those already stupid enough to contemplate spending their Saturday afternoons looking for what the film's characters call 'a row'. And it seems possible that by watching such events on the big screen, they will find their activities further legitimised – because that, whether the film's director, Nick Love, admits it or not, is the way popular culture works on society.

"Love is also trying to pretend that violence is not the point of the film. Only five minutes, he claims, are devoted to scenes involving heads being kicked. But all the available cinematic tricks are employed to ensure that those minutes are the heart and soul of the enterprise. And five minutes of heads being kicked in certainly feels like a long time. Of course, a worthwhile film could be made about football hooligans, just as the American writer Bill Buford once wrote a genuinely enlightening book, called *Among The Thugs*, on the subject. *The Football Factory*, however, is emphatically not that film. To condemn the film is to run the risk of sounding humourless (although not as humourless as the film). But if *The Football Factory* encourages one idiot to transgress the bounds of civilised behaviour in Cardiff next week or in Portugal next month, the price of Love's right to make such a film will have been too high."

Dyer was aware of the concerns, but was not apprehensive about them. "I think they were worried about hooliganism kicking off again," he admits. "And it did a bit afterwards, to be fair. I mean, I wouldn't say it's totally down to the film, but it became quite appealing to people again. Them days were gone. In the late eighties and nineties it petered out, which it fucking should do because it's fucking embarrassing – grown men running around swinging punches at each other for no reason whatsoever. We did a whole tour of it round the country, and we showed it to a different hooligan firm in every city. In Cardiff, we showed it to the Soul Crew, we did the Red Army in Manchester. That was quite nerve-wracking, because if they don't like it… We had a bit of trouble with the Mancs because they wasn't mentioned enough, apparently. The Soul Crew were mentioned, so they was over the moon. So it was a weird one. We'd do a screening, then we'd do a Q&A, then they'd take us all out. Nick was obviously worried about that bit, because Nick wrote and directed it so they thought he was going to be a little hooligan himself, sniffing gear and taking drugs. He doesn't do anything like that, so they were a bit disappointed in him. Then there's me and Tamer – we embraced it."

Very few people know that – like *Back To The Future* – the film was actually started with a different cast. "It started out with a different director with a totally different cast," Dyer reveals. "They had stupid names in it or something. The character names were just ridiculous. It was fucked so they went to Nick for help. Nick went, 'Okay, I'll do it, but I want to rewrite it.' Which is what he did, and he recast it completely. One of the characters was called 'Fuck Off All The Time' because he says fuck off all the time. It was cringing."

The film was also the first time that Dyer worked with Tamer Hassan, a relationship that has now become infamous. "When I first met Tamer, he was a massive fan of *Mean Machine*," says Dyer. "We was in a pub round the corner during my audition, and I remember him going to Nick, 'Why haven't you given him a fucking part?' I was sitting there cringing. And he went, 'Well I got Tom Hardy,' and he went, 'You've got to be a cunt! You've got to give him the fucking part!' And I thought, I love this geezer. I love this man. He was absolutely in shock that I didn't get a straight offer. He was like, 'Don't worry boy, you'll get it, you'll get it.' Do you know what I mean? He's got that way about him. And I think he really respected me as an actor more than anything else. Obviously in the movie he is my nemesis, and he was asking me questions about whether he was doing it right, and I loved that because he's quite a powerful man. For him to be quite vulnerable around me and asking me for tips… I like that. It's a nice feeling. And he was a big part of the movie. He got a lot of the cast involved, because he was a hooligan back in the day, a part of the Millwall mob. He used his football club, and we had to shoot with little sets in there and I think for him, it was always about, 'I'll hook you up, but I want to be in it.' And he delivered. He's great isn't he? He's fucking petrifying in it. I loved working with him. I love the actor he has become."

One of the best things about the film is the ending. Having depicted most people's worst nightmare – namely being beaten up by football hooligans – our hero and the film's core and conscience Tommy refuses to repent and change his ways. It's a great moment, reminiscent of the closing scene of *Goodfellas*. Ray Liotta's Henry Hill has lost everything but he was still a mobster at heart. "We did two final lines," Dyer reveals. "We did one where he said, 'Was it worth it?' and I said, 'I leave that for you decide.' It didn't have the same ring to it. 'Of course it fucking was!' If you're going to make a movie like that you've got to stick to your guns. That's what Nick's good at doing. And that's why it works, because there was no bollocks. Nick's not a yes man. Later on he became a bit of a yes man, I feel, and I think he shit himself a little bit because it was a little bit too political and that's why it didn't work, but with *The Football Factory,* we was like, 'Who gives a fuck? We'll make this film. Who gives a fuck if a cunt's upset?' This is a powerful piece of work, and there hasn't been anything like it since Gary Oldman's *The Firm*. We were proud of it, I was proud of it, and I got a bounce in my step again. I was proud of being an actor. I watch it, and I don't really feel I put a foot wrong."

# TABLOID (2004)

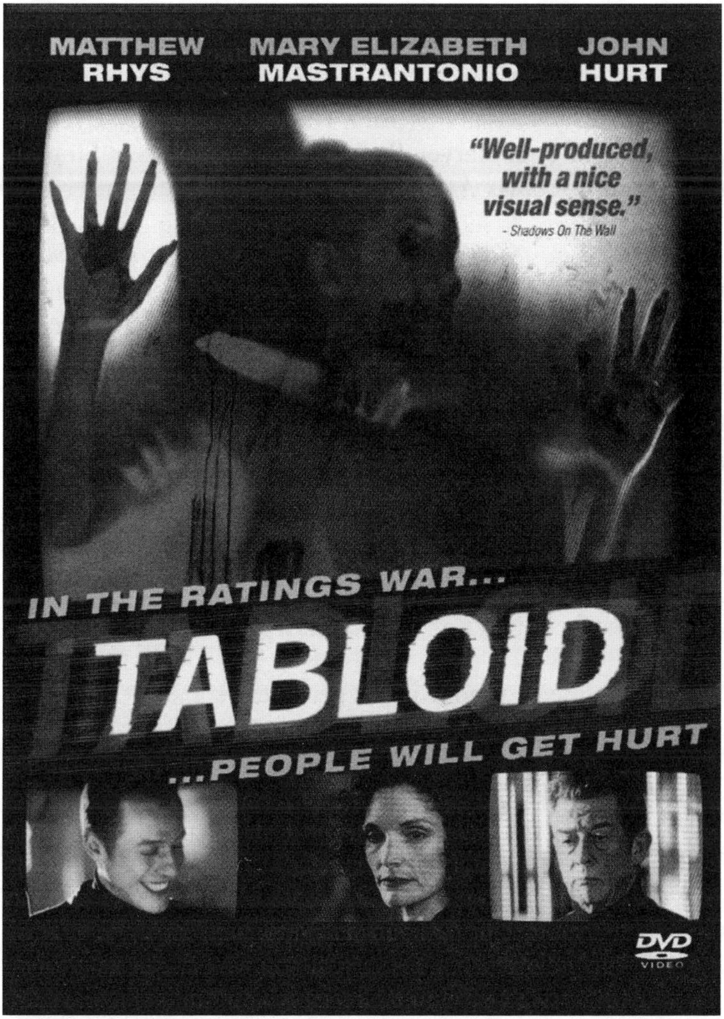


**"The disappearance of this film tells you all you need to know about the unpredictability of the film industry."**

**Director** David Blair **Producer** Mark Shorrock **Writer** Martin Stellman, Brian Ward **Costume Designer** Eleanor Baker **Music** Anne Dudley **Cinematography** Ryszard Lenczewski

**Matthew Rhys** Darren Daniels **Mary Elizabeth Mastrantonio** Natasha Fox **John Hurt** Vince **Danny Dyer** Joe Public **David Soul** Harvey **Stefano Accorsi** Lorenzo **Stephen Tompkinson** Lomax **Art Malik** Phillip Radcliffe

*Darren Daniels (Matthew Rhys) is the popular, good-looking, and heavily disingenuous host of TV show* Tabloid TV. *Celebrities desperately want airtime on the show, despite the fact that Darren regularly unearths troubling skeletons in their closets. One day, however, Vince (John Hurt) enters Darren's life, and leads him on a darkly sexual journey.*

Despite boasting an extremely impressive cast and a satirical script as biting as they come, *Tabloid* has never been released in the UK. A disturbing satire on the nature of celebrity TV, a decade on, it is startlingly prophetic, providing a unique insight into the modern obsession with celebrity.

In 2001, while in production it generated some press interest (ironically enough) mainly due to the rumoured casting of Billie Piper. On 12 January 2001, *Guardian Unlimited* reported that: "Newspaper darling and current squeeze of Chris Evans, Billie Piper, is set to make her acting debut in a forthcoming British film, appropriately named *Tabloid,* according to the *The Sun*. The 18-year-old singer will apparently star alongside veteran actor John Hurt, TV presenter Gail Porter and *Coronation Street* actress Beverly Callard in the £5m tale about a television show which unearths celebrities' darkest secrets. An insider on the project told the paper: 'As well as John Hurt, we have *Graduate* stage star Matthew Rhys, who plays a Chris Evans-style megalomaniac chat show host, so hopefully that will make Billie feel at home!' "

The rumour was unfounded, as revealed by *The Times* on 23 January 2001: "Guy Hands, the Nomura financier, and his wife Julia are providing the cash for a film about the horrors of tabloid TV. Starring Matthew Rhys as a repellent talk show host, John Hurt and Art Malik, the film, working title *Tabloid*, is being shot at Teddington and around London. Hands has invited 'the usual smattering of A list, B list and C list celebrities' (his words) to a party to celebrate it. The event will be filmed, and bits used in the eventual film, which is apparently one of those post-modernist things in which shots of real people are intercut with fiction. The film, costing a reported £5m, has already gained coverage in the, er, tabloids because of the non-inclusion in the cast list of a pop singer called Billie, now linked with Chris 'Ginger Whinger' Evans, so someone on the PR side is doing their job. But Hands's involvement has so far remained unsung. I wonder if his Midas touch will be enough this time. Small British films are usually a foolproof way to lose millions."

The following day, a party for the film took place. *The People* reported: "Last night, the producers of the film *Tabloid TV*, starring Matthew Rhys as an amoral talk show host, hosted a party, footage of which will be intercut with the scripted celluloid. In the film, Rhys's show uncovers the darkest secrets of even the most virtuous guest. Celebrities queue up to appear on his Russian roulette of talk shows, despite the high chance of humiliation. Already on board for the film are Art Malik, John Hurt, David Soul, Mary Elizabeth Mastrantonio, Stephen Tompkinson and Gail Porter (although Billie pulled out after boyfriend Chris Evans assumed the film was about him). James Hewitt, who was careful not to be photographed next to the portrait of Diana, will play a character very like himself in the satirical film. The evening was in aid of the charities Rainforest Foundation and Survival for Tribal Peoples."

Dyer himself has only seen it because a fan gave him a copy bought in Japan. "I don't know what happened to *Tabloid,"* he says. "David Blair directed it. Offered me a part. I read it, I loved it, I thought it was a really good idea. I was playing a stand-up comedian, and I remember he said to me, 'Listen, there's going to be a scene where I just need you to riff for three minutes,' which is what appealed to me. And I love Matthew Rhys, I think he's a great actor, and John Hurt – fucking hell. Mary Elizabeth Mastrantonio – being a massive fan of *Scarface,* I was like, 'Fucking hell, I'm all over this.' For me it was more about the idea of standing up in front of a group of extras and trying to make them laugh (which I did – they cut all the stuff I said because I was a bit filthy), but it was a weird little job, that one. It was a really strange one. It was trying to make a point of what fame can do to you. The main character played by Matthew Rhys is sort of based on Chris Evans, and he had a kind of *TFI Friday*-type show. He interviews celebrities and gets really whacked up in this world. This gangster blackmails him, and it's not a trick or anything but he thinks that he's killed these two girls at this orgy one night. But the gangsters pretended to kill them, and that sets him up and he goes on this weird journey. I don't know what happened. Again, it was a massive budget. I don't know what the politics was. It was shot here, mostly in a studio. I don't know. Maybe it's too controversial. The killings in it were pretty gory, but you later find out that it was all staged and it wasn't real, so it's a bit of a blur to me. I think a fan sent it to me in the post. It had Japanese writing on it. I did it then I didn't hear nothing more about it. It completely disappeared. Very, very strange. I think maybe it was something to do with David Blair directing and fell out with a producer or something. Something happened, a political thing. But they need to do a deal on it because it was over two million, easy. It was a massive budget. Lavish. Look at the cast, and their wages alone. I haven't even got a copy – this was a long time ago."

Given all the early Dyer works being repackaged and released, it does seems strange that the producers haven't managed to come to an agreement to get this released. Dyer is philosophical about it. "The disappearance of this film tells you all you need to know about the unpredictability of the film industry," he says. "Here's a good film with an intriguing plot starring a legend like John Hurt, and Matthew Rhys who is really hot right now and with all the crap out there, but you can't find this film for love nor money. You think it'd be quite an easy sell for a distributor. But in this game, anything can happen. Or not happen, as the case may be."

# THE GREAT ECSTASY OF ROBERT CARMICHAEL (2005)

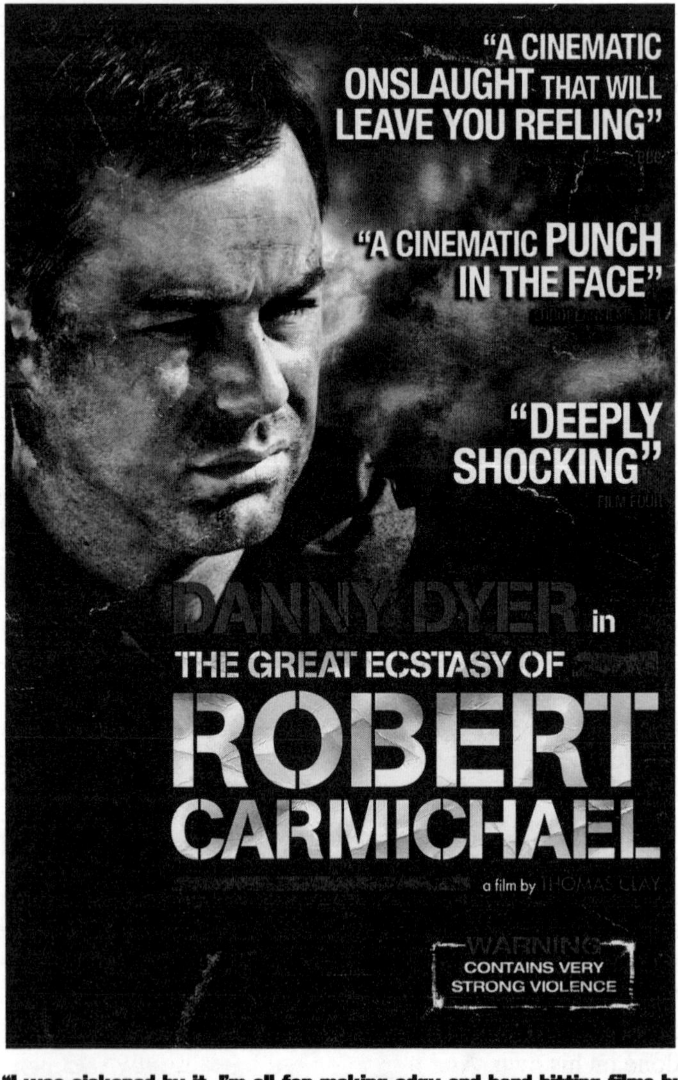


**"I was sickened by it. I'm all for making edgy and hard-hitting films but no one wants to see someone being raped with a fucking swordfish."**

**Director** Thomas Clay **Producer** Joseph Lang **Writer** Thomas Clay, Joseph Lang **Production Designer** Atilla Raczkevy **Costume Designer** Calandra Meredith **Music** Jonathan Henry Harvey, Amy Purcell **Cinematography** Giorgos Arvanitis

**Daniel Spencer** Robert Carmichael **Lesley Manville** Sarah Carmichael **Danny Dyer** Larry Haydn **Miranda Wilson** Monica Abbott **Michael Howe** Jonathan Abbott **Hilary Tones** Ruth **Ryan Winsley** Joe

*Robert Carmichael, a hugely accomplished cello player, is a lonely, introverted teenager unable to socialise in his home town of Newhaven. His mother (played by regular Mike Leigh collaborator Lesley Manville) dotes on him but also worries about his lack of interaction with others. Robert starts skipping school to hang around with a group of wasters and dropouts, taking drugs with them and sitting around parks talking misogynist nonsense. The scenes are often bookended with Iraq news reports to imply simmering violence stemming from boredom. After meeting Larry (played by Dyer), the activities of the group get more sordid, resulting in a truly disturbing home invasion in which the occupants are stabbed and brutally raped in a prolonged sequence.*

Without question the most controversial film of 2006, if not the entire decade, this has been variously described as the most shocking film ever made and one of the most repugnant pieces of fiction to ever tarnish the delicate peepers of the viewing public.

It is something of a pity that so much emphasis was placed on how shocking the film is, with little attention paid to the fact that director Thomas Clay funded the film entirely himself through private investors. No arts grant or lottery money, it was all done on his own. And it is a powerful, beautifully shot piece of work. Possibly the only positive review came from respected *Observer* critic Phillip French who commended the cinematography, stating: "The film has a rare poise, which derives from Clay's collaboration with Greek photographer Yorgos Arvanitis, famous for his association with Theo Angelopoulos. There are long takes in deep focus with no camera movement, smooth, lateral tracking shots, virtually no close-ups, no reaction shots and an occasional dissolve."

French's colleague Peter Bradshaw of *The Guardian,* however, thought that the stylistic mastery of the film only made it more offensive. "This is a deeply horrible and objectionable film," he ranted. "Its undoubted technical successes might simply extend and compound the offence. Critics have cited Kubrick's *A Clockwork Orange*: but perhaps it should be remembered that Kubrick's movie is also concerned with the effects and aftermath of violence. Nothing appears to interest Thomas Clay less than this. The combination of high art-house ambition, uncertain acting and brutal violence left me with a nasty taste in the mouth."

Comparisons to *A Clockwork Orange* were apt in terms of controversy but unfounded in terms of content. The controversy and lazy comparison stems from the film's final fifteen minutes, in which a group of youths break into the home of a wealthy couple and brutally attack them, culminating with possibly the most shocking and violent rape ever seen in a movie. This ending prompted mass walkouts at Cannes, critics were shouting abuse at the screen as they departed and rumours abounded that audiences were vomiting and fainting. Meanwhile, the normally unshockable and broadminded *Little White Lies* magazine – sounding more like the *Daily Mail* – railed against the film:

"It's vacant and dull and then, in a gratuitous final jab, Robert's sadistic desires play out to harrowing effect with the raping of a pregnant woman using a swordfish – before being glibly politicised by a hackneyed war montage. Plundering the emotive stockpile that is Iraq, Clay reveals a cunning get-out clause: label anything an indictment of war, and you instantly render anyone who objects a socially complacent prude. But pretension to a political agenda doesn't wash. Quite the opposite – it only leaves a dirty taste."

What surprised most was how critics normally accustomed to seeing such depravity seemed angry at the film, accusing it of being exploitative, sensationalist and giving it negative reviews for disturbing them so much. Was this the film doing its job and fulfilling its purpose in provoking a reaction, or was the uproar a justifiable response to a repugnant piece of filmmaking? Possibly a bit of both.

What makes the scene so surprising and shocking is that everything in the film building up to that moment is handled with real sensitivity, technical and visual brilliance. Earlier in the film, there is a horrific rape that is instigated by Dyer's character. This is no less shocking than the denouement but handled expertly in that none of the attack is actually shown on screen. A group of young men and young woman head to a drug dealer's house to score and sit around getting high while a wannabe DJ mixes records in the corner. A young female is led to a bedroom by Dyer and what proceeds is a horrific gang rape that is made all the more distressing by the sounds of the girl crying as the house music blares out. As the camera sweeps around the room in a circular fashion, the scene is shot in one take making it truly unbearable for the viewer. Reminiscent of the ear-cutting scene in *Reservoir Dogs*, it is made all the more disturbing by depicting the horrendous act just off screen. If anything, it is this that makes the later, graphic rape so unexpected and seemingly gratuitous.

"For me, it was a strange piece of work," Dyer admits. "The director was a fucking oddball, a fucking odd cunt. I had no rapport or relationship with him. He just seemed to be wrapped up in his own little weird world, obsessed with the idea of rape. Ultimately, rape is what the film's about. There's that rape scene that I do and it's weird! He did it in one shot that kept going round and round and round. It took forever to fucking do it. I felt sorry for this young girl. Obviously I wasn't raping her but she was seventeen or something – really young. She was a bit freaked out. There are young kids in the film and I was just thinking, 'Go on, you crack on! This is the start of your journey,' but as a piece of work, it's not really my cup of tea… I mean, fuck me! I'm only in it for five minutes!"

Dyer did not see the finished film before its release but was horrified when he eventually saw it at the Edinburgh Festival. "I couldn't fucking believe my eyes," he says. "I was sickened by it. I'm all for making edgy and hard-hitting films but no one wants to see someone being raped with a fucking swordfish. The films seems to be saying that these kids are living on an Eastbourne estate are so bored they resort to horrendous acts, well, I am from a rough background and I can assure you this is not normal. That kind of sentiment is an insult to all the poverty-stricken kids out there working hard to do well for themselves. Now all films need a happy ending. But ending with a horrific rape, murder, then the kids pissing on the body, leaving and lighting a fag – only for the film to end? It was so horrible and so depressing that I wanted to top myself after watching it."

Dyer admits that the reason he was so horrified by the film's ending was because he didn't read the whole script, just his pages. "I should have read the script," he says. "I just said, 'Okay, I'll do it,' and to be honest, that's entirely my own fault. I only flicked through it and didn't realise what happened at the end. I've not done that since because I've fucking learnt from it. That said, even if I had read it, I would not have expected for it to be shot in such a gruesome and horrifying way. The rape scene I was in was made more disturbing by the fact that you don't see anything but the final scene was much more graphic. You are watching it thinking, 'Why the fuck is he taking the swordfish off the wall?' Then you see it go into her as well. He could have done a shot of the swordfish being taken off and then we could hear a scream, but he wanted to show everything! It's very odd. It was the first time in my career that I'd been part of something I didn't really agree with. I'm not a prude in any way, shape or form, but I just didn't get it. I didn't understand it. But I ended up getting it in the neck from the papers and from my fans as well. It was the first time I'd started to get a bit of bad feedback and I wasn't used to it. I was used to people being nice and respecting me. They'd say, 'He's a good actor, a bit controversial, a bit mouthy and not very media-trained but we love him for that.' All of a sudden, I'm being blamed for people being sick in the cinema and walking out at the Edinburgh Festival. Fucking hell!"

This issue stemmed from many of his fans complaining to him personally and online that they had watched the film because he was in it and been horrified by what they saw. And this is a fair point. The marketing people at the film company chose to splash Dyer's face all over the poster and DVD sleeve despite him only playing a very small – if memorable – part. It was made to look like 'A Danny Dyer Film'.

"This was the first time I had started to experience this whole thing of what sort of clout I had in the business – I hadn't realised. You just don't think that way – you don't think that putting your face on the cover will sell a certain amount of units. I was only in it five minutes. I mean, my name comes up first – I've got the top billing! It's ridiculous because I didn't deserve that. Four days on a film set does not warrant that. I feel sorry for the other actors who put weeks of their lives into it."

Phillip French of *The Observer* also pointed out that the acting by the youths (including Dyer) far surpassed that of the (far more experienced) veteran adult actors. This perhaps stems from the naturalistic approach that director Thomas Clay appropriated. Often, more experienced actors struggle with this approach. Dyer is great as the convict, drug-dealing gang rapist who leads Robert astray. Chewing up every scene he is in, his character is truly repulsive but Dyer brings enough charm to it to convey how it is these kids are led by this Pied Piper of illegality.

Ultimately, this is a truly divisive film. Undeniably affecting, often unwatchable, but never forgettable, it has been debated at length whether this is a work of art or the worst type of video nasty. We would say find out for yourself, but only do so if you have an incredibly strong stomach and don't mind not sleeping for weeks afterwards. Dyer himself is no prude but stated firmly that after watching the film for the first time: "I felt like jumping under a bus when I left the cinema." But as Phillip French asserted, it is unquestionably, "A highly sophisticated and, many might think, sophistic film, and is technically extraordinarily polished."

# THE BUSINESS (2005)

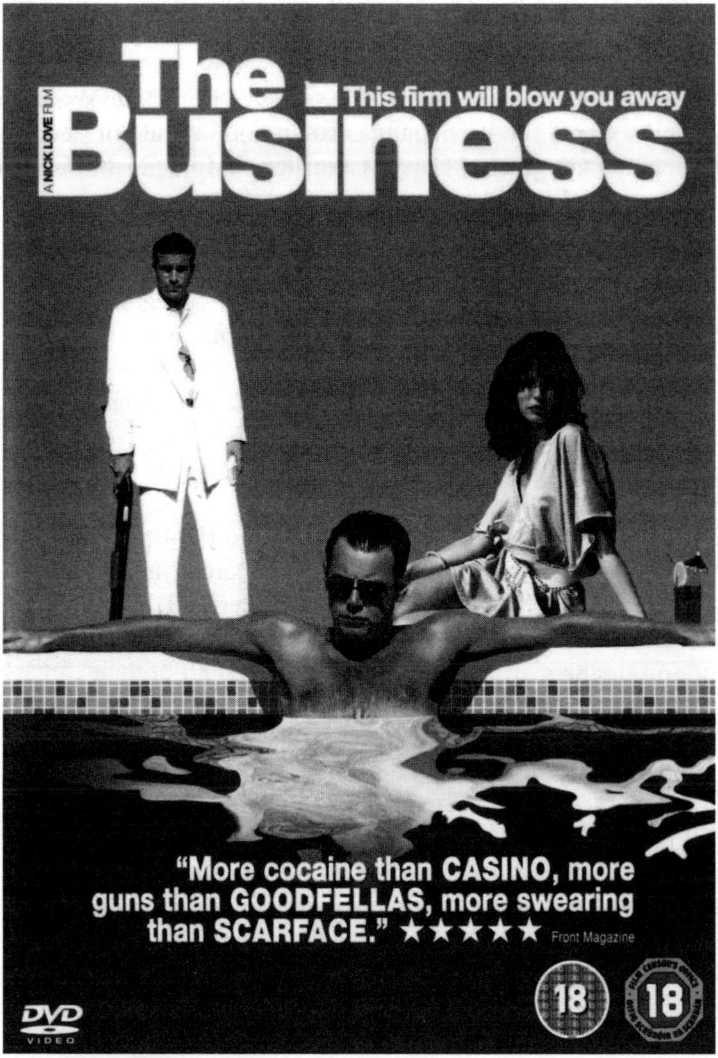


**"I think that what Nick did was to celebrate every gangster film he's ever fucking seen!"**

**Director** Nick Love **Producers** Allan Niblo, James Richardson **Writer** Nick Love **Production Designer** Paul Burns **Costume Designer** Andrew Cox **Director of Photography** Damian Bromley

**Danny Dyer** Frankie **Tamer Hassan** Charlie **Eddie Webber** Ronnie **Geoff Bell** Sammy **Roland Manookian** Sonny **Georgina Chapman** Carly **Camille Coduri** Nora **Tracy Kirby** Laura **Linda Henry** Shirley **Andy Linden** Joe

*After some trouble in London, naive lad Frankie (Danny Dyer) finds himself in Malaga – where smooth playboy gangster Charlie (Tamer Hassan) takes him under his wing. Charlie's psychotic partner Sammy(Geoff Bell) takes an instant dislike to Frankie, however, and when Sammy's girlfriend Carly (Georgina Chapman) takes a shine to Frankie it is only a matter of time before Sammy tries to set him up for a fatal fall.*

There are some films that are made by the right people at the right time and end up as collective career highs for all concerned. For Nick Love, Tamer Hassan and Danny Dyer, *The Business* is just such a film. If *The Football Factory* put the trio on the map, *The Business* catapulted all of their careers to the next level. For Nick Love, a card-carrying football fan with a Millwall tattoo on the inside of his lip, *The Business* was an opportunity to show a more vibrant side to his talent – and he wasted little time, as he explained to *Film4*: "I wrote it in a flat in Marbella. I was doing post-production on *The Football Factory* and I banged it out in six weeks. When *The Football Factory* was finished, I went straight into pre-production in Spain. I was totally knackered. I know I was a bit grouchy on set now and again. But no, I didn't do that much research apart from speaking to some people I know. It came much more from my subconscious. For example, I didn't find out exactly how they smuggled all the stuff but I knew from the folklore about the kind of things they did. So I wrote all the stuff about needing a full moon and waiting for the patrol boats to be far enough apart, knowing it was approximately what happened."

In an interview with *The Guardian* he offered a rare insight into his background, which explained the conflict in some of his films: "I'm a middle-class boy and I grew up in a working-class area. I think I had more to prove to everybody, so I always went that extra mile – more drugs, more violence. I think there is a lot of stuff rattling around there with my class issues. My mum is incredibly left wing and my dad was quite right wing – no surprise they didn't stay together – and so I had two very conflicting political opinions as a child, neither of which I was interested in taking any notice of, being a sort of little reprobate."

The little reprobate's masterful screenplay was drawn from his current life rather than his past, however, as Dyer explains: "This was another chance to work with Nick Love. Because Tamer Hassan and I had bonded so much on *The Football Factory*, he'd watched our relationship and he'd literally written a film around it: Tamer as Tamer and me as me. It was written for us. I was the young kid – a bit naive, maybe, with someone taking me under his wing. I think that what Nick did was to celebrate every gangster film he's ever fucking seen!

That's what it is: a culmination of all the movies he's ever loved. It was an original idea, but the setting, music and look just *worked.* When I read the script, it was such a beautiful moment. I thought, 'Fucking hell! I cannot wait!' I wanted to shoot it… tomorrow!"

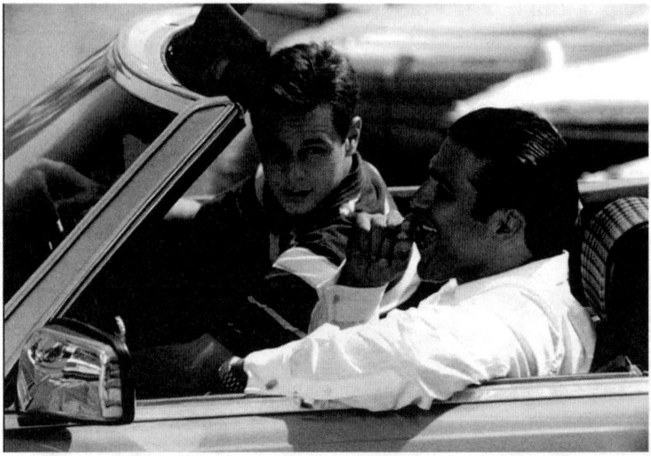

While promoting his film *The Sweeney*, Love explained to scriptlab.com why he liked working with a certain group of actors: "I think that you just ultimately work with people that you're comfortable with and that have a good way of interpreting what you say. Danny had a very good way of verbalising what I articulate on paper. Paul Anderson is another up-and-coming actor. I think they're all looking to make it easier as a job. If you know how to work with them, it makes the process easier. The motion of going into battle where you know their strengths and their weaknesses… you can then make a script tailored just for them."

Talking to cinema.com at the time of the film's release, Dyer explained: "We've got our own little clique of people, our little firm. That's the genius of Nick. I like to look at it like a *Carry On* vibe, he has a certain group of actors and he swaps the roles around. The great thing for me is that he's kept me as his leading man, he likes me to tell his story, you know. It just rolls off my tongue – he always says it's his brain and my mouth, and it's a great partnership. I look at him as my partner in crime, there's no two ways about that. He's the greatest director I've worked with."

Love was similarly gushing about Dyer when the movie was released, telling *Film4*: "We've got a shorthand now, we hardly did any prep. He came down to Spain a week before the shoot; we talked a bit about the character. We swam. There was technical stuff I took him through, but that was it. He knows I love him. Most of his stuff was done in just one or two takes."

Initially Love had planned to reunite all three leading men from *The Football Factory*, but as Dyer explains, Frank Harper proved an awkward fit with the material: "They originally wanted Frank Harper to play Sammy but Nick (being Nick) said, 'Listen, you've got to lose weight. In the opening scene, you've got to swim out to a fucking yacht. You look like a beached fucking whale!' Frank took that the wrong way... Nick said, 'I can't put you in a pair of Speedos, it'd be stupid.' and Frank said, 'Alright, I'll do it.' So they met again a couple of months later but Frank had put *on* weight! So Nick fucked him off and went to Jamie Foreman. Foreman was cast in Polanski's *Oliver Twist*, so he fucked us off. So we went with Geoff Bell, which was the fucking right choice. I remembered Geoff from the *Mean Machine*. I believe in fate and Geoff brought another dimension to the film." Bell was an inspired choice – and his sly, calculating playing of Sammy comes close to stealing the film.

With his three leads in place, Love faced a harder challenge – finding a sex bomb who could act to play sultry temptress Carly. Dyer enjoyed reading in at the castings but was ultimately surprised by the final choice: "I had to be at the castings for the role of Carly. This was one of my first moments of sitting in my 'throne'. People knew who I was now – *The Football Factory* was out and had been successful and now people were very interested in being in a film with Nick and myself. So we sat there and we saw fucking everybody.

Georgina Chapman was the second one in, which is why she got the part later on. I preferred Toby Stephens' wife – she was great. Georgina looks great but she just couldn't do it. I remember she was so nervous that she had a twitch in her eye, which I found really distracting. Nick and I discussed it and we never really mentioned Georgina either. Ultimately it was his decision. The scene was quite heavy and was later cut from the film but it was great for me to sit there all day with these fucking sexy birds. The line to me was, 'You know everyone wants to fuck you, don't you? Everyone wants to know what it's like to have your cock in their mouth!' I was like 'Oh my God!' It was nerve-wracking for her because it was difficult dialogue what with us sitting there, being lads and that."

As the cast headed out to Spain, Dyer quickly discovered how seriously Nick Love was taking the film: "I remember the first day that Geoff and I arrived. Our plane was delayed and we got drunk. We got off the plane and Nick was waiting for us at the airport. He fucking bollocked the pair of us. It was the first day, the first night, and he said, 'Is this how it's going to fucking be, is it? You fucking pair of cunts turn up, off your fucking nut?!' We were like, 'Fuck! We've got a week of rehearsal yet. We haven't even started shooting and he's on our case!' That was just his way of saying, 'Right! Don't forget – I'm the fucking boss here!' Tamer had flown out earlier and was laughing behind his back. It was a bit of a kick up the bollocks, which I think we probably needed!"

Filming on location in Spain was a dream job for Dyer, as he told cinema.com: "Where we were staying was very native Spanish, nobody spoke English, so they really didn't take that much notice of us. That was a shock. We were filming up in the mountains and were quite out of the way most of the time, because of the period setting we had to be careful where we shot. Every location had to be dressed. We found a great little port which was identical to Puerto Banus before it got all poncey. It was untouched. And we just got on with the job. We got a bit obsessed with it, me Tamer and Geoff. Every night we'd go back to the hotel and discuss what we'd done and what we were going to do the next day. We were constantly talking about the film for two months. It was great, but you have to get that way."

For Nick Love, it was a gruelling shoot but rewarding nonetheless. He told *Film4*: "It was stressful and, as I said, I was knackered. I tell you where I really loved: La Linea. It's a small fishing village, pretty poor and dusty. This is where the kid ends up when he's lost everything. The crew wanted to get back to the nightclubs and stuff – in fact, they wanted to carry on shooting forever. I loved La Linea though, because it had an air of sadness. I think my films are a lot to do with male sadness."

One surprise during filming was the implication that Georgina Chapman had been cast because she was married to movie mogul Harvey Weinstein. Dyer recalls: "Later on, I learnt that Georgina had got the role because of Harvey (Weinstein), which actually backfired. Harvey was on set for our sex scene – he was obsessed with her. He flew fucking sushi over from France for her! I didn't play the game with him and I didn't suck around his arse... I didn't really like his energy: 'I'm Harvey Weinstein. Don't fuck with me!' The power of the man was impressive but Bellsy and I weren't really that fussed. He thought I was a great actor but I didn't go to one of his dinner parties and he hasn't spoken to me since. That's why James Corden is now working with him and I'm not! They're working together because Corden went out and played the game. He would never turn down an invite to a dinner party but I just couldn't be bothered with it all and obviously Weinstein must have taken that as disrespectful. I didn't lack respect, though; I was just knackered and wanted to get my nut down. Geoff went, but he was caught skinning up in the corner and got thrown out! So he fucked it as well!"

It is hard to believe now that *The Business*, regarded as a modern classic, received a decidedly lukewarm critical response from the British press upon its release. Writing for *Empire* magazine, Kim Newman dismissed the film as nothing new in a blistering two star review: "With its postcard-coloured visions of package-holiday luxury, inside-the-good-old-days-of-the-drug-biz plot arc and soundtrack assortment of backlist hits, *The Business* shamelessly scrambles elements from *Sexy Beast*, *Blow,* and *Layer Cake*. Unfortunately, its nostalgia for a decade most want to forget makes it feel horribly like desperate

'Eighties Brit efforts like *Buster, Dealers* or (at best) *The Hit*." *Time Out*'s 'DC' was similarly dismissive: "It's a classic – hackneyed? – tale of a gangster's speedy rise followed by his even speedier, coke-fuelled downfall. But *Goodfellas* it ain't – more like a Day-Glo, budget version of De Palma's *Scarface*. Love papers over a by-numbers plot and cartoon acting with ample voiceover, back-to-back 'Eighties music and yards of casual clobber (Fila, Sergio Tacchini)."

Released across 279 screens, the film took a healthy £1.5 million at the UK box office, ensuring a monster first week on DVD, in which it shifted over 75,000 units. *The Football Factory* crowd had no interest in the critic's opinions and strong word of mouth about the film has ensured that its reputation has only grown. To date, it has sold over 816,000 units on DVD in the UK.

In America, the film fared less well, as Dyer recalls: "Harvey bought the film and then he canned it. He put it on a shelf and it was never released in America. I don't know why but it might have something to do with Georgina – perhaps he didn't want people to see his bird being slutty. It was a shame, because it was quite a sexy movie and I think it would have had a shot at success in the US."

For years, a sequel was mooted and Love wrote a script, which would have returned stars Dyer, Manookian and Hassan, but after establishing himself as a leading man in his own vehicle *Dead Man Running*, Hassan was reluctant to reprise his Charlie character in what he saw as a supporting role.

To Danny Dyer, *The Business* remains a film he is justifiably proud of: "The other night, I watched *The Business* for the first time in a couple of years. It's interesting because it brings back waves of memories. I can remember exactly what I was thinking at any time during any scene. Tamer and I had a bit of a fall-out on the scene with the mayor because I had a real cigar and he had a fake one. He wanted to know why he didn't have a Cohiba as well! So I said 'Just take the fucking Cohiba, then!' Then he lost it with me and we had a bit of a fucking argument. We didn't talk for a couple of days, so that whole scene where we're sitting at the table and then we're in the toilets sniffing, I wasn't talking to him. It was weird! I'm so proud of *The Business.* I think it's a sexy film and I'm really happy that I'm in it. I'm so *on it* in that film. Every scene, I just tried to bring it alive in my eyes and it set me up nicely for whatever I was going to go on to next. I was just pent up. I learnt about the whole 'reacting' thing: you have to *listen* to what's going on in the fucking scene and react accordingly, if you need to react at all."

Followed as it was by variable cash-ins such as *Freerunner*, *Dead Man Running* and *City Rats*, *The Business* perhaps feels fresher today than it did upon release. Nick Love never misses a trick and expertly teases out fantastic performances from Dyer, Hassan, Bell and the supporting cast. The locations, costume design and thumping eighties soundtrack all contribute to a classic lads' movie that never puts a foot wrong, one which all concerned can gladly call a career high point.

# SEVERANCE (2006)

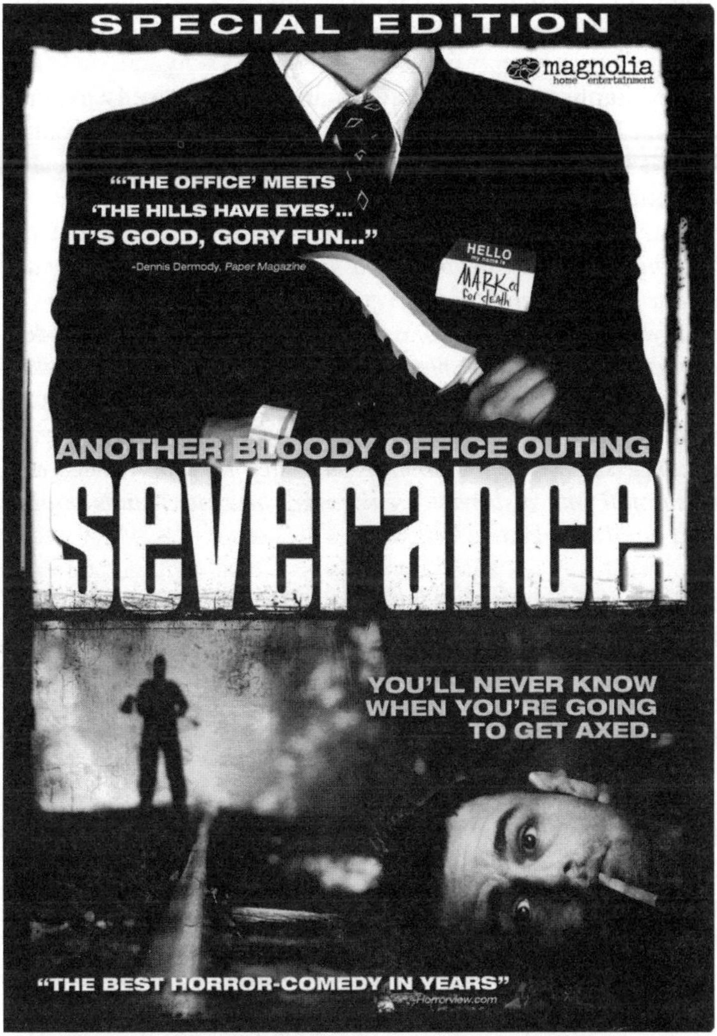


**"I needed to become the action hero but blend it with the comedy. To combine the two was a beautiful fucking thing for me."**

**Director** Christopher Smith **Producer** Jason Newmark **Writer** James Moran, Christopher Smith **Costume Designer** Stephen Noble **Production Designer** John Frankish **Music** Christian Henson **Cinematography** Ed Wild

**Toby Stephens** Harris **Claudie Blakley** Jill **Andy Nyman** Gordon **Babou Ceesay** Billy **Tim McInnerny** Richard **Laura Harris** Maggie **Danny Dyer** Steve **David Gilliam** George **Juli Drajko** Olga **Judit Viktor** Nadia

*A group of employees for a well-known arms-dealing company embark on a team-building retreat in the Matra Mountains of Hungary. In the middle of a deserted forest, the road heading towards their resort is blocked by a fallen tree, leaving only a dirt track to travel on. When the bus driver refuses to take his vehicle off road, the group decide to walk the relatively short distance remaining. As soon as they step off the beaten track, things fall into disarray: they quickly become victims, hunted by a band of unknown killers.*

In short, this is Dyer at his best. The comeback he needed. Danny not only nailing a performance in a part uncharacteristic of him, but also in a genre unexpected of him. Even his fiercest critics could not deny their enjoyment of this exceptional horror comedy.

British director and screenwriter Christopher Smith had impressed critics and audiences with *Creep* in 2004. A tense, low-budget horror set in the claustrophobic confines of the London Underground, it was atmospheric filmmaking at its finest. So two years later, the release of *Severance* was eagerly awaited by genre fans. It did not disappoint, even those who were apprehensive about the presence of Dyer in the cast, which included the producers of the film.

"The script blew me away, but originally, they wouldn't offer me the part because they didn't believe I could be funny," Dyer admits. "Chris Smith fought and fought for me. He loved me, but the producers were like, 'Nah – he's in *The Football Factory*. He's aggressive – he's not going to be able to be funny." I was up against Ralf Little who was hot because of *The Royle Family* and he was known for being funny. I had four auditions and I made myself go back to basics because I really wanted the part. It made me really fucking try to get rid of that little bit of complacency that had set in with a few films – fucking off to Lisbon because I wanted to go and watch the football and what have you! I'd got a bit lazy – but that can easily happen. You're getting offered parts left, right and centre and you think it's never going to end."

Dyer knew this film could be a real game-changer for him.

"I'll be honest, I needed *Severance*. And it put everything back in perspective because I earned it. Properly fought for it and earned it with hard work. However, I always knew the producers were not happy. I did the pie scene for the audition and my speech about the 'sex lodge'. I smashed it! I absolutely smashed it, so they had to give me the part because Chris was saying, 'Look – he's funny, he's funny!' But I always knew that they weren't happy. I was under pressure throughout the job, which was what I needed. The part hadn't been a given and I felt like I could be sacked at any point. This made me behave myself – I wasn't drinking and was completely focused. We went out to Hungary and I kept myself to myself. It was a strange cast, a real ensemble of very different people. I was used to the 'lad culture' of *The Football Factory* and *The Business* but these actors all had very different styles. That's why it worked – there are no two similar characters in the film and the director spins the traditional slasher plot on its head.

My character should be killed first – I'm the one on drugs at the start and I'm the one seeing shit in the fucking woods. Toby Stephens should be the fucking knight in shining armour, the last survivor. But it doesn't quite play out like that. It does the unexpected. That's what I loved about it."

Dyer has been the first to admit that he has partied on film sets, sometimes allowing himself to feel somewhat worse for wear when on the job. But this time it was not an option. "It was the first time I was asked to go to the gym and get fit," he says. "Chris wanted me to have a bit of muscle because I had these fucking fighting sequences. So I needed to become the action hero but blend it with the comedy. To combine the two was a beautiful fucking thing for me, as I'd never really had the opportunity to do that. And it was a lavish fucking production. Decent budget. For example, we had fucking swordfish for lunch."

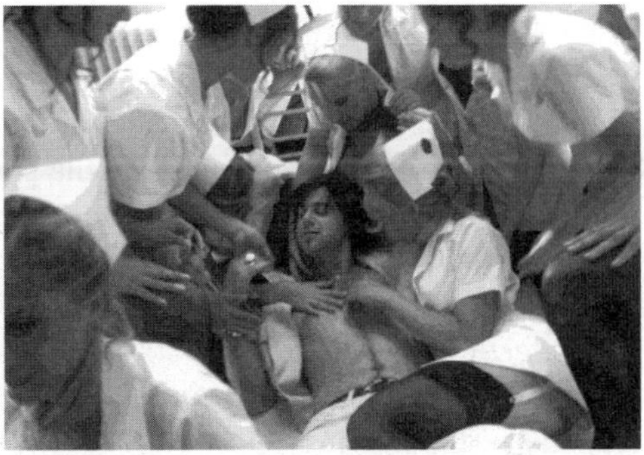

Christopher Smith's reputation in the film industry is an impressive one and Dyer holds him in high esteem. "We needed a good leader of the pack and Chris Smith was a fucking genius," he says. "Such a lovely man as well as great with actors. He would do these weird things with me – he'd tell me to play a scene one way and then he'd tell me to play it completely differently in the next take. So he'd say, 'Do this take with a smile,' and then, 'Now do it really angrily.' I'd start to get fucked off with him and wondered what he wanted from me. Then he'd say, 'Now I want you to combine the two.' He was probably the best at tweaking me. Nick Love gave me stillness and opportunities, whereas Chris really fucking twigged me. I really felt that I was being directed. I know that maybe some directors see me as intimidating but I'm not at all. I just need clarity and I need to be told straight. I don't need to be pussyfooted around. Chris really fucking pressed my buttons and he got a fucking performance out of me that I couldn't have done without him."

It paid off. A cult success in the UK (375,746 DVD sales to date) and a critical triumph Stateside. Peter Travers (the renowned *Rolling Stone* film critic), like many critics, referenced *The Office* in his review and raved that: "The jolts are juicy and so are the jokes as the office leader (Tim McInnerny) watches his team get picked off in increasingly hairy ways. Director and co-writer Christopher Smith, mischievously blending *The Office* with *Friday the 13th*, keeps things fierce and funny enough to give Steve Carell ideas."

High praise indeed. Industry bible *Variety* agreed and singled out Dyer for compliments. Writing for the magazine, Derek Elley stated: "As the violence mounts, the film's comic shock value comes as much from the way in which no cast member is spared as from what's actually shown onscreen. In that respect, *Severance* is a long way from formula slasher fare. One gag in particular, involving the gung-ho George and a rocket launcher, is a guaranteed roof-raiser for its sheer audaciousness and political cheekiness. Dyer (*Human Traffic*, *The Great Ecstasy Of Robert Carmichael*) and Harris slowly dominate the goings-on, but it's the increasingly outrageous action that becomes the real star of the movie."

Stephen Rea at the *Philadelphia Inquirer* did not like the gore too much but did find Dyer amusing. "*Severance*, for all its deft moves and jokey references, occasionally goes so far into *Saw* and *Hostel* viscera that a bad taste starts forming in the mouth," said Rea. "But then Smith comes back with a killer sight-gag involving an anecdote about death by guillotine, and you can't help but smile. (Even the decapitee can't help but smile.) Other employees of Palisades Defence that *Severance* runs through its gore gauntlet include a randy stoner (the funny Danny Dyer), a yuppie type (Toby Stephens), a sensible office manager (Babou Ceesay) and a ditsy secretary (Claudie Blakley). Why they're all being tortured and terrorised by a silent crew of Hungarian loonies isn't explained until *Severance* comes to its tricky, time-twisting end. Suffice to say it's got plenty to do with corporate karma. And the word *severance* is more than just a double play on words – it's a triple whammy."

In 2012 *Total Film* magazine ran a feature on The 50 Greatest Indie Horror Films. On a list that included *Henry: Portrait Of A Serial Killer, Eraserhead, Shaun Of The Dead,* Peter Jackson's *Braindead,* John Carpenter's *Halloween,* Sam

Raimi's *The Evil Dead* and George A Romero's *Night Of The Living Dead*, *Severance* is in good company. And rightly so. Calling it a "high point in Danny Dyer's career", they go on to say that, "*Severance* is a black comedy equipped with a very British sense of humour. A group of co-workers go on a team-building exercise only to get targeted by bloodthirsty killers." Also adding that if they had a bigger budget "they could've paid for Ricky Gervais to make a cameo as the group's hideous boss". Despite the fact that Tim McInnery not only nails that role but is also a far more accomplished and versatile actor and comedian than Ricky Gervais, on the basis that he has played more than one character in his career. An accusation that even his fiercest critics cannot level at Dyer after this career-changing film.

It wasn't all positive during the production, however. "We shot it during the 7/7 bombings and I lost the plot that day," Dyer says. "We were in Hungary and news was coming through that there were bombs going off in London. I've got a kid and a missus so I just downed tools. All the phones were down and I couldn't get hold of anybody. Everyone else was saying, 'Look – we've just got to shoot it,' and I was like, 'Fuck that! I need to know if my fucking kid's alive!' For some reason, I seemed to be the only one concerned. We were actually filming the ending – it was the railway part, where I turn up with the two girls and a machine gun. I had a lot of prosthetics and couldn't see out of one eye. I was a bit ratty, had the teat of a dummy up my nose and was wearing false teeth. It probably added to my performance, actually. When I finally got hold of my missus, she told me that they were fine. It was a beautiful piece of film that we shot that day, but the genuine horrors of that day really freaked me out."

Creatively this was a home run for Dyer. A horror comedy that was both scary and laugh-out-loud funny. A balance many have attempted but very few have achieved.

# THE OTHER HALF (2006)

**"They weren't offering much money but they were telling me I'd be able to watch all the England games. So I went out there for completely selfish reasons!"**

**Director** Marlowe Fawcett, Richard Nockles **Producer** Marlowe Fawcett, Ali Goldstone, Richard Nockles, Tiffany Whittome **Writer** Marlowe Fawcett, Richard Nockles **Music** Jim Hunt, Adrian Meehan, Tam Nightingale **Cinematography** John Behrens

**Danny Dyer** Mark Lamanuzzi **Gillian Kearney** Holly Lamanuzzi **Jonathan Broke** John Smith-Jones **Mark Lynch** Alan O'Luan **Vinnie Jones** The Boss **George Calil** Alex **Katie Corner** Suzie **Tracy Miller** Jack Schaeffer **Kristin Lindquist** Christy Schaeffer

*Mark and his bride Holly go on a romantic honeymoon to Portugal. They arrive to discover that a major football tournament involving the English team is playing. Holly suspects that Mark arranged the honeymoon just so that he could watch the football. Mark's odd behaviour, their whirlwind romance and complications involving Holly's father's vast wealth all begin to add up to a terrible conclusion.*

Yet another Danny Dyer film that harmed his reputation due to a ruthless marketing department. The DVD artwork depicted Dyer and Vinnie Jones looking tough (see page 116) and used the black, red and white colouring that was by this point ingrained on his fan base's subconscious. The cover implies football hooliganism and criminality. The film is not that. So what is it? Essentially, it is a romantic comedy.

The presence of Vinnie Jones as Dyer's conscience was simply a last-minute add-on shot for commercial reasons and was never part of the original script.

"Vinnie was pulled in later to play my conscience," says Dyer. "He did it as a favour to me but as soon as he'd completed his shot, he fucked off. So when it came for the cameras to be on me for my angles he wasn't there."

This perhaps explains Dyer's performance. He is barely convincing as the newly married football fan who miraculously finds himself travelling to Portugal for his honeymoon where England are playing. He has tickets for all their games, unbeknownst to his bride, and it was his plan all along. We learn this through the clunkiest exposition imaginable as Dyer's character talks to himself in the airport mirror in between miming headers during the opening credits. His bride is played by Gillian from *Shameless*, who does her best with what she's got. Dyer's reason for accepting the part was not dissimilar to his character's behaviour.

"I met the directors and I liked what they were about," Dyer says. "The script was unfinished and the idea was that we would fly out to Lisbon, where the European Championships were being held, and then the script would be developed according to England's progress in the football. My character was using his honeymoon as a front for the chance to attend England matches and I was doing the film for similar reasons. I'd started to lose the plot a little bit – it wasn't the best script in the world and it wasn't even finished! They weren't offering much money *but* they were telling me I'd be able to watch all the England games. So I went out there for completely selfish reasons!"

The plot is slight, more of a subplot in a bigger movie, so it's padded out with the aforementioned bizarre dream sequences featuring Jones, as well as animation, montages of cheering fans, and a pair of commentators who follow the leads around providing a supposedly comedic overview of the events unfolding. Sporadically fun, but overall it misses the mark. But that isn't what prevented it from being a success.

Shot against the backdrop of the 2004 European Championships, the aim of the film was for it to be a celebration of England's victory and a movie to be enjoyed by men and women alike. Broken up into each qualifying game and Dyer's attempts to get to the games without his wife clocking he was planning to go all along. There are many fan-pleasing shots of genuine crowds, clearly filmed separately, even when the protagonists are supposed to be in the shot. The film could have done good business were the country in a jingoistic mood. After all, in times of national pride we're willing to overlook any amount of awfulness. Take William and Kate dolls. Not to mention *Three Lions* staying at number one in the charts for three weeks. However, when England put in such a pitiful performance and were knocked out of the tournament early doors, no one wanted to be reminded of what had occurred.

"I went to every England game, but we got knocked out in the quarter-finals and the script had to be changed. Ideally, we wanted England to get to the final and win, so that they could make up, go to the final together, she loves it and we could film them celebrating together in the middle of the pitch surrounded by England fans. How stupid were we? We should have known an England win was never going to fucking happen!"

Dyer remembers vividly the game that England got knocked out. "We had the England-France game, what a beautiful thing. What a big, massive game against the mighty French – the guvnors, the European champions. I was sitting right in the corner where Frank Lampard scored and he ran over. I was thinking this is just the best job ever. And then soppy bollocks David James threw the game away for us. After half time when they changed ends, I was then right beside our goal when that mug let two goals in. It was absolutely devastating."

The low budget is unfortunately visible throughout, despite some nice camerawork and the lush location of Lisbon. Dyer recalls: "It was an extremely low budget – it was proper guerrilla filming! There were no call sheets, every day we got up and asked what was going on, we were just winging it. But that meant we never knew what was going to happen. All the press were saying the England fans were going to kick off and there we are filming right in the middle of them all. Who knows what's gonna happen. Are we going to get battered and have all our kit taken from us? I can't stand up and kick off for everyone. We've got no security, no permits. If it had kicked off. We were going into Rossio square which is where the hooligans would meet and it was terrifying, this wasn't a documentary, we are doing a film with dialogue. A proper movie. It's amazing that we pulled that off. It was so unpredictable. We really pushed our luck, but Richard (the director) milked it for all it was worth and shot the fuck out of it and he pulled it off. The next game was Switzerland and we had to leave Lisbon and go to Coimbra which was a mission because no one knew where they were going. And I'm depressed because we've lost to France. It's the end of England's journey and the end of the film! But I couldn't give a fuck about the film; all I wanted was for England to win the fucking match. And the kid Rooney really came to life. That was the point I really fell in love with him. We shamed them three nil. So by then we've been all over the country and England are still in the tournament. The next game which everything is riding on was Croatia. Which we have to win – and if we don't we are out of the tournament. Richard had just one ticket and gave it to me which kept me sweet. What a great match, the best I've ever seen England play. And Rooney was amazing again. So we won. And the film can carry on. Then it's the quarter-finals and of all the teams we get Portugal. We are there in their manor. Lots of the film crew were Portuguese and my character is wearing an England shirt the whole time. I started to feel like I was getting an odd vibe and dirty looks. By this point I really wanted to win, both for us and for the film. It was a major fucking game. If we had won this game we could have gone on to win the whole tournament. I mean look who won. Fucking Greece. But obviously we all know what happened. Sol Campbell's goal wasn't allowed. David James fucked up again. Portugal won. And the Portuguese were so happy. They are wonderful people, but that night I fucking despised them. Me and Richard went and got hammered and were proud that we got the film done with no money, no help. We went there and we did it. A rare achievement."

Dyer, as ever, is honest about his reasons for accepting the part. "I did it for all the wrong reasons as I had become tempted to take advantage of my fame," he admits. "I knew I was doing the filmmakers a massive favour but we were cutting every corner in the book. We never had any locations and we just had to film until the police threw us off. It was a bit of a fucking nightmare and my heart was never really in it."

Fans' comments on IMDB.com demonstrate that this was apparent to everyone who saw it.

Neil268 said: "With Danny Dyer and Vinnie Jones in this movie I assumed it would be decent. how wrong I was! This could be THE WORST movie I've ever seen in my life. the storyline is awful, the acting is terrible and just the whole movie sucked!"

DVDMANU said: "I have had this DVD in my collection for a while now and was really looking forward to watching it. How could it miss, you've got Danny Dyer (who I think is a very underrated actor), the England football team playing in Euro 2004, and a half-descent story line involving Danny Dyer's character trying to see the first three England group games (on their honeymoon) without his other half finding out he already had the tickets before they left. How about: I am thinking this could be Is Harry On The Boat?-meets-Football Factory, a cocky lads' film, a real Brit classic. How wrong I was. I was gutted, a real let down."

These were real Dyer fans feeling stitched up by the film's DVD sleeve – and there were many, with it shifting 183,348 copies to date. *The Other Half* was a nice idea, poorly executed and grossly mis-sold. An own goal for Dyer.

# OUTLAW (2007)

**"Nick made changes and fucked around with Outlaw so much at the editing stage that ultimately, I don't think the final product was the film that he had wanted to make."**

**Director** Nick Love **Producer** Christopher Bates **Writer** Nick Love **Production Designer** Marcus Wookey **Costume Designer** Andrew Cox **Music** David Julyan **Cinematography** Sam McCurdy

**Sean Bean** Danny Bryant **Danny Dyer** Gene Dekker **Lennie James** Cedric Munroe **Sean Harris** Simon Hillier **Rupert Friend** Sandy Mardell **Bob Hoskins** Walter Lewis **Sally Bretton** Kelly **Joe Jackson** Subaru Kid 1 **Igor Breakenback** Subaru Kid 2 **James Farbell** Subaru Kid 3 **Emily Maitlis** Herself

*Five interweaving stories of ordinary folk who become victims of crime and take the law into their own hands, doling out their own vicious form of justice*

Fans of Love and Dyer's first three films thought they knew what to expect here. It's Nick Love giving the gloss and thrills he gave to hooliganism and the Costa del Crime to vigilantes. The reality was very different, however. Love had different ideas and felt like he had something to prove to critics. Big mistake. In the process, he garnered the worst reviews of his career, and alienated all the fans who made him such a success in the first place.

Olly Richards of *Empire* magazine hit the nail on the head with his one-star review: "Nick Love has always had a love of geezers, but they've previously had a few redeeming features to counter their thuggishness. In this appallingly simple-minded film, however, Love portrays violent vigilantism as heroism, as a group of men who feel let down by the authorities take the law into their own hands. It's a volatile set-up with interesting questions to answer, but quickly descends into a sickening sludge of childish politics, brutality and creative swearing. To have such a bold statement hit home, Love needed to ensure all the details were impeccable, but frequent clunkers in the script and a fanciful take on the realities of the media make a pathetic, boorish rant."

Dyer now acknowledges that it didn't work but at the time was somewhat blinded by ego and opportunity. "I remember seeing the poster and buzzing off that – me, Sean Bean and Bob Hoskins," he says. "I was always excited when Nick put a script in front of me but when I was told that Bob Hoskins and Sean Bean were in it, I was like, 'Fucking hell! Wow!' When I asked who else was, he said, 'Listen – I'm getting rid of all our mob apart from you.' He upset a few people by doing this, but he doesn't owe anyone a career. Later on, of course, he did the same thing to me.

"He was used to working with the same people and in the same 'laddy' thing. All of a sudden he's got 'proper' actors and it brought out a different side to him. I think he overindulged as a filmmaker and I think he tried to make the same statement with the shooting as he did with the cast. I could see what he was trying to do, but it just didn't work. I think he should've been braver, as he had been previously. We were meant to be vigilantes and in the original script, we were supposed to go on a real rampage. Instead, he just focused on one gangster and it ended up being all about one guy. That guy was actually a grip on set – he wasn't a fucking actor! He used to pull the dolly along and had worked on *The Business* and *The Football Factory*. We based the whole thing on his being the ultimate, scariest character. He certainly looked the part – a bit like a little bulldog – but it all got out of control."

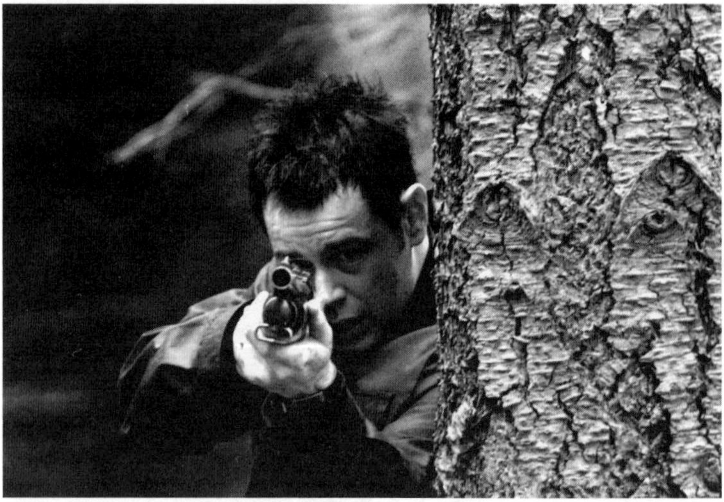

Pandering to one's perception of what critics want can only end in disaster and also suggests some overwhelming insecurity. "Even though our films had been very successful at this point, Nick was being mocked for apparently only being able to do one thing," admits Dyer. "He always said, 'Fuck the critics!' but I know it really hurt him… as it did me. You can't help it. It's really hard to just *wear* it because you find yourself asking, 'Who are these cunts? We're just earning a fucking pound note and doing what were doing and they're sitting there, the snivelling little cunts, absolutely assassinating us!' I think it got to him more and that's why he wanted to try something completely different. He wanted to try to do an American type movie, shot like *Heat* or something. The grading and the colour were a bit weird and it just didn't work."

As well as being visually odd, the casting was also a bit off. "Originally I was going to play the Sean Harris role," says Dyer. "Nick wanted me to play the nutty little fucking nail bomber, a Stuart Copeland type – a weird cunt. Then he changed his mind at the last minute, which I was a bit gutted about. I had no choice in the matter, though. I was very willing to go down that original route and I was going to have a different look – maybe just a moustache… I wanted to try something completely different and then he said, 'Look Dan, I can't find anyone to play the lead. You know you are the everyman to me. I've found this other actor, Sean who's going to be brilliant…' He trusted me to do that again. As much as I was proud and privileged to be in the film, I was a bit disappointed because I felt it was time to try to do something different. Although I was the lead, it felt like a nothing part and it didn't test me."

The plot also confused many, which, according to Dyer, was due to editing complications. "Nick made changes and fucked around with *Outlaw* so much at the editing stage that ultimately, I don't think the final product was the film that he had wanted to make," states Dyer. "I think that's probably the first time he had done that. I can't speak for him, but the other movies he made were *his* fucking movies. He made them how he wanted to make them, he cut them together and he added the music that he wanted. Then he fucking put it out there and said, 'If you don't like it, then fucking suck my cock!' This time I think he held back and thought, 'This isn't really the movie I wanted to make and this was supposed to be my big fucking Guy Ritchie moment!' It just didn't work."

The DVD commentary featuring Dyer and Love has now become infamous, thanks to a YouTube clip featuring five minutes and seven seconds of the most outlandish moments of their rants. Slamming the critics who refuse to see it is a work of art that will one day be recognised as a state-of-the-nation masterpiece like *Taxi Driver* and swearing ever more inventively, it does make for amusingly blinkered listening. It became such a viral hit that Peter Bradshaw of *The Guardian* was compelled to comment on it, writing: "Reportedly, Peter Cook and Dudley Moore liked to record their encounters after a good lunch, and it could be that Nick Love and Danny Dyer's discussion happened in, ahem, comparable circumstances. If you are squeamish about the C-word, then don't listen to it. The irony about this, for me, comes in two parts. The first is that, beneath the bluster, Love and Dyer have got some points. Clint Eastwood's *Dirty Harry* was indeed described as 'fascist', notably by Pauline Kael, although there is no real evidence that Scorsese's *Taxi Driver* was 'cunted' on first release – on the contrary, despite continuing misgivings about violence, that film was surely widely praised from the very first, getting the Palme d'Or at Cannes. But the difference is that these films are fizzing with life and passion and I've got to repeat my view that Outlaw is crude and dull and just horrible. Irony No 2 is that I liked Nick Love's latest film, The Firm, a reworking of Alan Clarke's classic football-casual TV drama from 1989. So did many of the hated broadsheet snarks that send Love and Dyer into a frenzy. The reason was twofold: the ending of *The Firm* was dramatically controlled and plausible – unlike the ending of *Outlaw,* which spiralled off into violent and crass absurdity. And the second reason was that it had that most welcome of things: a sense of humour, a lightness of touch which recurred, despite the subject matter, throughout the script. It sent me back to Love's likeable 2001 debut *Goodbye Charlie Bright* and reminded me that Nick Love is still a real film-maker. In fact, I wondered if some of the praise unhesitatingly lavished on Shane Meadows over the years might perhaps rightfully belong to Love. Anyway, let's hope the peace process between Nick Love and the critics stays on track."

Dyer would like to correct this much-claimed assertion that they were drunk, not least because Nick Love does not drink or take drugs. "People think I was drunk for the DVD audio commentary, but I wasn't," he says. "I was late and Nick bollocked me for that. I wouldn't have turned up drunk for him – he'd have fucking killed me! It was always weird doing those commentaries, because he and I did have this weird thing going on. We'd just sit there and blag it – talk complete fucking bollocks. I'd talk about me Nan's tits and stuff. It's complete random shit, but it did show how close we were. It's just us talking. You hear some of these commentaries and they're so boring! We'd made a decision to just sit there and show people our relationship as mates. I suppose that's why it hurts now that our relationship has completely broken down."

At the time of writing, Dyer and Love are no longer on speaking terms. "I don't know why it broke down," Dyer states. "Probably because I'm not cool enough! There's no other possible reason. I was gutted about not getting *The Sweeney* but it didn't mean he had to stop calling me. I'm still a friend. I rang him up and congratulated him about *The Firm* and he said, 'Dan; do you know what, mate? That means so much to me.' It was never discussed, though. He had a little attack on me in the press because I'd done *Deadliest Men*, a football hooligan documentary. I was performing in *Kurt And Sid* at the time and someone said, "Have you read *Loaded*?" I bought the fucking magazine, read it and was fucking disgusted with him. They asked why I wasn't in his new film and he said,

'Danny was never going to be in this. He's become too much of a celebrity now.' I thought, 'What the fuck does that mean?' and rang him up. He completely denied it. He came to watch me in the play and brought Paul Anderson with him and little Callum, but it was all a bit fake from then on. It was all a bit weird because he knows me as a human being, yet he clearly did say those things. I thought, 'Why did you say that?'

Dyer is sure that it was his decision to do the *Deadliest Men* and *Real Football Factories* documentaries on Bravo that made Love drop him. "He never really agreed with me going off and doing the hooligan things, but I needed the money," he says . "I was doing *Outlaw* for ten grand. I got fifteen grand for *The Business*. I got fifty or sixty grand for *Severance*, but with Nick they cut every corner. It was all like, 'Thanks mate, thanks for letting me be in your film.' For *Outlaw*, they offered me ten grand and I was like, 'What? That's ridiculous! It's embarrassing!' So they said, 'Well, give him another ten in cash but don't tell the other actors.' I thought, 'Hold on a minute, I don't do it for money, but it's like you're throwing me a bone again… at this stage in my career!' So when I was offered two hundred grand for running round the world in a fucking hooligan documentary, I had to go and do that. I didn't want to do it but I've never *seen* money like that. Nick resented it and asked why I was doing it. I said, 'Money. That's why I'm doing it. Do you think I give a fuck about hooligans? You think I want to run around the fucking world – Brazil, Poland – standing under archways, waiting for balaclava'd fat cunts? No, but I'm getting paid two hundred thousand pounds for six weeks' work and it's bought me a house!'

"I'm uncomfortable with it, of course. I hated every second of it! It's a really controversial subject and it was just a case of blagging it. I was going to meet these fucking nasty cunts and I had to be mates with them while they were talking about chopping earholes off and fucking gutting people. Then I'd have to say, 'Oh really? You raped him? Is that what you did? Yeah? Is that what you do here in Prague? You don't beat them up, you gang rape them?'

"In a way it was a sell-out. I gave away 'me'. Tom Hardy isn't going to do that, Fassbender isn't going to do that. I gave 'me' away and I think I became a bit of a parody in some people's eyes. I watch some of those documentaries and I cringe a bit because I'm talking off the cuff and that doesn't necessarily suit a documentary. As a presenter, my style is far from Vernon Kaye's. People either lap it up and love it or say, 'Fucking get him off my TV!' I'm letting people into who I am and not just through interviews. In a film, it's a script and I'm playing a character. If the audience don't like it, they don't like that character. With the documentaries, it's me – it's called *Danny Dyer's Deadliest Men*; so if you don't like it, it's me you don't like. It's the assassination of me. I'm no longer a blank canvas. Ultimately, I couldn't turn the money down. It wasn't a journalistic thing – I never wanted to be a presenter. People think you're a millionaire if you make a film, but I made fifteen grand from *The Business* and five hundred quid a week for the fucking *Football Factory*.

"In the documentaries, I was talking to guys with no substance. *The Deadliest Men,* for what? I'm not a deadly man at all! It's not what I'm about. I put myself in that bracket and Bravo milked it for all it was fucking worth. Four series! I was the face of Bravo for a while – hardly a cool fucking channel, is it? Nick didn't want to be associated with it. He was saying, 'I want to be a proper filmmaker. How dare you go off and do that? I can't really use you now because you've become 'Danny Dyer'. If I could change things, I probably would.

"As much as I had the fame and credibility of being an actor, I had never been rich. I made low-budget independent movies, I wasn't Tom Cruise. The fact that my films made over eighteen million at the box office makes me wonder where my fucking slice is! Actors like Jude Law and Ewan McGregor are in this bracket of making silly money, but the rest of us are not. If you make independent movies, you'll get a wage and a fucking producer's point of a producer's point later on. I still get three or four hundred quid now and again for *The Football Factory* but that's not going to fucking set me up for life, so I've had to go off and do these other things. I wish I hadn't had to do it, I really do."

# STRAIGHTHEADS (2007)

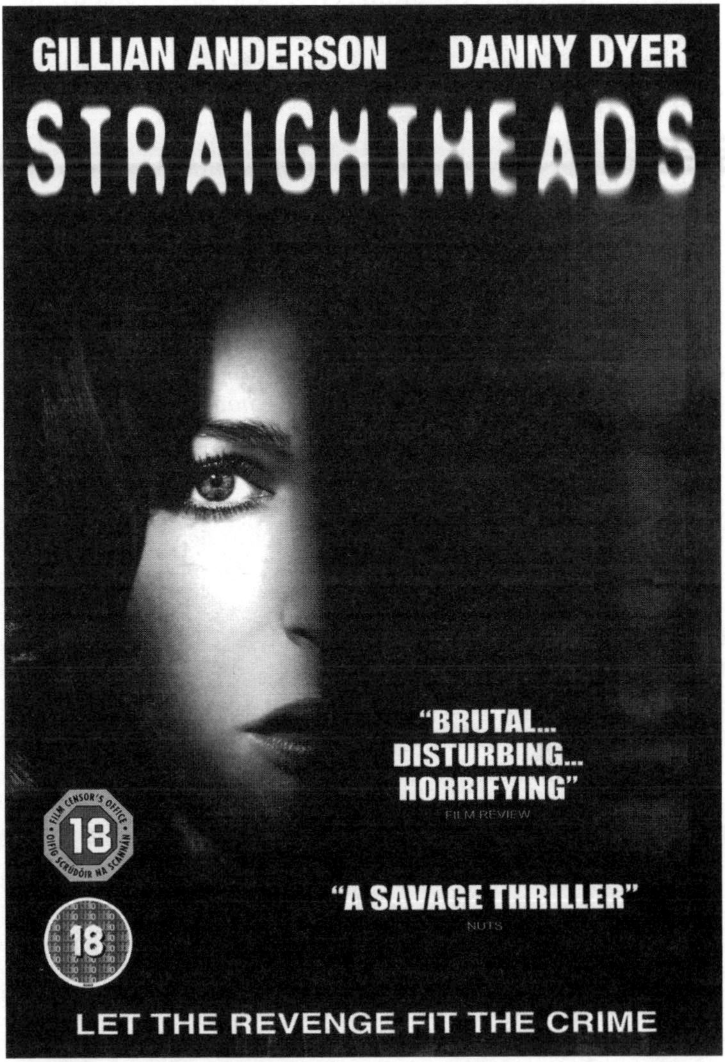


**"It was a beautiful experience as an actor to go two handed with Gillian Anderson, in my eyes a real acting pro."**

**Director** Dan Reed **Assistant Director** Jack Ravenscroft **Second Assistant Director** Harriet Worth **Producer** Damian Jones, Kevin Loader **Co-producer** Alexander O'Neal **Writer** Dan Reed **Production Designer** Simon Bowles Film Four **Costume Designer** Justine Luxton **Music** Ilan Eshkeri **Cinematography** Chris Seager

**Gillian Anderson** Alice **Danny Dyer** Adam **Anthony Calf** Heffer **Steven Robertson** Bill **Ralph Brown** Jamie **Francesca Fowler** Sophie **Adam Rayner** Jago

*When security installation technician Adam (Dyer) meets wealthy high-flying businesswoman Alice (Anderson), he can't quite believe his luck when she invites him to a lavish housewarming party at her boss's house. After having passionate sex in the woods near the house, they are driving home when they hit a deer. A gang of locals – who they earlier had a road-rage incident with – attack them, beating Adam and brutally gang-raping Alice. A month later, a twist of fate brings the pair into contact with their attackers again, and Adam and Alice find themselves dishing out a revenge they could never have predicted.*

Director Dan Reed was a documentary filmmaker for fifteen years prior to *Straightheads*, his big-screen debut. Specialising in documenting warzone conflict, it is perhaps unsurprising that, like Sarah Kane's *Blasted* and Sam Peckinpah's *Straw Dogs,* he chose to address notions of violence and our capacity for it.

For Dyer, there was one very good reason he was chomping at the bit to get this part. "I was a massive fan of Gillian Anderson," he states. "I had to audition, and she was in the auditions because she had already been cast. I remember the scene was an odd one, because it was a scene where I had to touch her tit, it was a scene where I'm crying and she cradles me while I slowly put my hand on her tit. So I did it and she pulled away, but I think I got this instant respect from her. She made the ultimate decision; it was out of me and Ashley Walters, so were they going to go with me or a black guy? So it was very, very different actors. I was very hot at the time, Ashley wasn't – Ashley is hot now obviously, so at that time I think a few actors were resenting me a little bit, thinking I was getting all the work and stuff. I get it because he's a good actor but he got really close. I just thought, 'Fuck it, this is the scene you've put in front of me, it's the beat of the scene, it's quite important," because it's a very sexually driven film and I've always been a fan of hers and I just couldn't wait to show off in front of her and go toe to toe with her. It was a weird one, because I'm quite submissive in this film – she's almost playing the man and I'm playing the little one who keeps moaning and whining about everything – she's the one who's good with the fucking gun. I think maybe it was just a little bit too dark. It was a beautiful experience as an actor to go two-handed with Gillian Anderson, in my eyes a real acting pro. I stood toe to toe with her and I learnt from her, but the whole subject was too dark. The rape thing again comes back to haunt me: it's based around gang rape and then our whole motivation for getting revenge is fuelled by closure, she needed closure. The fact that we raped this guy at the end with a gun in his arse… for me the last image is the most important image you leave in a movie, what people take away from it. It was brave. Quite arty, I thought."

Reed had profound reasons for the strong content of his film, but unfortunately it simply resembles an exploitation film rather than a searing indictment of modern warfare and horrors experienced away from our comfort zones. And as such it was a tough sell for the distributor, Verve Pictures. "I don't know how you would sell it, it's a strange one isn't it?" admits Dyer. "It's like a switchblade romance. The fact that it got funded, the fact that investors saw this script and thought, yeah… I mean nothing changed from the off, it always the same story. It just got darker and darker. I remember *Bizarre* magazine loved it, they gave it five stars. But it was a strange one because I really wanted to celebrate the fact that I was working with one of my heroes, someone that I grew up watching and someone I used to wank over and all of a sudden she's in front of me naked. It was driven by sex, our relationship was driven by this sexual energy that was all wrong. It was all wrong and if we'd have met at another time it would have been perfect because we were just on the verge of falling in love, and then this horrendous thing happens. So then our relationship takes a totally different turn and all that stuff where I can't get it up. It was up by the way."

Monisha Rajesh of *Little White Lies* magazine took the film as Reed had intended and gave it a mostly positive review, stating that: "Anderson adopts a highly commendable British accent in a gutsy performance that adds a little more lustre to the mid-career surge she's been enjoying recently. Dyer's woebegone Cockney is a little predictable, but he redeems himself in the last 20 minutes. It's here that director Dan Reed goes all out to twist the knife, in a convulsive display of cinematic shock and gore that feels very close to personal abuse. *Straightheads* is not to be taken lightly. It's dirty, horrific and upsetting, but it hits you in a way that, sometimes, cinema should."

Regardless of how the film is remembered – and while it got mixed reviews, it did okay commercially, more than recouping its budget – Dyer's pride in the work stems from playing outside his comfort zone and holding his own against one of his favourite actresses. "I just love the fact that I was good enough to stand up with her and have it and not play the laddy alpha-male role," he says. "I was completely the opposite of that. But it fucked my head up, that role; I came out of it quite depressed. Because of the role, I only had one eye in it. Every day I had to put this contact in that made me blind in one eye. It was so fat, it was my whole eye. It took so long to put it in that I'd have to wear it for the whole day because then I didn't have to put it in again. It really got me down and I really got depressed. It's a depressing film, there's no light-hearted moments in it, and my character – he's an especially dark character. So I suppose for the first time I started to experience taking my work home. I'd never done that before, I could always after action and cut be Danny Dyer. It was the first time that I was really fucked in the head. I was literally unapproachable, I was ratty, I was snapping at everybody, I was just a pretty miserable person. It wasn't like method at all, it really affected me. But that's no one involved in the film's fault. That's just me. After all, it was a great job, and it's a good piece of cinema. It's just not for the masses, unfortunately."

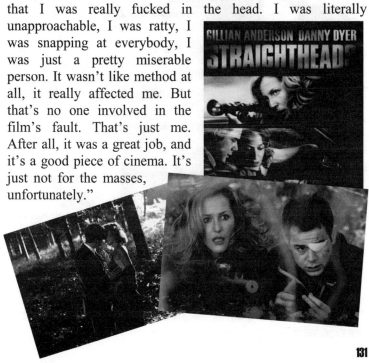

# THE ALL TOGETHER (2007)

"It was doing the cliché gangster thing in a comedy sort of way so it was a nice experience."

**Director** Gavin Claxton **Producer** Marion Pilowsky, Annabel Raftery, **Writer** Gavin Claxton **Music** David Blair-Oliphant, Richard Blair-Oliphant **Cinematography** Orlando Stuart

**Martin Freeman** Chris Ashworth **Corey Johnson** Mr Gaspardi **Velibor Topic** Bob Music **Danny Dyer** Dennis Earle **Richard Harrington** Jerry Davies **Amanda Abbington** Sarah **Jamie Kenna** Keith **Charles Edwards** Marcus Craigie-Halkett **Jonathan Ryland** Barnaby Winbow **David Bamber** Robin Swain **Fenella Fielding** Mrs Cox **Nicholas Hutchinson** Kenny Tinsel **Alexandra Gilbreath** Prue Swain

*After leaving his troublesome roommate Bob in charge of answering the door and letting estate agents into the house for viewings, TV producer Chris returns home to find Bob has followed his instructions a little too literally. He is greeted by four estate agents, two Jehovah's witnesses, and a children's entertainer – as well as two armed and dangerous gangsters... and a dead body.*

As Martin Freeman's Chris says in the opening seconds:

"First thing I'll do when I write this movie is make sure it doesn't start with a voiceover. I hate movies that start with a voiceover. Especially English ones. Some wanker trying to convince you he's worth eight quid and two hours of your life because he's working class and mixed up with gangsters and setting up all the tedious shit that's gonna happen because the idiot that's written it can't do dialogue. Either that or he's some upper-class prick who has just woken up in a panic because he's late for some wedding. TV's not a business, it's barely a career. It's just a way of keeping useless people out of everyone else's way."

Self-referential and witty, the film has more laugh-out-loud moments than most Hollywood comedies. But *Empire* magazine slammed it, calling it: "A vacuous, directionless Brit-com with spurts of self-referential narration which do nothing to distract from the laborious plot," however, it conceded: "A Brit-com that does nothing for the reputation of the industry although there are a few charming performances."

There is a charming performance by Martin Freeman, not unlike his *The Office* character, and well-observed stabs at the TV industry – especially presenters – estate agents, Dyer as an up-and-coming gangster, poo jokes, sick gags, a taxidermist who arranges his dead prey in sexual positions: what's not to like?

Take this exchange:

**Dennis Earle (Danny Dyer):** I'm not a kidnapper. Do I look like a fucking kidnapper to you?

**Marcus Craigie-Halkett (Charles Edwards):** What are you talking about? You are holding us here against our will. We've been kidnapped. Ergo, you are a kidnapper.

**Dennis Earle (Danny Dyer):** Now you listen to me you fucking ponce. If you kidnap someone you don't just 'old them against their will, you take them somewhere against their will. Then you ask for money or whatever. We haven't taken you anywhere. We are not kidnappers. Ergo, you are a cunt.

Sure, it's a bit overlong and sometimes the budget limitations are visible, but it's an honourable effort, slammed as usual by the country it was made in by sycophants in the pockets of the Hollywood studios.

Writer/director Gavin Claxton self-financed the film and shot it in eighteen days with a cast and crew of just 28. It is testament to the script that he managed to attract both Dyer and Martin Freeman to a zero-budget project.

As such, Claxton did not write the character of Dennis with Dyer in mind. "The only role written with an actor in mind was Martin Freeman's character, Chris," he says. "Danny actually auditioned for an entirely different role, that of Jerry, the odious television presenter. When he came in I'd never even heard of him. At that point I hadn't seen *The Football Factory* or *Human Traffic*. But I instantly liked him very much. I suspect I liked him for many of the traits so disliked by many of his critics; he was very confident, down-to-earth and had a swaggering presence. His audition – as Jerry – was very good and we could easily have gone with Danny in that role. Then firstly, I met another actor called Richard Harrington who I really fell in love with for the Jerry role, and secondly I watched some of Danny's other work and it was obvious he was building a very vocal and enthusiastic fan base of people who really wanted to see him in 'hard man' roles."

"I offered him the part of Dennis, the young British comedy gangster, instead and – even though he was disappointed not to get the part of Jerry – he accepted. He was reluctant to play another of what American's call a 'hard-on' character but as I explained, Dennis was written as a *send-up* of all those very familiar young British film gangster types (something most critics failed to grasp) and it was a chance to therefore poke fun at the sort of characters he's always being asked to play, albeit straight versions played for drama rather than for laughs."

Dyer concedes he was wary of playing a gangster. "At this point I'm still trying to do something different. It's so obvious that I would play that role, I didn't want to do the obvious gangster bollocks. But it was doing the cliché gangster thing in a comedy sort of way so it was a nice experience. They sent me the script and offered me the role straight away. Originally I wanted to play the little fucking divvy flat-mate, but he said he'd already found someone who was amazing, who was Velibor Topic, who I've got to say is fucking brilliant, I mean I obviously would have played it very differently. I could see why he wanted me to do it, it's not a bad role it's just a bit obvious and so I thought if that was the way it had to be, then that's the way it had to be."

Claxton was extremely pleased with Dyer's work. "Danny was terrific and I think brought both comedy and menace to the part," he enthuses. "In some scenes he's hilarious and in others he really makes you feel something like sympathy for what is essentially a rather pathetic and unpleasant character."

Dyer's lack of experience in the comedy field did not worry Claxton. "As soon as I met Danny, it was obvious he was a very interesting actor with many more strings to his bow than just petty criminals and football hooligans," he says. "Of course, with his natural swagger, working-class upbringing and Custom House delivery Danny can be so easily cast in those roles. Fine – I liked *The Football Factory* but Danny can play a much wider spectrum of roles than the vast majority of people give him credit for, or directors the opportunity to take on. Good actors, actors who are more usually associated with dramatic roles, can always play comedy. *Always*. Even ones with no obviously sharp personal sense of humour, because as good actors they know how to inhabit a character and, crucially, to trust the script. Take Gene Hackman for instance; there's a superbly gifted leading actor-come-Hollywood superstar who avoided taking 'comic' roles for years because he truly believed he couldn't play comedy. But you only have to watch two minutes of *Get Shorty* to see that is plainly not the case."

How was Danny to work with? "Danny was a good as gold. Mostly! Never late, always knew his lines, open to suggestions and easy to get along with. He was fond of starting the day in make-up by walking round naked from the waist down. Not in a sexually provocative way – in a mischievous 'let's see who I can shock' way. Some people may read that and think 'of course it was sexual' but I assure you it wasn't. In the current climate we're in danger of losing some perspective about what was once called 'high jinks'! It's still okay to laugh heartily and applaud tales of similar antics from Burton, Harris and Reed, but not others apparently."

There's always a story where Danny is concerned though. "One more thing – one day we went to a pub near our location for lunch. It was the first day Danny had meet Richard Harrington, the actor playing Jerry (a hideous TV presenter) and they were bonding, getting on well and inevitably competing with one another. Normally, of course, drink is off the menu during a shooting day but – unbeknownst to me – they had decided (or I suspected Danny had suggested) they have a few shorts. By the time we got back on set both were a bit tipsy. Which sounds rather unprofessional, perhaps but not on Danny's part. Because it was only then that Richard realised that Danny's entire workload for the rest of the day involved lying on the floor playing dead! Richard on the other hand had lines and a key scene to play. Not great for Richard (or me) but a source of endless amusement for Danny as he lay on the floor for the rest of the afternoon, chuckling between takes."

The poster of the film depicted a buddy movie between Martin Freeman and Dyer. This was not the case. It was, put simply, a con job. "Well contrary to what the film poster would have the audience believe, Martin and Danny share no screen time together whatsoever. Danny's character is shot dead before Martin's arrives home. Again – actors, directors, producers are often at the mercy of distributors and in the case of bigger budget films, the 'studios'. When Lionsgate (or rather Redbus as was) bought the film for UK distribution at Cannes in 2005 they purchased a very low-budget British comedy starring two actors whose profiles were rapidly growing. The trouble for them was that Martin (Freeman) and Danny never once appear on screen together. But they didn't want that. But we'd shot the film, so what could they do? At one meeting they said to me… 'Does Danny's character have to die?' 'Er', I said, '… not if you're going to give me a wad of cash to rewrite the screenplay and then go and re-shoot the second half of the movie, no.' But they were less keen on that idea. So they released it as it was… with the two actors they wanted to see play opposite each other not sharing a scene. That didn't stop them trying to heavily suggest they did by putting just Martin and Danny together on the poster, hinting that the entire story revolved around their character's (non-existent) rivalry. But when they did meet, they got on well. Both Martin and Danny are excellent actors and good men; they were never going to be bezzies but they shared a mutual respect so got on just fine."

For Dyer, Freeman was the whole reason he wanted to do the film. "The appeal was, for me, Martin Freeman, all day long. I liked the idea of the film, but it was like a play. I don't think it should be a movie. I thought it would make a better play because it's set in one room – it's set in a kitchen – but being a massive fan of *The Office* and Martin Freeman I thought, 'Fuck, I've got to do this.' Again, it was something very different, I had just done the Gillian Anderson thing and now I'm to go toe to toe with Martin Freeman, and Martin really wanted to work with me as well. Again, it was a buzz because he knew who I was, and I was a fan of his and he was a fan of mine, a bit of a lovey up."

Dyer is frank on why the film wasn't a huge success, with just £7,553 at the UK box office on eight screens and a mere 31,882 DVD sales to date. "I just don't think it was a film, like I said, I think it should have been maybe a play," he says. "I think if you set it in one room people switch off, if you want to just rely on dialogue then you go to the theatre. It was a nice experience; it was me just getting a bit bored playing the same old thing. On set I was thinking 'same old bollocks, same old bollocks'. I was losing a little bit of passion at this stage."

# ADULTHOOD (2008)

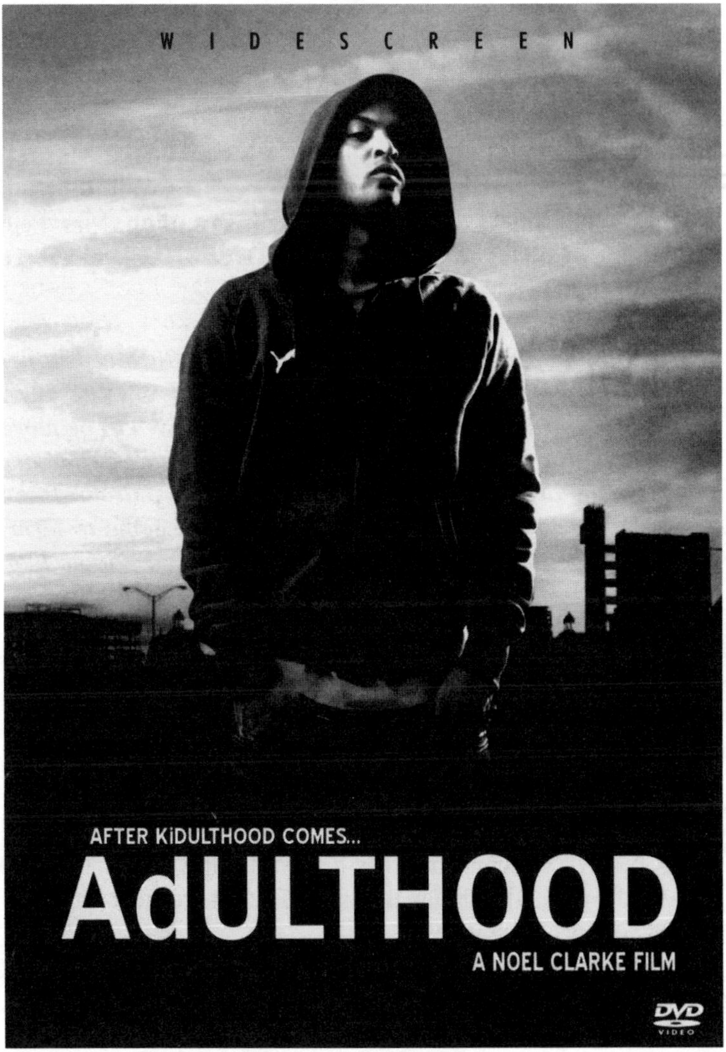


**"What part of me looks like your fucking blud?"**

**Director** Noel Clarke **Producer** George Isaac, Damian Jones **Writer** Noel Clark **Music** Chad Hobson **Production Designer** Murray McKeown **Costume Design** Andy Blake **Cinematography** Brian Tufano

**Noel Clarke** Sam Peel **Adam Deacon** Jay **Scarlett Alice Johnson** Lexi **Femi Oyeniran** Robert "Moony" **Red Madrell** Alisa **Jacob Anderson** Omen **Ben Drew** Dabs **Wil Johnson** Big Man **Nathan Constance** Ike **Adjoa Andoh** Mrs Peel **Madeleine Fairley** Claire **Danny Dyer** Hayden **Pierre Mascolo** Andreas

*Following the tragic events of* Kidulthood, *Sam (Noel Clarke) is released from prison for the murder of Trife six years later. However, confronting the people of his past proves to be more testing than life inside: though many have moved on to better things, many are still trapped in lives of crime and hardship. As Sam tries to put his life back together and come to terms with his wrong-doing, his circumstances become darker than ever before.*

A small part for Dyer, but a scene-stealing performance in a film jam-packed with them. Having played the lead in *Kidulthood*, Clarke took the helm for the sequel and delivered a real tour de force about the reality of life for kids on London's estates. Shocking and honest but also inherently moral, a fact that *The Observer*'s legendary critic Phillip French highlighted in his review, stating that: "It's a hard-driving thriller, violent and foul-mouthed, about the stupidity of respect and the hollowness of vengeance."

Dyer was not overly enamoured with taking such a small part at this point in his career, but was aware of the film's potential. "*Adulthood* was a strange one, because obviously I'd seen *Kidulthood* and it wasn't really up my street because I just felt old watching it," he says. "It was the sort of stuff my daughter was into, but she wasn't old enough to watch it, I could see that whole mentality. Noel wrote me a letter bigging me up and saying how much he thought I was great, and how he's always wanted to work with me, so would I come and do him a favour in *Adulthood.* I read it and realised how fucking small the role was and that he only needed me for a day, so I thought, 'You know what, he seems like a good kid. I'll go in and do it.' It was that line that sold it for me, 'What part of me looks like your fucking blud?' I suppose Noel loved this hoodie-in-our-blud stuff, and he needed to put the iconic London white man into that."

Dyer's first scene in the film is unforgettable, due to it boasting possibly one of the most graphic depictions of cunnilingus ever committed to celluloid. "It was an odd one because in the opening scene I was licking the girl out. I walked in, shook her hand – she was in the first one – and I was literally between her legs. You have these moments where you think, 'Fuck, what a mad job I've got.' 'Hello babe, how you doing?' And I'm straight between her legs. It's very odd. We banged that scene out and then we went outside and smashed that scene and it was a piece of piss. I never thought it would do the business that it would do. They put me on the back cover and stuff to sell it. Again, you feel privileged and honoured that someone like Noel would trust me and would want me in it because it makes the film cool. It was just one day on set."

Dyer does not claim to be a part of the world the film depicts but all experiences are good experiences when Dyer's working. "That world is quite alien to me, and the dialogue is weird because no one talks like that in a film normally," he says. "And Noel is nothing like his character in real life, he's the complete opposite to that. This put him right on the map to be fair, as a director. Obviously I'd later go on to work with him in *Doghouse*, which came about thanks to the good time we had working together here and the mutual respect we have for one another."

Young people loved the film because it talked to them, and they went in droves to see it. Often twice. And as a result, it did exceptionally well at the UK box office bringing in more than £3million. The DVD haul was even more impressive, shifting almost half a million units to date. The film was well received critically but not as heaped with praise as it should have been, for the simple fact that this is not a world the critics understand. Although the white, middle-class Philip French felt knowledgeable and streetwise enough to comment that, "it presents a pretty authentic account of life on the streets and in jail for young blacks."

*Empire* magazine were very positive calling it: "Tense, tough, troubling stuff. A *Rudeboyz N The Hood* loaded with British grit and energy to spare." And as well as comparing it to John Singleton's masterpiece, it also referenced some other Brit crime classics: "*Adulthood* already feels like it fits in the tradition of Great British Grit – Alan Clarke especially. Strip away the slang and tracksuits, and it compares well with the likes of *The Firm* and *Scum* (recalled in the brutal prison flashbacks) and the two (unrelated) Clarkes share the same anxiety over flash-temper alpha males and the searing subcultures that surround them. It ain't pretty, but it's a million postcodes from the fantasy geezer-land of Guy Ritchie, and a lot more vital. And, really, how could you possibly dislike a British movie that name checks Um Bongo?"

How, indeed.

# CITY RATS (2009)

**"I just loved the idea of me playing this really depressed alcoholic."**

**Director** Steve Kelly **Producer** William Borthwick, Dean Fisher **Writer** Simon Fantauzzo **Music** Julia Johnson, Mark Maclaine **Production Designer** Amy Spicer **Costume Design** Alice Walkling **Cinematography** Adam Levins

**Tamer Hassan** Jim **Ray Panthaki** Dean **Danny Dyer** Pete **Susan Lynch** Gina **Kenny Doughty** Olly **Myanna Buring** Sammy **James Lance** Chris **Natasha Williams** Carol **Jake Canuso** Marco Harper **James Doherty** Trevor **Philip Herbert** John the Cowboy **Katrine De Candole** Chloe **Vyelle Croom** Darryl **Emily Bowker** Carla

*An ensemble piece,* City Rats *tells the loosely linked stories of several Londoners as they make their way through a fragment of their lives. Jim and Sue meet as they simultaneously attempt to commit suicide; their chance encounter leads to a mutual decision to give life one more shot. Sue's ex-boyfriend, Dean, a poet and painter, is struggling to create anything that the critics love, until he discovers Gina, an experimental prostitute living next door. Olly is struggling to come to terms with his homosexuality when he finds himself looking after his deaf-mute brother Chris for the day. Chris, also gay, and far more comfortable about his sexuality than Olly, requires his brother's help to lose his virginity. Recovering drug addict Pete is being stalked by Carol, the grandmother of a friend of Pete's from his violent past. Each haunted character goes on their respective journeys, seeking solace from their disturbed urban lives.*

In the opening montage of this thoughtful study of London life, Dyer's character is seen working in a burger van, being harassed by an impatient customer. The man's insatiable desire for the fast food results in Dyer spitting in his meaty roll. This serving up of the unexpected can be used as a metaphor for what happened with the DVD release of *City Rats* itself.

Devised, written with a *Pulp Fiction*-esque structure, it was, conversely, marketed as a Brit gangster movie with Dyer and Tamer Hassan on the cinema poster and DVD cover and sporting the white, red and black packaging design atypical of the gangster genre. The slogan 'The explosive stars from *The Business'* ran across the top. This campaign essentially assured fans this was a fast-paced gangster thriller like *The Business.*

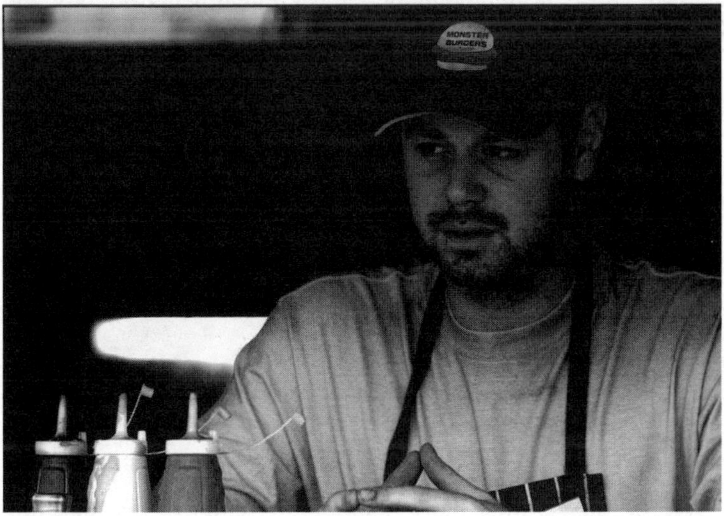


The result of this was the film became one of the most successful British DVDs of the year, with Dyer and Hassan fans clambering for a copy. Only for them to be horribly disappointed to be denied a fix of criminality and gangsterdom. And the art-house fans were put off by a cover that suggested it was the type of film they normally hate. From a commercial point of view the marketing tactic was a brilliant one, from a creative perspective a crushing error.

The film's cinema release was not well received by newspaper critics. Peter Bradshaw of *The Guardian* was particularly scathing:
"There really is no film as terrible as a terrible Brit-film, and here is a depressing example that I can only compare to

Madonna's legendarily abysmal *Filth And Wisdom*. It's an anthology of criss-crossing lives in the big city; individual plot-strands feature Danny Dyer as an ex-con working in a burger van, Tamer Hassan as a suicidal middle-aged man, Susan Lynch as a prostitute with a bizarre regular client – and many more. It is set in lowlife-bohemia Larndarn, which is neither remotely real nor in the slightest bit interesting. There is lots of leaden, self-conscious dialogue and a monumentally crass and fatuous view of prostitution. The scene where a troubled guy finds redemption in taking his gay disabled brother out on the town to get him laid is beyond excruciating."

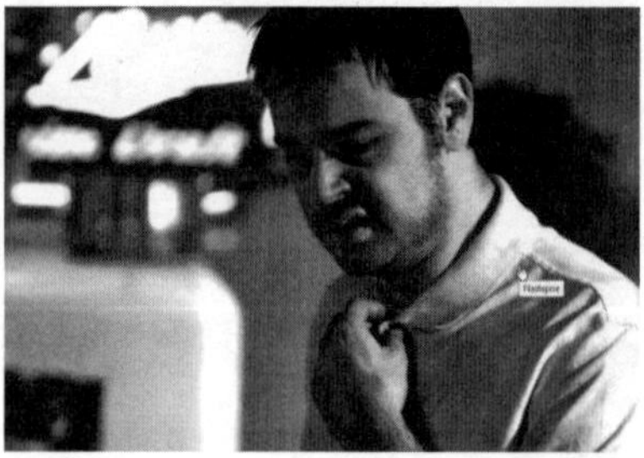

The cinema run was only intended to be short and the DVD rolled out in supermarkets and entertainment shops three days later, which is where it found its home. Albeit for the wrong reasons. FlickeringMyth.com said: "Looking at the DVD cover for *City Rats*, it would be easy to overlook this as little more than another entry in the long line of tired, low-budget British gangster movies, however I must admit to being pleasantly surprised by what the film has to offer. The feature debut of director Steve M Kelly and screenwriter Simon Fantauzzo, *City Rats* is a dark and gritty tale with four storylines that run concurrently and explore a number of depressing themes including suicide, murder, prostitution, homosexuality, loneliness and loss. Promising first-time director Steve M Kelly manages to make the most of his low budget and the film benefits greatly from impressive cinematography, with a slick and polished visual style that really brings the city itself to life. It will be interesting to see what Kelly could accomplish, given a larger budget and – despite its flaws – *City Rats* is an ambitious effort that certainly provides a refreshing change from the typical British gangster movie of recent years."

Shortly after spitting on the aforementioned greasy patty, Dyer's Pete meets the grandmother of an old friend. The scenes between Dyer and Natasha Williams are magnificent if you like thoughtful, nuanced acting. In short, it is a good film that found a huge audience, but not the audience it was made for.

Respected website *DenOfGeek.com* stated that: "The film is starkly shot, probably to show how grim and gritty the whole affair is, and there's some interesting camera work, particularly in Jim's storyline (and even more so when it's raining melons). Any creativity in the camera work is hampered by clichéd and lazy direction – lots of cuts and long, drawn-out shots to accompanying music and staring into the distance from the cast. Sadly, it's got a script where characters, particularly Dyer's, sound pretentious more often than they sound meaningful. Despite this, Dyer's section is actually the most interesting in the film, possibly because it walks a well-trodden path of friendship, loss, violence and darkness. Carol, played ably by Natasha Williams, has little to say, but when she does speak she is totally believable as the imperfect mother of a lost son."

*"City Rats* again was another little small role and I got sent the script," says Dyer. "It came through Tamer actually, someone that Tamer knew. It was never ever from the off thought of as a Tamer and Danny film. We were both going to be in it, but we never had any scenes together and he had different days to me. I was very surprised when I read it – the fact that they wanted us in it – because it was unlike anything we had done, which

excited me. I thought that it was going to be quite 'gangstery' but it was just the complete opposite. I just loved the idea of me playing this really depressed alcoholic. It really excited me to get involved in that, and having this whole two-hander with this 50-year-old black lady. It just really intrigued me because it was just so completely different. Again, it was really low budget, and I only had about three days on it. When they shot my bit they still had three quarters of the film left to shoot so we didn't know how it was going to pan out. I just did my bit and I really relished it. I went a little bit method on that as well: I was drinking on set. It wasn't just for the sake of it; I just really wanted to get this lazy eye thing going on. I'm just such a sad case in it, where I work in that burger van, and I wanted my whole physicality to change. I was gagging to do something good at this point, I was just dying to have an opportunity to just try and show people something different. By this point people knew who I was as an actor, and they either thought I was a good actor or they didn't like me but I never really got an opportunity to do different things like I did at the start of my career. In *Straightheads* I sort of did because I wasn't the alpha male, but I didn't have enough to do, I felt, physicality wise. In this I could really milk it, because it had some really nice little speeches in it. You actually warm to me by the end. I have a good heart and I go out on a limb. It was the first time that I started to notice that I didn't even think about that, I just went and did it."

The film was the breakout DVD success of 2009, selling 371,056 units. A huge haul by anyone's standards, with 26,354 in the opening week alone. Dyer had conflicting emotions when it transpired how well the film had done commercially, because he knew it was to the detriment of his loyal fans who believed they were buying one thing and getting another. Revolver Home Entertainment simply couldn't resist. They had seen how many copies of a film they could shift by depicting it as a Dyer gangster flick when they packaged *Borstal Boy* as such. "I was frustrated but at the same time I was on cloud nine, with the fact that I still had power and clout," he admits.

"This is why my phone didn't stop ringing. You can imagine people in the industry were looking at *City Rats* and going, 'Fucking hell, what's he done really? He's just put Danny on the cover of a fucking film.' And Tamer to an extent. I was fucked off, I couldn't believe the front of it, why would you do that? It's not the fucking film. Okay, I do actually hold a gun in it, but it did also say something about *The Business* on the cover. Also, who gets the blame for it? Who does the white van man blame? It's me, it's my fault. It's like, 'How dare you do that to us? Wasting our hard-earned cash.' So as much as the fact that I'm buzzing, because of the fact that this movie has fucking smashed it because I'm on the cover, I'm also getting a little bit of, 'Fucking hell, Dan, what was that all about?' Just in the street – I wasn't doing Twitter then, it was just that general thing of, 'Fucking hell, Dan.' During that whole thing I got really disappointed, and I couldn't explain that. *City Rats* is an interesting film but wasn't what my fans wanted. I can assure you they won't be conned again. With *Vendetta* we have delivered on everything the artwork promises, everything the fans want, it's all there. There's no bullshit."

# DEAD MAN RUNNING (2009)

**"It was a nice part, I enjoyed it, it was fun, it was good to be around people like 50 Cent, and it's quite a credible film."**

**Director** Alex De Rakoff **Producers** Pikki Fearon **Writer** John Luton and Alex De Rakoff **Production Designer** Matt Button **Director of Photography** Ali Asad

**Tamer Hassan** Nick **Danny Dyer** Bing **50 Cent** Thigo **Monet Mazur** Frankie **Phil Davis** Johnny Sands **Brenda Blethyn** Mum **Alan Ford** Sol **Bronson Webb** Smudger **Joe Egan** Big Joe **Jeff Stewart** Client **Adam Saint** Cockney Red **Esme Bianco** Herself

*Ruthless American loan shark Mr Thigo decides to make an example of one of his debtors, London blagger Nick, to show that he won't be messed around. He gives Nick 24 hours to repay £100,000 or he'll murder his mother. With only his partner in crime Bing in his corner, Nick shuttles around Britain collecting money through gambling, robberies and bare-knuckle fighting.*

A bona-fide modern lads' classic, *Dead Man Running* is probably the closest Dyer ever stepped into Guy Ritchie territory. But the film wasn't conceived as a tongue-in-cheek caper movie, as screenwriter John Luton recalls: "I wrote the original version of *Dead Man Running* in 2002. At that time a major producer was going to do the movie, with Michael Caine as the ruthless loan shark Al Thigo and a number of 'names' up for the role of the man on the run. It was going to be a very tough and realistic *Long Good Friday / Get Carter*-style movie." Luton, a film-maker and editor, eventually found another, less traditional party interested in the property: actor Tamer Hassan. "Unexpectedly, the project did not go ahead, and it was not until several years later that Tamer Hassan and his agent Camilla Storey saw the script," says Luton, "They loved it. I remember Tamer saying that the script was a real page-turner."

Since *The Business*, Hassan has flitted between leading roles in indie films and solid supporting parts in bigger movies but he and his indomitable agent Storey, a vivacious redhead, had been scouring Soho for a script that could solidify Hassan's leading man credentials. *Dead Man Running* was undoubtedly that script and Hassan took it to Pikki Fearon, who had recently produced urban crime film *Rollin With The Nines*.

In the original script there wasn't really a role for Dyer, but adding him to the mix effectively underwrote a UK deal, allowing Hassan to concentrate on packaging the picture with Fearon.

In the film's press kit, Hassan gave his take on his on-screen relationship with Dyer: "It is always brilliant working with Danny, who plays Nick's best mate, Bing. We are great friends in any case, so we bounce off each other and our characters have a great chemistry, the strength of their friendship is actually very endearing. Danny brings the light relief element to this film. He has this fantastic dry humour and I'm playing Nick completely deadpan, the combination works so well, it's hilarious. It's during rehearsals that we can really tell it is working because the crew can laugh out loud. I can't wait to watch it in the cinema because I know people are going to be crying with laughter all the way through. The genius of the script and the relationship between Nick and Bing is that Nick's mission is very serious and stressful as he desperately tries to get this money together. Then, just when it is almost unbearable, Bing turns up and makes you laugh. It is almost a Morecambe and Wise partnership, the chemistry works so well."

Hassan drew together a number of high-profile Executive Producers to finance the film including footballers Rio

Ferdinand and Ashley Cole. Screenwriter John Luton was excited by Dyer's involvement: "A new producer came on board. Tamer and Danny Dyer have appeared in a number of movies together and have great 'chemistry' as an on-screen team, so Danny's role was created as Tamer's loyal mate, trying to help him get out of the life-or-death situation he is facing at the hands of the loan shark, which was now to be played by Curtis '50 Cent' Jackson instead of Michael Caine – quite a change! The mood was changed to a lighter, more jokey approach. Tamer and Danny worked really well together."

Dyer recalls, "It was Tamer's project. We wanted to work together again; the last outing we had was *City Rats* which was a fucking major success. So this time we got to be fucking pals again and do it that way."

Hassan also attracted a high-calibre director – Alex De Rakoff. Perhaps best known for directing smash-hit video game *Grand Theft Auto 2*, De Rakoff had worked with Hassan on boxing comedy *The Calcium Kid* and saw star quality in the Turkish giant. Dyer was full of admiration for the director: "I loved Alex De Rakoff. Just a real good energy, reminded me of Nick a little bit because him and Nick were really good friends and they were very similar sort of people. But Alex needed a shot, he did *The Calcium Kid* which died a death, with Orlando Bloom. So he needed another way, and he was living in LA with his missus, and his missus is in the film, she plays Tamer's wife. She was a bit of a star in America. Incredibly sexy. Her accent wasn't too good, she was from Billericay or something. It was a really good vibe on it though, it was good to be working with Tamer again and it was good to be with Alex."

If Dyer was the icing on the *Dead Man Running* cake, Hassan pulled off a major coup by drafting in US music legend 50 Cent for a chilling cameo as gangster Thigo. Dyer chuckles, "It came to me and 50 Cent was on board, which I didn't believe to be honest, I didn't believe it until I saw him on the set. I was like, 'Fuck off, you haven't got 50 Cent!' and lo and behold the cunt walks on the fucking set, with his entourage. 50 Cent was very professional, he's not like you'd expect him to be, he didn't drink, he didn't smoke, never fucked up any lines ever. He was completely on the ball. He was fine; his entourage were the fucking problem. I remember he came on set for four days and the crew doubled in size. There were just geezers standing around like they've just walked off death row. But once you had a chat with him he was lovely."

Hassan and Fearon surrounded Dyer and 50 with an unusually strong supporting cast which included Phil Davis, Alan Ford and Brenda Blethyn. "Brenda Blethyn told me she turned down other roles because she'd never had the opportunity in anything to hold a shotgun," says Dyer. "She never thought she'd get that opportunity again, especially at her age and stuff. I remember her being an absolutely fucking joy to be around, another sort of Helen Mirren character."

Dyer was only too aware that his role was little more than Hassan's sidekick, but he relished supporting his old friend's venture: "It wasn't a stretch for me, it was Tamer's vehicle, I was like, 'Go on son, you crack on, you do what you've got to do.' It was a nothing part really, even though I'm playing his mate. It was not really anything that was going to excite me. It was a nice part, I enjoyed it, it was fun, it was good to be around people like 50 Cent, and it's quite a credible film."

Interviewed for the film's press kit, director Alex De Rakoff was enthusiastic about the physicality of leading man Hassan: "It is great to be working with Tamer again. There are a fair amount of stunts in this movie but the biggest was the bare-knuckle fight scene. We were very lucky with Tamer because you don't have to double him. He used to be a boxer so he is game, if anything you have to pull him back a bit because you still have five weeks to shoot and you don't want him bashed up! Tamer was fantastic in that scene because he is athletic and he is a fighter so he did all his own work. Rocky (Taylor – stunt coordinator) helped us put this scene together and work out how we could get the most impact whilst making it feel as real as possible. I was really pleased with the outcome."

In February 2009, Pathé announced that it had acquired UK distribution rights to *Dead Man Running*, but when the company decided to refocus on larger theatrical movies, indie Revolver – which scored a smash hit with *City Rats* in 2009 – stepped in, closing a deal to buy the rights from Pathé in August.

Promoting the UK release, 50 Cent, free of preconceptions about Dyer and his work, was sincerely flattering about his co-star: "He's one of the best actors I've ever worked with, and I've worked with a lot of great actors – like Al Pacino, Robert De Niro and Sharon Stone," he enthused, "he just has charisma and bounces off the screen." For Dyer, this was a huge compliment: "He said some beautiful things about me in the press as well, which was really nice. He couldn't understand a word I was fucking saying but I think they said it was *Severance* and another film of mine that he buzzed off so he agreed to do the job, which was a buzz for me. He said I was like the English version of De Niro or something. I think it's because I didn't drive him mad as well, because Tamer was all over him whereas I just sort of kept my distance and looked at him from afar. It was a strange one, because it's almost like he's got all these people around him and when you approach him they step away, it's only when you're in the scene with him that you can approach him. It was a real buzz for me and I was really chuffed with that, I'll never forget that. I think he gave me his number and said give me a call if you ever need anything but I never rang him. It was purely about acting, it was nothing else, he'd seen me in a couple of movies, and he really was impressed with me."

*The Guardian*'s Peter Bradshaw, despite only awarding the film two stars, admitted: "for all the sub-Guy Ritchie clichés, it has its moments. Hassan and Dyer have a reasonable double-act going as dodgy heroes Nick and Bing, and there's a funny contribution from quivery-voiced Brenda Blethyn playing the mother for whom Nick is trying to go straight. It'll shift serious DVD units, and is not as bad as it could have been." *Empire*'s Kim Newman, rarely a fan of the genre, also gave the film two stars, dismissing it with the comment, "Nothing remarkable or noteworthy about this Brit gangster-by-numbers effort, except the cast." Derek Adams, writing for *Time Out*, stuck the boot in too: "Partly financed by footballers Rio Ferdinand and Ashley Cole, this budget-conscious, simplistically plotted and often cringingly performed crime caper is not quite as inauspicious a producing debut as one might have expected. Granted, its message is contradictory – on one hand it drums home the old 'crime doesn't pay' adage, while on the other it demonstrates exactly the opposite – but its lighthearted, comic tone proves relatively genial. And Blethyn's a right laugh as the gaga mum with a mite more gumption than first meets the eye." In retrospect, the critical mauling the film suffered seems particularly unfair, as while it might not hit the heights of *Lock, Stock* or *Snatch* it is most definitely at the high end of the genre.

Released across 80 screens on 30 October 2009, *Dead Man Running* took a respectable £513,120 at the UK box office. In its first week on DVD it shifted a whopping 45,702 units, bolstered by a nationwide signing tour for Dyer. To date, lifetime DVD sales in the UK have topped 235,000.

After the film performed so strongly on DVD, little time was wasted in announcing a sequel. Taking its cue from the first film's best gag, the sequel was tipped to be set in Dubai and budgets of £10 million were bandied about Soho. According to Entertainment site Digital Spy, Girls Aloud singer Cheryl Cole (then married to *Dead Man Running* exec Ashley Cole) was in line to play the female lead in a proposed sequel: "Cheryl Cole will allegedly be offered a six-figure pay cheque to star in the sequel to crime thriller *Dead Man Running*. According to a spokesman for Revolver Entertainment, the firm behind the project, plans are afoot to recruit the pop star for the follow-up. "There is a character Cheryl is perfect for and we are holding meetings over the next few weeks to discuss exactly what we can offer her, it will be a sizeable sum," the spokesman said. *Dead Man Running* starred 50 Cent, Danny Dyer and Brenda Blethyn and was produced by Cole's estranged husband Ashley and his England teammate Rio Ferdinand. It is unclear if Cole or Ferdinand will be back for *Dead Man Running 2*."

Reflecting on his venture into film production with BeyondHollywood.com while promoting Essex Boys film *Bonded By Blood* in 2010, Hassan noted: "Yeah, I produced *Dead Man Running*. I don't like the physical, hands-on side of production, but I do enjoy raising money, I do enjoy being the glue, I do enjoy putting the line producer with the producer and then getting the director on board and helping the cast out – the whole process of film-making, I love it. But the actual hands-on side of it – not for me, I'd rather be in front of the camera."

As late as December 2010, Hassan still nursed ambitions to make a sequel, but sounded a note of caution about flooding the market, as he explained to BeyondHollywood.com: "Well we've got *Dead Man Running 2* coming up and there's also talk of *The Business 2*. We've just been offered a few comedies here and there – you know, people writing stuff for us. But what we don't wanna do is saturate the market with Danny and Tamer movies! I think if we do one every two or three years people will enjoy them more, so we've got to be careful of that."

It's easy to dismiss *Dead Man Running* simply because it isn't *The Business*, but then it never set out to be. But as ticking clock London caper movies go, it's up there with the best of them and is a major return to fan-pleasing form for both of its stars. There is no doubt that Tamer Hassan knew exactly what he was doing when he tailored the role of Nick for himself and it fits him as well as one of his cashmere coats. He delivers a satisfying, charming performance, aided and abetted by a particularly cheeky Dyer. Their late-night, bickering cab ride up north is one of the great unsung comedy scenes in British movies and because they are clearly having such a good time, it's hard for the audience not to as well. Skilfully directed and decidedly glossy, *Dead Man Running* is essential post-pub viewing.

# JACK SAID (2009)

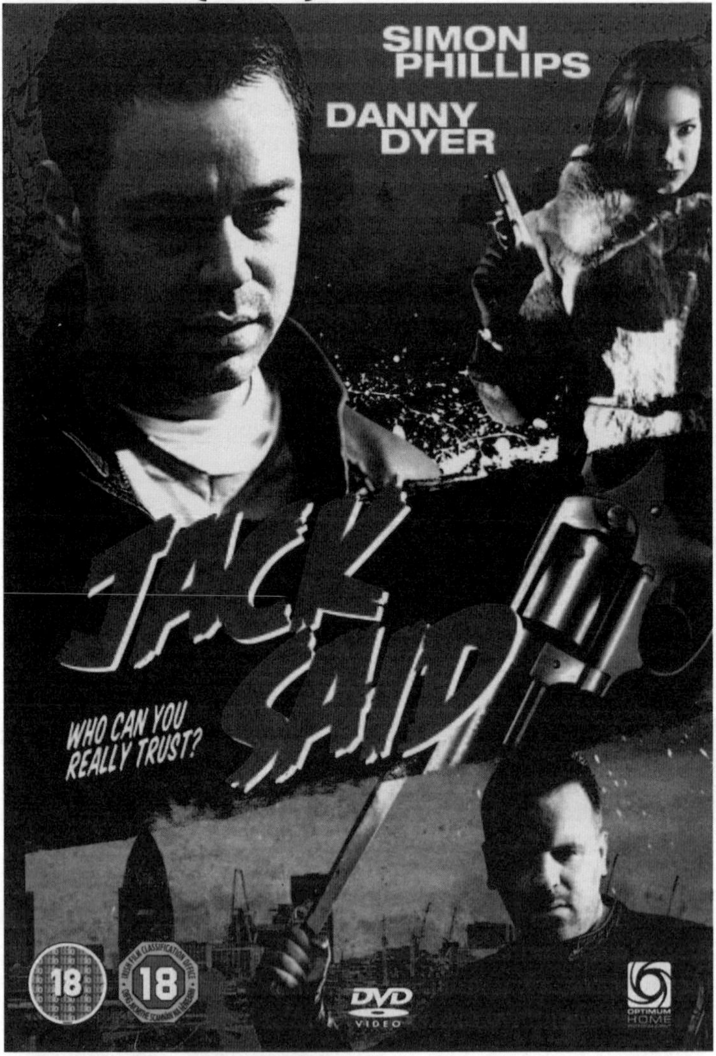


"Jack Said... I'd rather say nothing about Jack Said. Do you know what? I've never seen it. I've never watched it."

**Director** Lee Basanavvar and Michael Tchoubouroff **Producers** Simon Phillips, Toby Meredith **Writer** Paul Tanter **Production Designer** Sophie Wyatt **Costume Designer** Suzy Peters **Director of Photography** Bob Komar

**Simon Phillips** Jack Adleth **Rita Ramnani** Erin **Danny Dyer** Nathan **David O'Hara** The Boss **Christopher Fosh** Dave **Terry Stone** The Fixer **Ashlie Walker** Natalie **Steve Lawson** Ozzy **Dominic Burns** Yianna **Stuart Brennan** Valuev

*Unlikely undercover policeman Jack Adleth has worked his way into a notorious London criminal gang but his past is catching up with him – and his situation becomes even more complicated when he meets and falls in love with Erin, his friend's sister.*

Danny Dyer has appeared in some truly wretched films, but this one marked the lowest point in his career – an amateurish, self-indulgent mess that completely fails to engage the audience and lives up to every cliché critics cite when dismissing British gangster films as rubbish.

*Jack Said* star Simon Phillips' twin careers as actor and producer have been inextricably linked from the beginning, as he generally only appears in his own movies. His first feature, *Jack Says*, had drawn some minor press attention for uniting the unlikely onscreen duo of *EastEnders* icon Mike Reid and footballer Eric Cantona. The film had been promoted as Mike Reid's last film but had done virtually no business on DVD. Phillips had drawn ridicule for his ham-fisted lead performance as undercover cop Jack Adleth, not only because of his obvious unsuitability for the role but also because of his bizarre decision to saddle himself with a decidedly dubious Scottish accent. Despite this, Phillips and long-time cohort Paul Tanter had conceived a prequel and enlisted no less than 36 producers and two directors in order to bring it to the screen. At one point, the producers were even running eBay auctions to buy parts in the film.

When Dyer was approached to appear as Jack's friend Nathan for a few days he was at a low point – he'd seen the aborted *Rapture* project fall apart and the likes of *Malice In Wonderland* and *Doghouse* were some months away from filming. Dyer recalls how he tried to justify the project to himself: "I've always been a massive fan of Mike Reid, I love him in *EastEnders*, I just love his old-school Cockney way, and my dad loves him. So I was aware of the first one, *Jack Says*. Eric Cantona was in it. they sent it to me and I watched it, and I thought, this is not ground-breaking but it's got something about it. So they asked me to do it, and I thought because of the Mike Reid association (and he's dead in the second one) I did it. Probably not the wisest decision. It's not the creative thing, it's just because I was a fan of someone that I'd like to be associated with. But it was not a good experience for me at all. This was when I started to lose the plot a little bit. I didn't really realise what I was worth. I was down. It was horrible, a really horrible experience. I got paid nicely for it. The guy who won the lottery was in it and I had a scene with him. It was just a moment for me to think, 'Fucking hell what am I doing? I really should not be here.' And it's not an ego thing or arrogance, but I just felt that I'd lost my way. I don't think I was being managed in the right way. I always make my own decisions but I had no one there in my ear hole. My agent would go, 'I don't want you to do it' and I would go, 'Why? There was never a reason, so I'd go, 'Fuck it, what else have you got in the pipeline? What's the alternative?' So I'd just go and do it."

Filmed early in 2009 on location in Essex and London, *Jack Said* seemed to capture every bit of the monotony that Dyer was beginning to feel with the quality of the films he was being offered. Dyer found twin low points working opposite Simon Phillips and 'lottery lout' Michael Carroll: "The lead actor's a joke. Simon Phillips is just not an actor, and he wants to play a tough Scottish copper. He really wanted to test himself but it was just cringey. Michael Carroll, bless his fucking heart, I just remember fucking torturing him in the scene. Like really fucking going, 'Alright cunt, you want to be a fucking actor? Okay I'm going to show you what it's like to be an actor.' So I was chucking lines at him that weren't in the script and he was just panicking, he was petrified; he was standing there shaking. He paid his way to be in it, and he hated every fucking second of it. He just wanted a photo with me. I think he just wanted to meet me and have a photo so he paid twenty grand to be in it. I don't blame him; I blame the people who put him in it to take his fucking money."

Perhaps because of Dyer's brief screen time, and his wise decision not to promote the film or attend the premiere, or perhaps because he looked so embarrassed amongst a sea of am-dram day players, the majority of the critics let him off gently after wasting an hour and a half of their lives. "This aims for the stark graphic look and hardboiled noir feel of *Sin City*, and misses by a mile," wrote *Time Out*'s Nigel Floyd. "If writer Paul Tanter's voiceover and dialogue had been delivered with any conviction, it might have distracted us from the dull visuals, over-complicated flash-back/flash-forward structure and TV soap opera-style acting." *The Guardian*'s Andrew Pulver singled out Dyer for praise, however: "There's not much to be said for this overcooked, overheated Brit gangster thriller – a sequel, apparently, to a film that appears to have made almost no impact in the first place… it's only enlivened by a brief cameo from Danny Dyer – but it's safe to say this won't be featuring in the Dyer retrospective we're already all looking forward to." *Little White Lies* magazine also found little to cheer about: "cack-handed… British geezer flicks have (thankfully) moved on and a Steadicam, some leather-faced ex-cons and a vacant lock-up in Barking are no longer enough to cause a buzz."

Released on one screen, *Jack Said* took £1,240 at the UK box office but the red, white and black cover, which misleadingly promoted Dyer's cameo as a lead role, and TV spots trumpeting it as "the new Danny Dyer film" prompted 12,736 people to buy the film on DVD in its first week. It is likely that the majority were bitterly disappointed. To date, the film has sold over 58,000 DVDs in the UK, thanks to endless point-of-sale campaigns and the striking cover.

To the horror of audiences and critics alike, a third Jack film was released in 2011 – *Jack Falls*. With a much bigger budget and higher production values, this outing boasted an all-star supporting cast – including Tamer Hassan, Adam Deacon, Jason Fleymng, Dexter Fletcher and Martin Kemp. Unfortunately, it still featured the insurmountable problem of Simon Phillips in the title role. By this point, Dyer was starting to realise that appearing in bad films was hurting his career and passed up the lucrative opportunity to reprise his role, this time as a ghost. In a hilariously awful bit of shark-jumping, *The Football Factory* actor Neil Maskell squeezes himself into Nathan's vacated leather jacket to play Dyer's part instead. Without Dyer, the *Jack* name meant nothing, and the third film in the trilogy bombed spectacularly.

Dyer, always a realist, knows exactly how bad the film is: "*Jack Said*… I'd rather say nothing about *Jack Said*. Do you know what? I've never seen it. I've never watched it. I've never brought myself to watch it. I don't know if I'm bad, I don't know if I'm good in it. I was depressed. So I was just trying to lift myself to get something out of it, but it's really hard you know."

The best way to describe *Jack Said* is as a mistake on every level – it truly is an ugly blot on the copybook of British cinema. A horrible mess of a film, ill-conceived and appallingly executed. Even Dyer can't make this rubbish watchable and the tired, sad look in his eyes is reflective of how you feel after viewing it. Thankfully, after this monstrosity the only way was up.

# DOGHOUSE (2009)

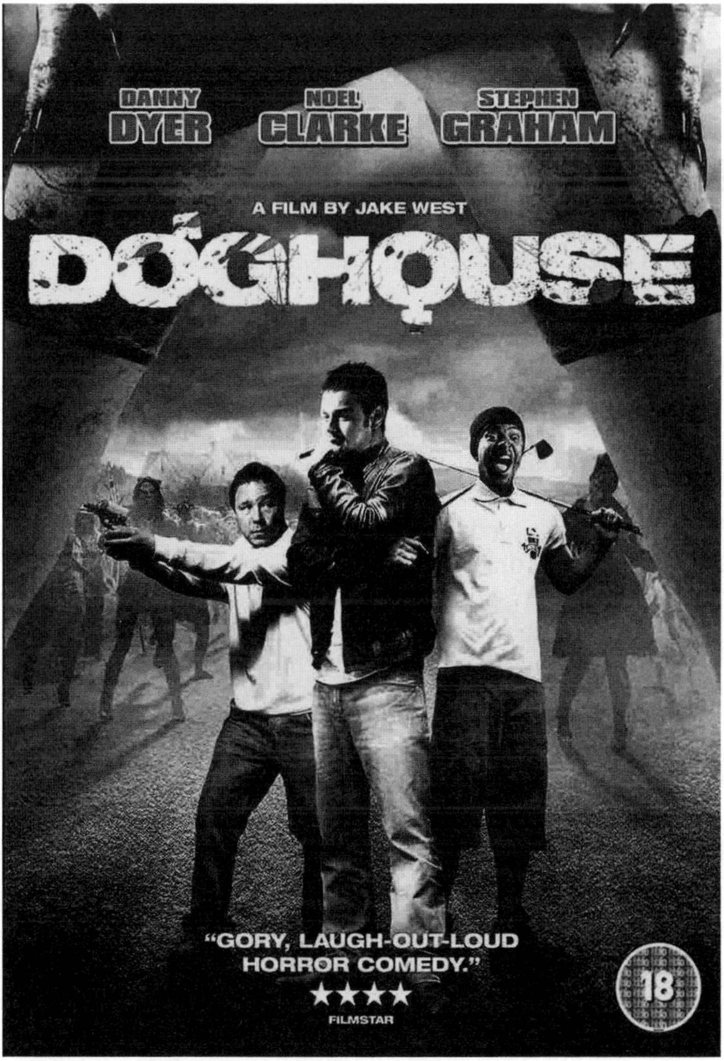


**"I just thought we should get a fucking good cast together of real fucking actors and let's try and make this funny."**

**Director** Jake West **Producers** Mike Loveday **Writer** Dan Schaffer **Production Designer** Matt Button **Costume Designer** Hayley Nebauer **Director of Photography** Ali Asad

**Danny Dyer** Neil **Noel Clarke** Mikey **Lee Ingelby** Matt **Christina Cole** Candy **Stephen Graham** Vince **Adele Silva** Bex **Terry Stone** Sgt Gavin Wright **Emily Booth** The Snipper **Neil Maskell** Banksy **Keith-Lee Castle** Patrick **Emil Marwa** Graham **Billy Murray** Colonel **Alison Carroll** The Teen **Dani Dyer** The Ballerina

*A group of lads head to a remote village to help one of their friends, Vince, get over his divorce; when they get there, though, they discover that all the women have been infected with a virus that has turned them into man-hating cannibal monsters – zombirds!*

Cult movie director Jake West had been on the cusp of a big movie for some time – the darling of the Frightfest scene for low-budget crowd pleasers such as *Razorblade Smile* and *Evil Aliens*, his striking visuals and wacky style had earmarked him for bigger things. West recalls the film's genesis: "*Doghouse* was an original script from Dan Schaffer and it has a very comic-book style feel and is true to his comic-book writing style in terms of both themes – in this case, the battle of the sexes and an ironic look at 'lad culture'. Also the film has a very designed, visual look that stays true to a comic-book style. I'm a huge fan of Dan's comic work, especially *Dogwitch* – which is one of my favourite all-time comics, and we both share a similar sensibility and sense of humour, so it was a joy to work with him. We became friends and discussed the possibility of doing a film project together and thus *Doghouse* was born, barking and screaming. We spent a good time developing the script ideas and really enjoyed the process. Dan is a terrific writer and produced one of the most entertaining and enjoyable screenplays I've read. He has an authentic and intelligent understanding of a genre that is actually very tricky to write in, and few get right – hence everyone always comparing these types of films to the same old benchmarks. I thought the script itself had something extra to any of the normal scripts I've read... It had a quirky Britishness, an original spin to a tired zombie genre with a clever provocative subtext (that of the idea of the virus only affecting one gender) and some great characterisations. The fact that the story therefore had an interesting edge to it beneath its zombie-action veneer, with this subtext of the whole gender politics issue that was going to stoke up the PC brigade and bound to ruffle a few feathers, excited me and I hoped would take a number of viewers and critics out of their predictable comfort zones, and that's why the horror genre is cool because it can still do that. It's not bland and still has a bit of danger too it. All that combined made it an irresistible prospect for me."

As West explains, finding producers interested in the script took little time: "We'd finished writing the script and we'd done a couple of drafts of it before we were ready to show it to people. Just by pure chance I got invited to a photoshoot for a magazine about the UK's rising film talent. Somehow I got recommended by somebody! I don't normally get put on those kind of things. Ironically, I think the magazine went bust before they did the article. But on that shoot I met Terry Stone, who was one of the executive producers of *Rise Of The Footsoldier*. He had done that with Carnaby Films and he was looking for some other projects. He knew that I'd done *Evil Aliens* and he knew I had a bit of a following with the horror audience and he was interested in any kind of horror stuff that I had. And I said, 'Your timing is pretty good because I've just finished developing this with Dan Schaffer,' and told him about Dan and what we had done. He said, 'That sounds fantastic,' and I said, 'I'll tell you what, I'll give you first look at it and you can decide yourself whether you like it and whether you want to get involved.' Because he was saying that he felt he may be able to get some money together, he had a company called Hanover Films that raised money for stuff. Basically, he read the script and the next day he got back to me, which once again is very unusual in the film industry. Normally when someone says they're going to get back to you, you never hear from them again. And he absolutely loved it and he said, 'Look, my company Hanover can put some money in towards the budget of this. And I'd like to take this into Carnaby,' who he'd worked with on his previous film. They loved it and they fast-tracked it."

Hanover Films, owned by Stone, former soap actor Billy Murray and businessman Toby Richards, had co-produced *Rise Of The Footsoldier* with Carnaby Films, a financing and production outfit which used government EIS schemes to raise money for films. *Footsoldier* had bombed at the box office but had quickly gained a huge cult following on DVD and, unhappy with how the campaign panned out, the producers wanted more control of the release of their next film. A deal was soon struck on the *Doghouse* script and Carnaby set up a deal with Sony Pictures to release the film in the UK. Sony had cast approval and the man at the top of their list was – perhaps unsurprisingly – Danny Dyer.

Dyer picks up the story: "By the time I get to *Doghouse*, they're begging me to be in this fucking film, because obviously after the *City Rats* thing, you get Danny in it and the film gets made. I got sat down with Michael and Andy Loveday and they basically said, 'Listen, we can't make this film without you. What do you want?' This is literally the thing, I went and met them at the Peacock Gym (which is weird), and they said, 'Look, what do you want? We cannot make this film without you. Who do you want in it?' I was like, 'Hold up mate, slow down, let me read it.' They'd let me play whatever the fuck I wanted in it, they'd give me completely free rein. I didn't have a clue about what it was or what it was about, so I was like, 'Thanks, I'm chuffed and flattered, but I've got to read the cunt. I can't make a decision here.' They were like, 'What do you want, one hundred grand? One hundred and fifty grand? Do you want one hundred grand now, and we'll put fifty as an investment of yours?' I was like, 'Listen, just let me take this home and I'll fucking read it.' I went home, I fucking read it and I pissed myself. I thought, 'Fuck me, this is not what I expected to be picking up.' I knew they'd made *Rise Of The Foot Soldier* so I was assuming it was going to be some gangster hooligan thing, and it was the complete opposite. As an actor I thought, wow. They did give me free rein to play the lead, which would have meant Stephen Graham's part. But I read it and it was the scene with the fat bird where I'm tied to the chair crying that sold it for me, and I thought, I've got to play that role, I just have to do that. Again, I love comedy."

Initially, producer Terry Stone had seen himself in the Neil part but was flipped over to play a rather unlikely soldier when Dyer chose that part over the obvious lead. So keen were the producers, that they essentially gave the actor carte blanche to nominate the rest of the cast, as he recalls: "They just said, 'Who do you want in it?' And I said, 'I want John Simm as the lead,' because John was going, 'I really want to work with you, we haven't worked since *Human Traffic.'* I offered him it and he fucking turned it down, it was probably his agent saying, 'I don't want you to be associated with it,' or whatever the fuck it was, which fucking upset me. It was the same with Sean Parks for the Noel part, because I wanted to get the old team together. He fucking turned me down as well! So Stephen Graham, who I've always been a fan of, and he's always been a fan of mine, we got him. And I thought, 'Wow, we got fucking Stevie boy.' And then Noel came in to read and I thought I'll just let him roast for a bit, because he just thought he deserved the part. But he was probably the best man for the job, there's no two ways about it. Then you start thinking, that's a pretty fucking good line-up. That was the only thing they did say, 'Listen, do what you want, have who you want in it, but Terry Stone's got to be in it.' It was because he produced it, and he said he wanted to be in it. So I basically handpicked the cast. Lee Ingleby was someone I worked with on *Borstal Boy*. I was racking my brains thinking, 'Who did I really enjoy working with, whose going to be good in this?' Lee Ingleby is fucking great. Andrew-Lee Castle, fucking brilliant, he came in for a reading. So I almost took a kind of producer role. I sort of sat back and they really got me involved. They were shit at poker to be honest, they completely laid all their cards on the table, I will completely control everything. But I didn't do it in a Vinnie Jones way, I just thought we should get a fucking good cast together of real fucking actors and let's try and make this funny."

West, a fan of Dyer's work in *Severance* and *The Business*, was initially cautious about his star's profile: "My main worry about Danny was that to the public at large he has a 'you either love him or hate him quality'. If I had a worry, it was that some people wouldn't give the film a fair chance because they would be distracted by the casting, and miss the ironic subtext of the film, which was taking the piss out of lad culture and the characters' unreconstructed attitudes and inability to understand women. Ultimately some viewers got it and some didn't, and I think Danny brought lots of great moments to the role."

With Dyer topping the bill, attracting a heavyweight ensemble cast became an easier job, as director Jake West recalls: "Once Danny was on board we read a number of other actors against him as we wanted to see that the combination of blokes would play and we'd believe them as friends. Ultimately we spent about three months on the casting and really saw hundreds of people to get the balance right. We worked closely with casting director Jane Frisby who got some great people in for me to see. Originally we had Jimi Mistry (*East Is East, The Guru*) cast to play the role of Graham and we had him read with Danny Dyer, and he was fab but we lost him to *2010* and Roland Emmerich, who offered him loads more money and his filming dates clashed with ours. Noel Clarke came in just for a meeting to discuss what part he might be interested in and I was thinking, 'I don't know if he'll really dig it.' But he came in and he absolutely loved it. He was so enthused about the project, it was fantastic. Because he had just directed *Adulthood,* which was very different and obviously had done very well at the UK box office. So he came in and he just loved it, then we got him back to do a reading with Stephen Graham and Danny Dyer, to see how the chemistry would work. So he was great and from there we had our bigger names in. The hardest part to cast was Vince because in many ways that's the hardest role in the film. He's the one who's depressed because he's getting divorced. So we needed an actor who could handle that, but it wasn't a showy role. There was a big development, a big character arc on Vince. So we wanted someone really solid for that and it was only finally the week before shooting that we finally managed to do the deal with Stephen Graham. Stephen came in at the eleventh hour really because we were talking to people who had other commitments. By which point we then lost Jimi Mistry because Roland Emmerich was shooting his movie in Vancouver and offered him silly money to go out and do that but that interfered with our shooting dates. So we then had to recast the role of Graham and Jimi had kindly recommended Emil Marwa who was also in *East is East* with him. He came in and did a fantastic reading so we got Emil involved. But I think two of the real finds for the film were Keith-Lee Castle and Lee Ingleby. Obviously they've done stuff before but they're not names and they're both fantastic actors. I've seen Keith in *Seed Of Chucky* and his *Urban Gothic* thing."

Shooting began in July 2008 at an abandoned hospital in Sussex. Finding the right location was a challenge, as West remembers: "It was about nine months of searching and despair. We eventually got lucky and it was production designer Matt Button who happened upon the hospital when he was doing another job and he called excitedly saying he thought he'd found 'The One'. And he had! We went on numerous location reccies, trying to find Moodley with Matt, and he's the one who eventually found the hospital for us. He was doing another shoot for a Sky job and he found this place. No one had ever shot on it before until he arrived there and he went, 'Right, we could turn this place into a village,' because we've been looking all over the place. We had been inspecting disused airfields. Just trying to get permission for what we wanted to do would have been impossible in any normal town or village. They don't want you blowing stuff up at night, a huge amount of noise, zombirds screaming and attacking. It became a practical thing to try and build a real village. It was really nice and quite magical to see this place being built before you. That was a really great thing but that took a long time to sort out as well. It meant that we could do things properly and we could think about them and plan it so it would work for the shoot, which was really nice."

Dyer enjoyed the shoot: "They put most of the money into the prosthetics because they needed to make these zombies look good, otherwise it breaks the spell. It was a mad shoot, we hired this old hospital where Alec Guinness died, it was haunted. It was South London, across the water. What they'd done was brilliant. They built a little village on the grounds and we all slept in the rooms. We all had single rooms, and they opened a bar at night. It was all a night shoot, a very surreal shoot, and it was 30 birds dressed as zombies every night. It was a very odd, weird experience."

For West, working with a cast of leading British actors at the top of their game lead by an enthusiastic Dyer was an experience he cherished: "Danny was great to work with. He was prepared, knew his lines and always full of energy and upbeat about getting the shot. He really helped set the tone on set and helped galvanise the other actors. I thought Danny brought a great energy to his performance as Neil. He has great comic timing and it was great to see him riffing on his media stereotyped Jack-the-lad persona. I particularly think he was great in the scene where he's tied up and gets his finger cut off by 'Bubbles', who fancies eating him and has a fetish for men's fingers, as Danny had always highlighted this scene as the reason he wanted to do the film and it was really something to see him reduced to tears pleading for his life and trying to use his charm – especially when you understand Neil's character and views on women. Also I love the fact we managed to get *Female Of The Species* licensed for this scene. I think it's one of the highlights of the movie. Stephen Graham who plays Vince is a powerhouse performer who's worked with some of the best directors out there, from Martin Scorcese and Michael Mann to Shane Meadows, so to have an actor of his ability trying his hand at this genre for the first time was really special. His passion and instincts are spot on and he's an actor that challenges you to look at a scene and character beats in a much closer way than I've ever had the opportunity to before. Noel Clarke is currently one of Britain's most exciting talents. I respect him not just an actor, but a successful writer and director who proved his popularity by winning a BAFTA – 2009's Orange Rising Star award. Working with Noel was great because he is a joy to work with. Because of his additional experience of directing he has real insight and sympathy for a director's day-to-day problems on set and is a very patient and focused performer. Horror films are very technical and require the cast to really get into the world you're creating. What was important is we believed in this group of actors as a gang of real friends. All I can say is they worked so well as an ensemble that this was never even a question and now they are all firm friends! This theme of 'friendship' is the heart of the why I think the film works and is what *Doghouse* really celebrates – so I hope this touches a nerve with the audience."

When West delivered his cut of the film, it was considered to be too long and Carnaby brought in Julian and William Gilbey to recut it. "My 94-minute director's cut got cut to 84 minutes," notes West, "I believe we had a stronger film before it was shortened."

Reviews for *Doghouse* were stronger than for other recent Dyer outings but were, as ever, mixed: *Empire* gave the film four stars, noting: "This is the sharp, laddish, creepy, funny war-of-the-sexes horror-comedy *Lesbian Vampire Killers* wanted to be. A major step forward for British horror director Jake West, of *Evil Aliens* fame, and one of the freshest, most overlooked UK films of recent years. Make sure it's huge on DVD." *The Guardian*'s Catherine Shoard was less forgiving: "The acting's just awful, the misogyny undeniable, but the odd flash of *Shaun Of The Dead*-style inventiveness means you forgive it buckets." This may have seemed like damning with faint praise but these notices were considerably better than those accorded the less-polished contemporary Dyer films, suggesting that at this point the critics were generally still prepared to give him a chance. Fate, however, had other ideas.

*Doghouse* was released theatrically across 99 screens on May 18 2009, the same day as *The Hangover*. There was only one blokey comedy that audiences went to see that summer and it wasn't *Doghouse*, which never stood a chance against the wolfpack. *The Hangover* went on to gross over £21 million in the UK alone.

*Doghouse* fared better on DVD, shifting 28,255 units in its first week of release, with UK lifetime sales currently over 175,000. These were the kind of numbers that reinforced Dyer's position as the king of DVD, but would soon be undermined by a series of misfires, mis-sells and misdemeanors.

Perhaps because of the strong ensemble cast, high production values or universally popular genre, *Doghouse* has travelled wider than many of Dyer's other films. Abroad it has been through a number of titles including the amusingly misleading *Zombie Harem*.

There's a lot to like in *Doghouse* and there's no doubt that Jake West knows and loves his genre, bringing Dan Schaffer's memorable characters to life with style and humour. Dyer gets all of the best lines ("bird flu") and enjoys the chance to flex his acting chops as well as his star power opposite high-end contemporaries such as Clarke and Graham. Watching the film, it is so easy to see how Dyer became such a big star and his swaggering, cocky turn would – ironically – not have been out of place in a big American comedy such as *The Hangover*.

The supporting cast is solid, though there's no denying Terry Stone, dependable in the likes of *Bonded By Blood* and *Rise Of The Footsoldier*, is out of his comfort zone as a terrified Special Forces soldier. Production design throughout is excellent and the creepy village is perfectly realised. Taken on its own terms – it's the geezer's zombie movie – *Doghouse* is a minor classic.

# MALICE IN WONDERLAND (2009)

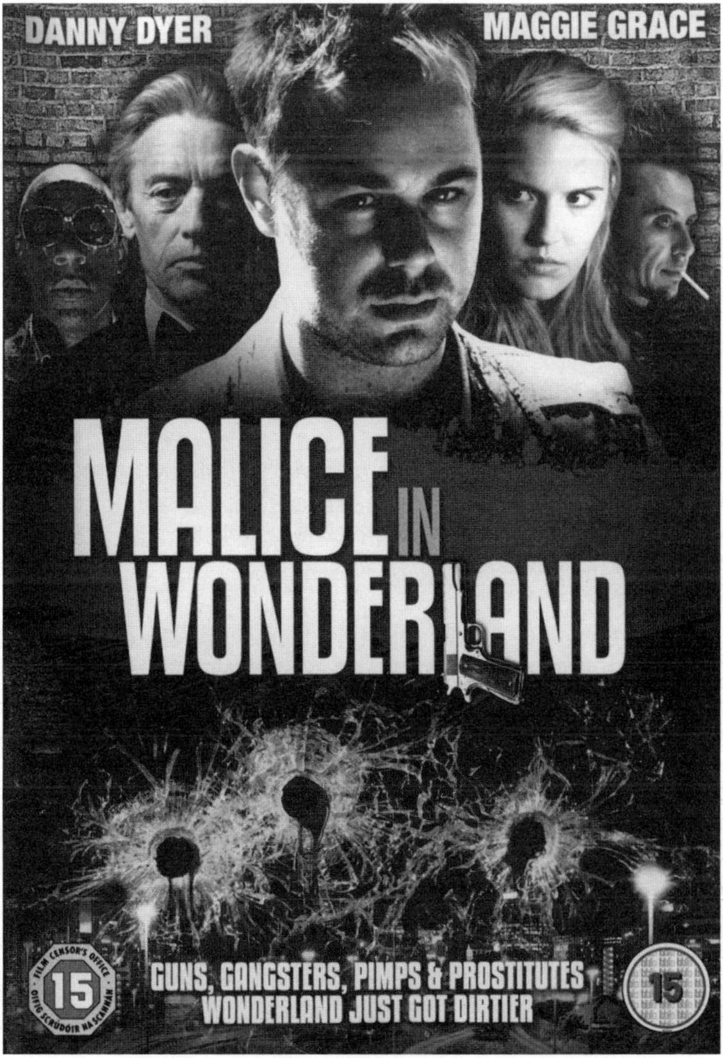


**"I loved the character; I loved the trippyness of it, the surrealness of it."**

**Director** Simon Fellows **Producers** Albert Martinez Martin, Mark Williams **Writer** Jayson Rothwell **Production Designer** Lisa Hall **Director of Photography** Christopher Ross

**Maggie Grace** Alice **Danny Dyer** Whitey **Matt King** Gonzo **Nathaniel Parker** Harry **Bronagh Gallagher** Hattie **Anthony Higgins** Rex **Gary Beadle** Felix Chester **Paul Kaye** Caterpillar **Sandra Dickinson** Mother **Steve Furst** Mo **Pam Ferris** Doochey **Steve Haze** Midge

*A contemporary retelling of Lewis Carroll's classic tale, with gangster's daughter Alice suffering from amnesia after being knocked over by a black cab. The driver, Whitey, is in a terrible hurry and drags Alice into a terrifyingly bizarre underworld.*

The one truly tragic example of Dyer's films being mis-sold, *Malice* is perhaps the only time his fans bought one of his films on DVD and were pleasantly surprised by the film not matching the predictably gangsterish packaging.

Director Simon Fellows had cut his teeth on glossy action films starring Wesley Snipes and Jean Claude Van Damme when the inspiration for what ultimately became *Malice In Wonderland* came to him. Fellows recalls: "I became involved with the film *Malice In Wonderland* from its inception. I was working with the writer Jayson Rothwell and we were brainstorming ideas. I basically wanted to work with a piece of existing classic text and contemporise it. We focused on *Alice In Wonderland.* A week later the writer called me and said, 'how about *Malice In Sunderland*?' After laughing for a while it clicked and that was our start. Although we had to drop the Sunderland aspect as it felt a bit region specific. Interestingly, though, Lewis Carroll actually wrote some of the original story when he spent time in Sunderland. Curiouser and curiouser!"

The landscape of the British film industry in the early noughties had few stars and Dyer was always in Fellow's mind to play the male lead: "I always felt Danny was right for the part of the White Rabbit, especially as the script evolved, and I had watched his career develop. The casting directors Ros and Dan Hubbard, who were involved in the project at one point, also felt Danny was right. I never have preconceived ideas, as I've learnt having worked with several names that you never really know how someone is going to be, and if someone can act then they should be able to achieve the character the script screams for and that I need. I was, of course, aware of Danny's films and general style and felt that he had the right charisma, charm and screen presence for this role, and I always get excited about casting outside of what others feel is an actor's box."

Dyer explains the project's gestation and how he very nearly wasn't in it: "It had been around for a long time, it goes back to around *The Business* time that this script came to me and they originally offered it to me. Then they fucked me off for Andy Serkis. Then Andy Serkis, when he gets *King Kong,* fucked them off, so they came back to me. So then I had this dilemma of, 'Okay, you did want me, and then you didn't want me.' I had to get over it, I loved the character, I loved the trippyness of it, the surrealness of it. I thought, 'How is he going to get this made?' It wasn't a big budget but how is he going to make this work? Because it is *Alice In Wonderland* but in a really fucked-up version. It's quite a visual film so I had to get over it, I was going to fuck them off to be honest and go, 'Fuck you, go and get Andy Serkis! Oh, can't you get him now? Go get some.' But I thought, 'You know what man, he's a nice geezer, he's just going with his heart.' Serkis at the time was I suppose cooler than me, because I was obviously going through this weird stage."

When Dyer finally committed to the picture, the hunt was on to find an American star to play Alice. Step forward *Taken* star Maggie Grace, then best known for cult TV show *Lost*. Dyer recalls: "It was also, of course, Maggie Grace who was the thing that did it for me. Originally it was going to be Mischa Barton. It was going to be her originally and I didn't like her. But Maggie Grace, I was like, 'Yeah, sign me the fuck up.'"

Fellows, too, was impressed with his female lead: "Danny was first. Maggie Grace was a total professional and more than that had a very smart understanding of British humour. I think it kind of fascinated her and she was in for the ride. Danny and Maggie connected brilliantly on screen, I feel. They both are cinematic and the camera loves them. Both are very competent actors and again came to set every day or night, up for the challenge, well rehearsed and nailed their lines – which helps! Danny bought his own unique humour to the set on and off and Maggie integrated extremely well into the fold. She arrived only a few days before the shoot and was thrown deep into the wonders of the British seaside town, Great Yarmouth, which for me and the purposes of the film is Wonderland, and provided the perfect off-kilter backdrop. Again Maggie adapted very quickly to the environment and people around her and Danny made it comfortable for her."

For Dyer, *Malice In Wonderland* was a welcome change of pace: "This was an opportunity to have a different look with a leather jacket, looking cool. It was a chance to have a different look about me that I didn't have before. It was like the idea of being told not to act all the time, to be really animated, to really take it to a fucking weird level because I'm not a real character. I'm playing this weird cunt who speaks at one hundred miles an hour and he's really bitchy, I'm basically the rabbit from the movies. It really excited me."

Filming began in Great Yarmouth in the summer of 2008 with a budget of £1 million. Fellows recalls his crew with fondness: "It was just over £1 million budget. I felt it looked a lot more, thanks to the graft and craft of all departments, especially the DP, production designer, costume and make-up talent. It was that interesting thing that I find always happens with the right crew that when you're faced with a limited budget it is the limitations that always drive smart solutions to problems that don't necessarily compromise the look of a film – and at times enhance it."

The shoot was a fun one and Fellows recalls one particularly funny Dyer escapade that left the star bereft of his tough guy image: "We were shooting through the night at the end of Great Yarmouth Pier. It was the carousel scene where Alice meets Gonzo (Matt King) the fairground owner and his minions and is then rescued by Whitey (Danny). We had full control of the fairground and obviously it was all switched on for lighting and functional. During a break I saw Danny and Matt King slink off together towards the ghost train/haunted house ride. The crew were all drinking their hot soup as I watched them both step cautiously through the black rubber doors like two naughty boys and disappearing inside the ride. Silence and the sound of the ocean crashing beneath the pier, then a massive spooky klaxon sounded, the classic one from all our childhood memories whenever a cart enters the ride. Both Danny and Matt flew out of the black doors, running for their lives and scared shitless, not realising the rides were working. I think there was the green glowing skeleton on some fishing line that jumped out in front of them when the klaxon went off. Very funny and not very 'hard' of them both, if you know what I mean!"

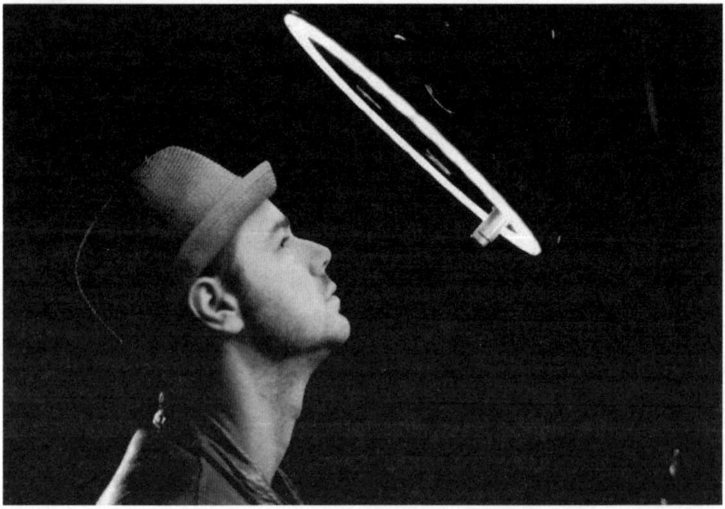

One problem the production encountered was that, despite playing a taxi driver, Danny didn't actually hold a driving licence. Fellows recounts: "Yeah I only got wind of that one halfway into the shoot! Mind you, typical Danny, he went for it with a shot, driving and skidding up on the pavement outside of a corner store, and he nailed it in the first take. The rest of the London taxi shots were pretty much shot against green screen, which worked beautifully. It's sometimes not easy to make fake driving look right, but he did it."

Fellows enjoyed working with Dyer: "He's a very talented actor. He always knew his lines, he plays well off other talent and when asked can bend the performance a little this way or that with ease, he's a bright boy. He's very classy in my opinion and a nice bloke to boot."

The director was happy with the finished film: "Yes, very happy. I always knew it was going to be tough to make a visual and contemporary *Alice* film on a tight budget and also knew the script had that Marmite factor (you either love it or hate it). I think the film is very different and impressive on its budget and I really loved the emotional themes running underneath the plot. I find it very touching at times."

But once again, fate conspired to sink the film. Sony acquired the film for the UK and in light of the success Revolver had enjoyed by mis-selling *Borstal Boy* and *City Rats*, decided to jump on the misleading sleeve bandwagon.

*The Guardian*'s Peter Bradshaw singled Dyer out for praise in his otherwise dismissive two-star review: "Dyer has some funny lines, and he makes the most of them, proving that he is actually a good performer, all too often marooned in endless geezer knees-ups. But otherwise it's a bit pointless and heavy-handed." Cult movie doyen Kim Newman, writing for *Empire*, welcomed the film, calling it a "genuinely original interpretation of the Brit gangster and Lewis Carroll's surreal tale", and awarding a rare three stars. This cool, decidedly underwhelming reaction clearly indicated that the film was going to be a hard sell and influenced Sony's decision not to release the film theatrically.

Following a muted premiere at cult film destination The Prince Charles Cinema, at which a proud Dyer was visibly bemused by the posters which presented the wacky fairytale as some kind of gangster film, *Malice In Wonderland* was released straight to DVD with little fanfare in the hope that Dyer's name and a generic cover would ring the bell. Week one sales just north of 10,000 proved the distributors wrong and, as word spread that the film wasn't what it appeared to be, audiences dropped off and it has only sold 42,000 copies to date.

Simon Fellows was, of course, disappointed with Sony's release strategy: "It could have been a lot better, if only they would have gone with the film it is, then I feel audiences are for sure smart enough to embrace it. I think Danny playing a romantic lead basically is brilliant and he pulls it off beautifully."

"*Malice*, again I had really high hopes for it, I loved it," reflects Dyer, "Just the whole *Alice In Wonderland* thing, everyone knows that story so I thought everyone would be able to identify with it. I don't know what happened, I have no idea what happened."

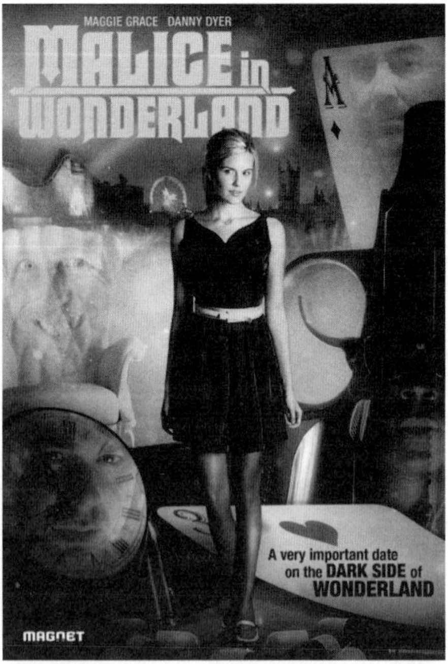


If you go out and buy one Danny Dyer film that you haven't seen after reading this book, make it *Malice In Wonderland*. Beautifully shot, skillfully directed and performed with passion, it is a genuine shame that it has fallen through the cracks. Quite unlike any other British film of the period, this really should have opened Dyer (who is superb throughout, as is Maggie Grace) up to a whole new audience, whereas in retrospect, the cheap mis-sell of the DVD only hastened the decline of his quality film career.

# JUST FOR THE RECORD (2010)

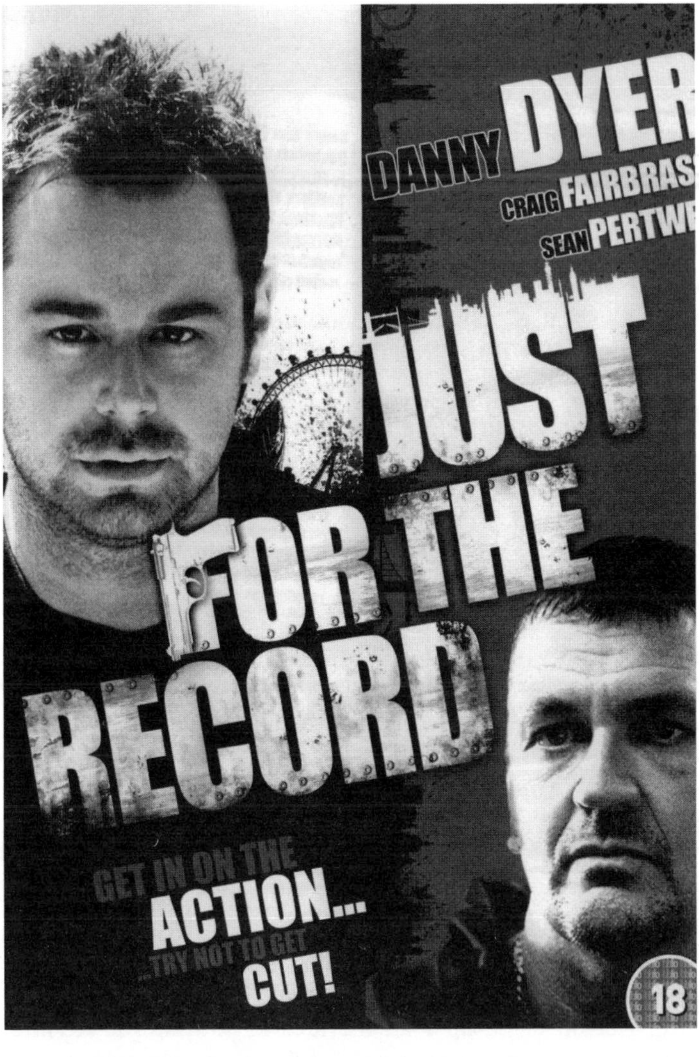


**"If you're going to make a film about a film failing you're setting yourself up for a major fucking fall."**

**Director** Steve Lawson **Producers** Steve Lawson, Jonathan Sothcott **Writer** Phillip Barron **Additional Material** Ben Shillito **Production Designer** Sophie Wyatt **Costume Designer** Alice Woodward

**Danny Dyer** Derek La Farge **Craig Fairbrass** Malcolm 'Mental Fists' Wickes **Rik Mayall** Andy Wiseman **Billy Murray** Wilson Barnes **Victoria Silvestedt** Sarah Freidrechs **Roland Manookian** Harlan Noble **Sean Pertwee** Sensei **Colin Salmon** Maynard Stark **Triana Terry** Lucy Smithfield **Steven Berkoff** Mike Rosferry **Ian Virgo** Flynn Beatty **Phil Davis** Ed Grains **Geoff Bell** Nicholas Johnson **Lisa McAllister** Rosie Frond **Ciaran Griffiths** Danny **Callum MacNab** Mark

*After a disastrous attempt at making a romantic comedy set in a second-hand record store, cast and crew are rounded up for a documentary by film-maker Andy Wiseman. As the accusations fly thick and fast, it soon becomes clear that most of the interviewees are at the very least deluded and in some cases insane.*

Perhaps unsurprisingly, *Just For The Record* has its roots in fact – in summer 2008 a micro-budget comedy called *Mixed Up* began filming at Beanos record store in Croydon. Among the cast were future *Just For The Record* stars Billy Murray and Lisa McAllister, alongside former *Hollyoaks* actor Lee Otway, Terry Stone (*Rise Of The Footsoldier*), Adele Silva (*Doghouse*), Sylvester McCoy (*Doctor Who*) and Faye Tozer (from Steps). After a few weeks of filming, relations between the producer and director broke down irreparably and the film was knocked on the head. A bitter round of recriminations followed and eventually producer Jonathan Sothcott and writer Phillip Barron came up with the idea of slotting the existing footage into a mockumentary about the worst film ever made, with the original cast playing themselves. Barron's screenplay was initially offered to Martin Kemp to direct while he was making horror film *Stalker* on location in Suffolk. Kemp, showing his usual good judgement, turned the project down, citing his belief that nobody beyond those involved in making the film would find it funny.

A visitor to the set of *Stalker* was Steve Lawson, an affable businessman from Essex who was trying to carve a career as an actor and had invested in both the abortive *The Rapture* and *Jack Said.* Lawson sensed that his ambition of becoming a leading man was not around the next corner and decided that he would like to try his hand at directing. He offered to fund *Just For The Record* on the condition that he could direct it. Lawson sensibly wanted to drop the idea of using the *Mixed Up* footage and fictionalise the whole affair, starting from scratch and using assumed names to protect the guilty. Writer Phillip Barron notes, "Creating different characters was much more liberating. It amused me later on when people reviewed *JFTR* negatively and listed certain characters as stereotypes – usually the ones who were most closely based on real people."

Lawson's enthusiasm to throw everything he could at his directorial debut meant that he wanted Barron to considerably expand on the original 90-page script. Barron recalls, "The film was certainly very different from my third and final draft, the one where I was asked to open the whole film out, throw in lots of famous lookalikes and double the length of the script (obviously, that wasn't the actual instruction – but I was asked to take a script with no action lines and put an action line between every line of dialogue without cutting ANY of that dialogue. Seemed fairly obvious the script would double in length, but no one was interested... until they actually received the 170-odd page script they'd inadvertently asked for!)." Among the new additions were the UK's fattest man Barry Austin as a karate student and lookalikes of Brad Pitt and Sylvester Stallone, who producer Nicholas Johnson (Geoff Bell) meets in a strip club. There was even a part written for Simon Phillips as unlikely action man Jack Adleth's bank manager brother, Colin.

Still sore at his bad experience on *The Rapture*, Lawson drafted in most of the incomplete film's cast – Geoff Bell, Roland Manookian, Ian Virgo, Lucinda Rhodes, Lisa McAllister, Colin Salmon, Phil Davis and Steven Berkoff were all sufficiently eager to poke fun at the indie film scene that they signed on for *Just For The Record.* Lawson's penchant for British gangster movies saw him also offering the likes of Craig Fairbrass and Frank Harper roles.

At this stage, Lawson brought in his friend Ben Shillito to script edit and ultimately write additional scenes as required. Perhaps the biggest casting coup was much-loved funnyman Rik Mayall, the only accepted comedy movie actor in the film. Also attached at this stage was *A-Team* icon Dirk Benedict, who was scheduled to play Wilson Barnes (and is billed as such on early promotional art for the film). Eventually the dates didn't work and the search was on for a replacement Barnes throughout most of filming. Another tantalising prospect was Martin Kove – the villain in the original *Karate Kid* films – who was approached to play Harlan's sensei. Unfortunately, budget restrictions meant that he could no longer be accommodated, something he is no doubt relieved at today. Sean Pertwee stepped up to the part and almost stole the movie.

As production loomed, an approach was made to Danny Dyer to appear in the film – all of his peers were in it and he would be the cherry on the cake. Dyer was offered the role of suave executive producer Derek La Farge, the invention of Ben Shillito. Dyer agreed, electing to model the character's mannerisms on producer Jonathan Sothcott (he can be seen sporting Sothcott's pink tie throughout most of the film). Writer Phillip Barron recalls, "I was very confused when I heard Danny was playing the executive producer because I couldn't work out how he would fit into the story; but since that was made a feature of Derek La Farge's character and there was very little story to speak of... yeah, he works as well as anything else! I like the fact no one knew what he was doing there... but I do feel it probably confused most of the (tiny) audience. It also felt a bit odd that a lot of Danny's lines were ones I'd written for other characters – they didn't quite seem to fit in his mouth; but he definitely created the funniest moment in the film. Faint praise that, though."

Filming began on location in Essex in the summer of 2009 and new scenes and characters were added throughout the duration of the shoot. Eventually Billy Murray (upon whom the character was based) stepped up to play Wilson Barnes, giving one of the film's better performances.

Once the edit began, it soon became apparent that much of what was shot couldn't possibly make the final cut. Gone was Danny Midwinter's Rastafarian porn star. Gone was Jamie Foreman as a photographer who could top any anecdote. Gone was an ill-advised cameo from Z-list celebrity Jack Tweed. Virtually gone was Jenna Harrison as Sarah's alcoholic PA and Isabelle Defaut's paralytic production manager. Gone, too was what semblance of a story there was, as writer Phillip Barron reflects: "The film varies wildly from scene to scene and that makes it difficult to watch. There seems very little point or dramatic tension in the film either – I honestly can't remember if that's the script's fault or not. Possibly; but no one seemed to pick up on it at the time. Either way, the script which people (apparently) read and (claimed they) enjoyed somehow turned into a film which is almost completely unwatchable!"

Producer Jonathan Sothcott reflects: "I learned so much about comedy on that film – mostly that I shouldn't try and do it again. We all sat around splitting our sides laughing at how clever and hilarious we were, and of course the end result was just a ridiculous mess. One thing that became apparent in the edit very quickly, however was that some of the smaller

characters were much, much funnier than the leads – in fact the director, producer and writer characters were all pretty weak. Dyer, Fairbrass and Murray, on the other hand, who should have been supporting characters, were getting what few laughs there were to be had. In fact, there's no doubt that Danny steals the film." Writer Phillip Barron concurs, "I thought he was great. There are some great performances in that film and Danny's was one of them. Unfortunately, in a film *that* bad it's hard to isolate anyone and say they did a good job; but I do think there are certain actors who were incredibly funny. I think Danny's portrayal was spot on and if you just watch his scenes on their own you can see how funny, creepy and useless Derek La Farge is."

Danny Dyer recalls: "If you think about it, it was my first opportunity to do an accent, it was a bit nerve-wracking really. I remember some of the extras on that film couldn't believe that it was me playing that role. It was a completely different idea. I quite liked the script, and I thought it had potential. But if you're going to make a film about a film failing you're setting yourself up for a major fucking fall. The film's about a shit film that never really happened. I mean I'm really happy with how I did in it, and it was nice to be able to do something completely different, I really milked it, and it was comedy which was what I wanted to be doing, and it was doing it in a slapstick characterised way, I loved it. A weird job, man."

With the film assembled, London sales agent Moviehouse Entertainment took on the job of selling it to distributors. "I was in a pub when Gary Phillips from Moviehouse called to say there was an offer from Metrodome," recalls producer Jonathan Sothcott. "It wasn't big money by any means but it was money and the film wasn't exactly catching fire elsewhere. So I said, 'fuck it, let them have it.' Gary said they'd asked if we'd be flexible about which faces could be on the DVD cover – maybe just Dyer, Fairbrass and Mayall. That made sense – Danny and Craig would sell more DVDs than Roland and Geoff. Little did I know the significance of what I had just agreed to."

Metrodome – predominantly a minor art-house distributor which made the odd foray into commercial territory – had thought they'd spotted an opportunity to 'do a *City Rats*'. They packaged this silly mockumentary about the film industry as a gangster film, predictably with a red, white and black cover using an image of Danny from another film. Even the synopsis on the back cover bore scant relation to the movie:

*Danny Dyer (The Football Factory, The Business), Craig Fairbrass (Rise Of The Footsoldier, The Bank Job), Sean Pertwee (Dog Soldiers, Doomsday), Phil Davis (Dead Man Running), Steven Berkoff (The Krays) and Billy Murray (Rise Of The Footsoldier) come together as one of the greatest British casts in recent memory. Dirty dealings, back-stabbing, insults, threats, blackmail and deception – it's all in a day's work for this motley crew who have been assembled for a business venture more treacherous than any kind of criminal behaviour! As sparks fly, it's every man for himself, take no prisoners and, hopefully, get out in one piece with reputation still in one mangled piece!*

Knowing that the film-makers would carry the can for this, Jonathan Sothcott commissioned an alternative DVD cover and got Metrodome to agree to printing the cover double-sided, so stores could make the choice of selling the film as a comedy or as the gangster film Metrodome were pushing. Sothcott later went into supermarkets all over the country asking the DVD section staff to reverse the covers. Many were receptive to the idea (having no notion that the film was a comedy) but many had a policy that taking the discs out of the shrink wrap voided their returns policy and so refused.

Writer Phillip Barron was less than impressed: "So they came up with this for the DVD cover: a photo of Danny from a different film and emphasising words like CUT and ACTION. They even put a gun on the front cover. A fucking gun! This had the amazing effect of pissing off everyone who bought the DVD expecting it to be a Danny Dyer gangster movie. It wasn't a good film to start with, but setting up audience expectation for a different film really doesn't help. It's a bad film, they weren't going to make any money from it so it made (business) sense to alter the cover before word gets round that it's a complete turkey. There probably wouldn't have been any good word of mouth about it anyway; but all they did there was ensure everyone who saw the film would hate it."

Ben Shillito was equally unimpressed, telling film journalist MJ Simpson: "The *JFTR* sleeve came to my BlackBerry from Steve, forwarded from an original message from Jonathan. The design was attached as a jpeg, and the subject of the message was simply, 'You're not going to believe this'. Suffice it to say, we didn't believe it. My response contained the word 'mendacious' – most other personnel used stronger language. Arguments followed. Enough said."

Dyer, too, was disgusted: "It was really starting to bug me at this point. I mean for fuck's sake, it had me and Craig Fairbrass on the front with a gun. I thought, 'Fucking hell man, is this what the British film industry has come to now, is it just about numbers? Where's the creative aspect to it?' Of course, I'm the fall guy for that, so you're almost your own worst enemy. That was fucking bollocks. It's a constant fucking thing of laziness; it's really frustrating for me."

A far bigger problem than the cover was on the horizon, however, and the DVD cover byline "Get in on the action – try not to get Cut' was to haunt the film's brightest star for some time to come.

On 5 May 2010 the producers staged a premiere at the lavish Curzon cinema in London's Mayfair. Initial disappointment at a lack of press interest soon turned to concern as the film became engulfed in a very controversial story.

Dyer had, for some time, been contributing a weekly Agony Uncle column to lad's Mag, *Zoo*. In the latest issue – published the day before – Dyer apparently counselled heartbroken 'Alex from Manchester' to cut his ex-girlfriend's face so that nobody else would want her. *Zoo* had a weekly circulation in excess of 100,000 copies at the time but this appalling mis-step soon spread far wider. And the insane vilification of Danny Dyer as a violent misogynist began. Jonathan Sothcott picks up the story: "not to knock Danny's literary prowess, but he never wrote a word of that column. He'd have five minutes on the phone with a *Zoo* journalist every week and they'd cobble something together and not send him the copy to approve. The real story was how the hell this slipped by the subs and the editor himself – but journalists are often wary of bashing their own, and Danny is an easy target." As the premiere loomed just hours away, Dyer was trending on Twitter for all the wrong reasons and – unsurprisingly – the condemnation began in earnest.

Holly Dustin, manager of the End Violence Against Women coalition, told *The Guardian*: "Danny Dyer's advice to a *Zoo* magazine reader to 'cut' his ex-girlfriend's face is truly stomach-churning. Violence against women and girls is no joke but a dreadful reality for too many. Around half of women experience domestic violence, sexual assault or stalking in their lifetime. Worryingly, one in two young men think it's okay to hit a woman or force her to have sex in certain circumstances. We are calling on *Zoo* magazine to publish a prominent retraction and tell its readers what its stance is on violence against women. Furthermore, the next government must tackle media messages that condone or tolerate violence against women as a priority." *The Guardian* also quoted Ceri Goddard, chief executive of the Fawcett Society: "I can only assume that Dyer thought he was being ironic. But I would like him to explain that to a woman who is a victim of violence. I am worried that this does show an attitude that jokes about violence against women are fair game."

Jonathan Sothcott recalls, "despite the media frenzy – the cinema was absolutely surrounded by paps like a scene from *Zulu* – Danny showed up for the film. I never thought he would in a million years but that's a testament to his enormous professionalism. I met him in a hotel round the corner and he was absolutely in bits about the whole thing, he was just completely devastated. It was very obvious that he'd been a victim of malice or accident but that didn't make him feel any better." Sothcott ended up giving an interview defending Dyer to the BBC inside the cinema as the actor was advised not to comment.

*Zoo* magazine quickly issued a statement blaming a typo – "Due to an extremely regrettable production error, an inappropriate and indefensible response to a letter has appeared in this week's issue. *Zoo* editor, Tom Etherington, apologises unreservedly for any offence the response may have caused and has launched an internal enquiry to ensure lessons are learnt. *Zoo* and Danny Dyer condemn any violence against women. A donation will be made to Women's Aid."

But it was too little, too late. Would things have been different if Danny had issued a denial on the day? Maybe, maybe not. But press across the spectrum were now lining up to take pot shots at an actor whose seemingly unbreakable run of success they clearly resented. Reflecting on the debacle in a 2013 interview with *The Independent*, Dyer said, "It just makes me feel sick that people would believe that I'm this misogynist who would advise somebody to cut a woman's face."

*Just For The Record* was released across six cinema screens in the UK, showing in mid-morning slots. It grossed just £35, most of it from writer Phillip Barron, who went to see it with a couple of his friends. There were no posters for the film in the foyer and because an audience wasn't expected, the film had started ten minutes early.

In order not to expose the mis-sell of the DVD, Metrodome (perhaps sensibly) elected not to send out review copies of the film. One review surfaced on film blog HeyYouGuys.co.uk, but critic Emily Breen seemed to have been watching a different movie, laying into Dyer: "By way of contrast *Just For The Record* features a star appearance from DVD-shifting powerhouse Danny Dyer, in a surprising turn as sleazy producer Derek La Farge. His schmoozing, smooth-talking patter intended to offer hilarious contrast to his usual brand of "awright treacle" Ray Winstone charm. The problem: Ray Winstone can parody his caricature and play against type because he is a talented actor who understands nuance. Danny Dyer ought to play to his strengths – or play to the terraces – until he has mastered his art. His performance seems almost to be an in-joke with someone just off camera and, after an initial chuckle at the terrible accent, the joke wears wafer thin fast." Harold Pinter, of course, was more than happy that Dyer had mastered his art some time before *Just For The Record*, but online critics do often see things quite differently to the rest of us.

Released on DVD on 17 May without any kind of publicity campaign, the film bombed, shifting just 4,177 units in its first week of release, the worst result for a Dyer film since *The*

*Great Ecstasy Of Robert Carmichael* five years earlier. In its first month it sold just over 12,000 units in total and has now hit the 31,000 mark. The public were not as stupid as Metrodome had hoped.

Generally grouped with the likes of *Jack Said, The Basement* and *7Lives* as the nadir of Danny's film career, *Just For The Record* is a truly wretched and largely unfunny film, but buried deep amid the rubbish are a few things to love, not least of all what might well by Dyer's funniest screen performance. Looking totally unlike 'Danny Dyer', with slicked back hair, a moustache and a smart suit and tie, Dyer delivers a blisteringly funny performance that is part Leslie Phillips, part Terry Thomas and all so much funnier than a single frame of *Run For Your Wife*. There are other fun performances too – Craig Fairbrass plays it brilliantly straight as a hulking gangster, Billy Murray is on good form as a fading boozehound and Steven Berkoff rants away with aplomb, hamming it up for all he's worth. Ill-conceived and distinctly amateurish in places, *Just For The Record* is a misfire of spectacular proportions but – as with other ensemble pieces – it is completely unfair that it is regarded as 'a terrible Danny Dyer film' when he has less than ten minutes' screen time. On the contrary, Dyer's brief screen time serves to illustrate what a naturally funny comedic actor he is and while the film stands little chance of a critical reappraisal it can only be hoped that Derek La Farge will some day come to be appreciated as one of the actor's best-kept but most enjoyable movie secrets.

# PIMP (2010)

**"This was the first real opportunity to play a really nasty, fucked-up sociopath."**

**Director** Robert Cavanah **Producers** Crispin Manson, Robert Cavanah, Matthew Stradling, Royd Tolkein **Writer** Robert Cavanah, Jon Kirby **Production Designer** Simon Pickup **Costume Designer** Georgina Napier **Director of Photography** Steven Annis

**Robert Cavanah** Woody **Danny Dyer** Stanley **Gemma Chan** Bo **Billy Boyd** Chief **Scarlett Alice Johnson** Lizzy **Barbara Nedeljakova** Petra **Martin Compston** Zeb **Susie Amy** Tammy **Robert Fucilla** Vincent **Adam Saint** Vlad

*Soho pimp Woody is charged with finding a missing prostitute by his boss Stanley. The deeper Woody digs, the more it appears that the girl is involved in the underground snuff movie scene – but all is not what it appears and soon Woody finds himself in danger.*

In the broad cannon of Danny Dyer's films, *Pimp* might just be the most under-appreciated of them all. It is remembered mainly for its £205 opening weekend box office, which *The Guardian* et al latched onto with predictable fervour. Dig a little deeper, however, and there's an interesting and gripping thriller set among the Soho vice trade that has a genuinely different style and a lot to appreciate.

Star/director/co-writer/producer Robert Cavanah was a popular face on television on both sides of the Atlantic from shows such as *Taggart, Highlander, The Raven* and *The Royal* and had film credits including *Tomb Raider: Cradle Of Life* under his belt when the prospect of what became *Pimp* was first mooted. He recalls: "The idea for *Pimp* was originally Jon Kirby's. He and producer Crispin Manson approached me, probably around 2004 or 05, in Cannes. I knew Crispin from my first short film which he associate produced. Jon had written a script called *Scratched Inside,* about a week in the life of a pimp, more or less, and would I consider the main role. I read it and really liked the core premise, but thought the script needed work. I offered that I would play the role if we could rewrite the script first. Jon very graciously agreed and so over the next couple of years Jon and I would occasionally meet when time availed itself, but it eventually became clear we had different ideas of where the story ought to go and its tone. Jon finally felt it might be best if I took the script and ran with it on my own. I loved the tone of *Man Bites Dog*, and adored the visual style and Pinteresque dialogue of *Sexy Beast*. I went into Soho and interviewed people in and around the sex trade and garnered stories, detail and characters which began to inform *Pimp*. Pretty much everyone and everything within it was ultimately based on reality, including Gerald and his traffic cone; a scene which has come under some heavy criticism for being ludicrous. What can I say to that! I also wanted to make my docu device credible, so conceived that the film should have no stars in it, no titles and be virally linked and connected to real sex industry workers' online profiles, so we might really push the reality angle. However, the docu device and the release strategy meant a bespoke tack in marketing from both the distributors and the producing team to create a cultish product, which I really wanted to do. This just wasn't gonna happen, sadly. I think this would have created a very different legacy for us."

Cavanah had always intended to both star in the film and direct it, as he explains: "I was always intended to play Woody, Jon was to direct, with me assisting. However, ultimately, the script and the role became so close to me that it just made sense for me to helm it too, and since I had directed some short films and telly, it seemed a natural step. I wanted a debut feature project as a director, and since Jon felt that the script had evolved somewhat differently to his original conceit and that perhaps he did not have the right sensibility for the new script, with his blessing it evolved that I should do both jobs. It would save us money in the budget, too, since I wrote, directed, acted in and produced. Had we employed a director, they definitely would have needed to be paid. I received no fee for any of my roles. I should point out that while I received no fees, nor did the other producers. I was unpaid four times. They were unpaid once. However, for all of us, the outcome remained the same – we were unpaid. There was one point early on where we discussed if it was wiser to cast a name actor in the role, but given the level of budget and that Woody had been written to my strengths, plus that Revolver (our distributor) was not asking that I step aside, it seemed absurd not to leave me in the role of Woody. Further, I had written every scene with a clear vision of how it ought to look and feel, so it seemed that finding a director who had the chops but would also be willing to accommodate prior expectations may have been unfair and hard on them. It might have been interesting to see what another director would have done with it, and to see if I could have dodged a little of the flak I got. However, I wanted to direct my debut feature, and it got a national release – despite flak – which is still an achievement I am proud of."

Ironically given their 'home of Danny Dyer' positioning, UK distributor Revolver came on board before he was involved, as Cavanah explains: "I had a champion at Revolver in David Shear. Initially, we couldn't get distribution in the UK to even return our calls. However, my manager in LA called me one day and said he was at a party there with a guy from Revolver who had never heard of *Pimp* and was interested in chatting. I chatted with him and asked him to the negotiating table. He agreed instantly, and we met and thrashed out a basic deal. This was early on, before Danny and the other cast came aboard. David was great from start to finish and whenever things got stressful, he offered support, and ultimately he and Revolver loved the film."

Cavanah packed the cast with high-calibre friends and colleagues including Billy Boyd and Martin Compston, but the villain of the piece was not initially intended for Dyer, as Cavanah recalls: "I originally wanted Danny's character, Stanley, to be older and had written it thus. I had met and asked Brian Cox, at a couple of social occasions, if he would look at it when it was ready and he said yes. Brian and I are with the same agency, so when the moment came I asked them to give the script to him. That process took an inordinate amount of time because of various factors not necessarily within our agent's control, and ultimately it didn't work out. Time was now precious, so I offered it to about half a dozen big-name actors of similar age and standing to Brian, but they were all either too expensive or unavailable. Finally, I was watching *Adulthood* one day on DVD. I saw Danny and realised this was the legend that is Danny Dyer. I hadn't actually seen his other films before. I knew his name, of course, but not the man. If an actor isn't in drama on Radio 4, or history documentaries, I wasn't likely to come across them. I then watched a few of Danny's films to get up to speed, and excitedly rewrote Stanley for him. It worked far better than I had dreamed and I felt kinda dumb for not thinking of it before. Then we asked Danny; the litmus test. I might have done all this work for a swift, 'No thanks.' To my amazement he loved it and said yes. He loved the dialogue and thought it was bold, brassy and still credible. Though Revolver had committed to the film without a cast attached, Danny was the cream on a cake already baked, as it were. As Danny is simply an actor who wants to act in good material, he turned up, did a great job, was a gem to work with, then moved on graciously and left us to it; never less than a fantastic ambassador to the film's intention and to me. I am very proud of his input and his loyalty to me and the material too."

Dyer, was also enthusiastic about the role: "This was the first real opportunity to play a really nasty, fucked-up sociopath. I got sent the script and I was really busy at the time with shooting something else. I remember reading it and thinking that it had real potential and I loved the whole mockumentary style of it. I love London, and I love Soho – it's a really fascinating place. To delve into it with this was really interesting. We were on a very low budget again but I relished the role as it was a really good opportunity to play a nasty cunt. As much as people said I had, I'd never really done that before."

Revolver, still basking in the monster success of *Dead Man Running* and *City Rats* while *Pimp* was in production in the summer of 2009, must have thought all their Christmases had come at once when Dyer boarded the project and there was clearly a shift in thinking at the distributor as they lined up the film as a Dyer movie, continuing to promote themselves as 'the home of Danny Dyer'. "Again, I suppose it's the branding thing – I was in it for twenty minutes and I'm on the cover," reflects Dyer, "A 'Danny Dyer' fucking vehicle, a 'Danny Dyer' film. Of course it happened just after the *Zoo* magazine thing."

Cavanah fondly recalls Dyer's input and commitment to the role of Stanley, which was quite a departure from his usual casting: "Danny upped everyone's game. All he had to do for that was arrive, but he does more than just that; he comes to work like any actor, with notions of the role, ideas for amendments if necessary, a will to excellence, and the manners of a gentleman. He was very loving and supportive to all of us among the crew, or visitors to set. I could see from the first that he understood the mechanics of screen acting intrinsically, though his theatre experience too reminds you he is an actor with depth and earnest intention. My only regret with Danny is that I hadn't more for him to do, but it was already set to paper so all you can do is shoot it. There was one scene which wasn't in the script, which evolved because Danny's approach to the character inspired something other than I had anticipated. The 'Cuntbox 'scene. Danny makes profanity sound both onomatopaeic and opposite to its meaning all at the same time, which had us in hysterics, so I asked the art department to rustle up a money box to allow for a pound to be deposited every time his character swore; then simply filmed him swearing as much as he wanted, whatever words he chose. We then shot lots of money being dropped into the Cuntbox, edited it all together in a short, comic sequence, and thus one of my favourite moments in the film was born."

Cavanah also found directing himself to be a relatively painless experience: "Directing myself was fairly easy, because I was aware intrinsically what the role needed since I had created it. I trained at Drama Centre London and have acted in a considerable volume of TV, film and theatre, so I knew all I really had to do was know my lines, avoid bumping into furniture, focus more on everyone else, and naturalism would happen. If it were a more intense character journey which demanded a different set of preparations for me, I likely wouldn't have done both jobs; as with another film I am trying to get off the ground called *Invisible*. I recognise that this is a role which needs no other job to interfere with it."

Though the shoot was a smooth one, cracks begin to show in the production once the edit began. Cavanah reflects: "Production started smoothly, and the team seemed to be pulling in the same direction, but when we got into the edit it became fractious. There were signs of this in pre-production but I was too busy to really deal with it more astutely. I had people telling me how to edit the film in quite astonishing detail, taking it in directions that to me seemed against the original conceit, much of which, in my opinion, cheapened the final product. It was an experience I much regretted, not least because I ended up with a film that was barely 60% what I planned. I believe when you have the right people for the job, you let them do their job. The tail wagged the dog on this and I am sure we all regret that now. Would I have made *Pimp* without that team though? Perhaps not. So for that I am grateful."

Trade paper *Screen International* ominously foreshadowed the Dyer backlash that surrounded *Pimp*'s release, with Alan Hunter noting, "A small UK theatrical release is scheduled for May 21, but prospects seem slim in a territory where audiences may well be suffering from Danny Dyer fatigue after a surfeit of similar low-life wallows featuring this actor."

Following a lavish premiere in the West End at which branded condoms were given away to attendees, Revolver had booked the film a small platform theatrical release to qualify for VOD on 21 May 2010, ahead of the DVD release on the 24. Like never before, the critics lined up to shred the movie. Writing in *The Guardian*, a ranting Cath Clarke admonished, "There's nothing to recommend Danny Dyer's mock-doc about the Soho sex industry – it's just plain unpleasant... This really is snoringly predictable and Cavanah nonsensically presents it as footage filmed by a documentary team: a real doco unit would have scarpered to the nearest cop shop after witnessing five seconds of beatings and torture. With nil insight – into the sex industry or anything else – you might conclude *Pimp* is a film for men who get their kicks watching Dyer strut around leering at topless women who – in the parlance of the film – look like 'the basic pleasure model'. One for *Zoo* readers, then."

David Jenkins, writing for *Time Out*, was similarly outraged: "What with his writing, TV presenting and movie acting, one might argue that Danny Dyer has – like Peter Ustinov before him – become the counter-cultural media polymath of the age. He restlessly churns out content, but when it comes to film his name is fast becoming a byword for the unutterably dreadful. And so to *Pimp*, a cack-handed and joyless trawl through the grotty dives of Soho following a chaotic week in the life of scallywag sex trafficker Woody (played by writer/director Robert Cavanah). Offering a tired rehash of his stock wideboy persona, Dyer plays crime lord Stanley who employs Woody as muscle for his ongoing turf war against local rivals 'the Chinks'. With its excessive levels of casual racism, sexism and homophobia, the film feels like nothing more than a rejected *Derek And Clive* sketch that's been stripped of eloquence and irony and calibrated instead for cheap, leery laughs."

Quite what possessed film critic Mark Kermode to launch his ranting, free-form assassination of *Pimp* and particularly Dyer on the radio remains a mystery. Despite the fact that Dyer is known for his (widely imitated) deep voice, Kermode's 'impersonation' of him was pitched in an unusually high girly voice – and had nerds and keyboard warriors up and down the country calling him a hero for taking a pop at one of the cool kids. The downward critical spiral of Dyer's films had begun.

And then the inevitable happened. With no press or promotion for the theatrical release– which was intended solely to qualify the movie for Virgin Filmflex – and scathing reviews at every corner… nobody went to see it. The film scraped together a meagre £205 opening weekend ahead of a £658 total UK box office. Mark Kermode must have thought Christmas had come early.

Robert Cavanah highlights the stacked deck the mainstream

press were playing with: "I thought one or two of the bona-fide critics made fair points, which concurred with my own feelings, based on the final edit. However some critics made ludicrous claims, such as the much misinformed amount the film took at UK box office as though this was a true reflection of the film's calibre. These 'professionals' know all about the multi-platform release structure, and precisely what a limited cinema release is for, how much money is NOT spent to advertise the film, how few screens it actually is ever intended to play in, what anti-social times of day the film will screen at, the likelihood it may not even fulfil those times, and that it is pretty much a box-ticking exercise to put it in those cinemas at all. They understand that this structure helps low-budget indie films like ours to see the light of day, yet they hijacked this information to suit a diatribe which was mean and totally out of context. The film did really well on DVD and download, as it was always intended to, and sold confidently abroad too, so it is unfortunate the reviews were as vitriolic as they were."

Dyer, of course, was mortified: "When it came out it's almost like people wanted it to fail. It died a death at the cinema and the press were saying, 'Danny Dyer's fans are deserting him!' But it was only released in three or four cinemas – it wasn't a big release. It was a bad time for me, a horrible time for me. I was reading negative after negative after negative and there wasn't anything I could do about it. I wasn't used to it but that's all part of life I suppose – the world I'm in and the path I chose. In my early career, everything just seemed so easy and natural. It was just hit after hit after hit! I was working with great people and I couldn't put a foot wrong. Now, all of a sudden, I couldn't put a foot right! I really felt for the people that made it, because they got the backlash for the whole *Zoo* thing. Revolver just wanted to whack my fucking face on the cover and sell as many DVDs as possible. They were cut-and-shut merchants. It's great if it works, of course. If it doesn't, I'm the fall guy."

And the irony, of course is that *Pimp* did sell a lot of DVDs – a week one tally of 12,758 units belied a strong word of mouth, and to date *Pimp* has achieved lifetime sales of over 100,000 units, a credible success by any standard. But nobody wants to hear that and it will never be reported in the mainstream press.

As recently as August 2012, the Yahoo movies site was smugly proclaiming, "Everyone's favourite fake football hooligan Danny Dyer was forced to wolf down humble pie when his movie *Pimp* bombed at the British box office in 2010," in a list of 'Britain's biggest box office bombs'. Yet the fact remains that in its actual market, home entertainment, *Pimp* was an enviable and unarguable success.

The other surprise about *Pimp* is that it's actually pretty good – for anyone who knows and loves Soho, it has just enough of a hint of authenticity. The dirty, rough-and-ready camerawork keeps it interesting and Robert Cavanah is consistently watchable and convincing as harangued flesh peddler Woody. Dyer gets an unusually showy cameo as vice boss Stanley, decked out in outré Mark Powell tailoring and swearing like a Tourette's convention ("cunt bubble" is our favourite), his scene-stealing turn is a joy to behold. The supporting cast are good too, and the unusually dark ending is suitably satisfying. While it might not be to everyone's taste, *Pimp* is ripe for rediscovery as an engaging and sometimes shocking London film.

# THE LAST SEVEN (2010)

"I liked the idea of this 'end of the world *Armageddon*-type thing."

**Director** Imran Naqvi **Producers** Simon Phillips, Patricia Rybarczyk, Toby Meredith **Writer** John Stanley **Production Designer** Stuart Kearns **Costume Designer** Natalie Egelton **Director of Photography** David Mackie

**Tamer Hassan** Sgt Jack Mason **Simon Phillips** William Blake **Rita Ramnani** Isabelle **Danny Dyer** The Angel of Death **Daisy Head** Chloe Chambers **Sebastian Street** Kendrick **John Mawson** Henry

*Seven disparate people, including a soldier and a politician, find themselves stranded in a deserted London after a mysterious cataclysm. As they struggle to piece together what happened, they are picked off one by one by a demonic entity stalking the empty streets.*

By normal standards, *The Last Seven* is an unremarkable low-budget horror film with hit and miss casting and a predictable conclusion. However, given that it was made by the producers of the execrable *Jack Said* it is a huge step up on every level, and while it shares a fatal flaw with that film, it is at least consistently watchable.

"*The Last Seven* was another favour," recalls Dyer, "Tamer was in it and I liked the idea of this 'end of the world *Armageddon*-type thing. I liked the idea of playing the grim reaper – walking around with a blindfold on, taking people's lives. I don't speak at all; I just come in and take their eyes from them. It was quite weird and arty, which is why I did it."

Producer Simon Phillips scored a major coup reuniting Dyer and Hassan, however spuriously, and as soon as Dyer signed on it was obvious that the film would end up being mis-sold as a gangster film in the wake of *Borstal Boy* and *City Rats*. The coup became an own goal, unfortunately, as Phillips cast himself in the lead, delivering another woeful performance. To his credit, he assembled another army of executive and associate producers, 29 this time, and managed to stage the eerily impressive deserted London scenes on a budget of around £100,000.

Dyer was insistent that there would be no stills of him on the cover, and given that his features are obscured by blood and bandages in the film, it seemed that he would have his way. When a deal was struck with Metrodome, who were predictably eager to promote the picture as a blokey gangster outing, a way around the lack of stills was soon found and an old stock image of Dyer was plastered front and centre on the artwork. "Again, I'm in it for ten minutes, they chucked me on the cover and it didn't work," reflects Dyer, "So you can see the downward spiral…"

"A violent post-apocalyptic fantasy is Danny Dyer's latest attempt at career rehabilitation – and has no visible effect," wrote Peter Bradshaw in *The Guardian*. "Danny needed some blue-sky thinking. What he has decided to do is take a role in a terrible British film opposite Tamer Hassan. Now, in terms of career redemption, that is not exactly thinking outside the box. It is thinking tucked well inside the box, with the flaps sellotaped shut over your head." *The Telegraph*'s Tim Robey was similarly dismissive: "This doomily pretentious low-budget Brit thriller is as low on scares as it is on sense."

Released on one screen to platform the film for press, *The Last Seven* took £309 at the UK box office, but still shifted a solid 11,209 units in its first week, as hopeful fans clamoured to see if the film was indeed a bona-fide Dyer/Hassan team up. To date, it has sold just over 38,000 units.

There can be little doubt that Dyer should never have agreed to appear in *The Last Seven*. It isn't a terrible film but his involvement could only ever lead to disappointed audiences as it is no hidden gem like *Malice In Wonderland*. But at this time Dyer's drawing power on DVD was so great that UK distributors were deliberately buying his films with the intention of misrepresenting them as crime/gangster pictures. Perhaps Dyer needed better advice. Perhaps he should have been less rash. Either way, if he'd actually appeared in some half-decent genre films in 2009 and 2010 there can be little doubt that they would have been hugely successful and his star would not have waned so quickly. He simply wasn't being offered the material. For every *Doghouse* and *Dead Man Running* there was a *Jack Said* or a *Dead Cert* – and ultimately the public blame bad films on the face looking out at them from the DVD cover. Dyer was the biggest star in independent films, but he was also a movie star living on a jobbing actor's wages and his bad career decisions were more often than not financially motivated. Despite his star power he never had the comfort afforded by the usual endorsements or glossy magazine spreads that film stars earn money from between carefully selected acting jobs. Instead, Dyer had low budget films offering him thousands for a few days' work. And for a while, his audience was so loyal that it gave every new film a chance. All of that, however, was about to change.

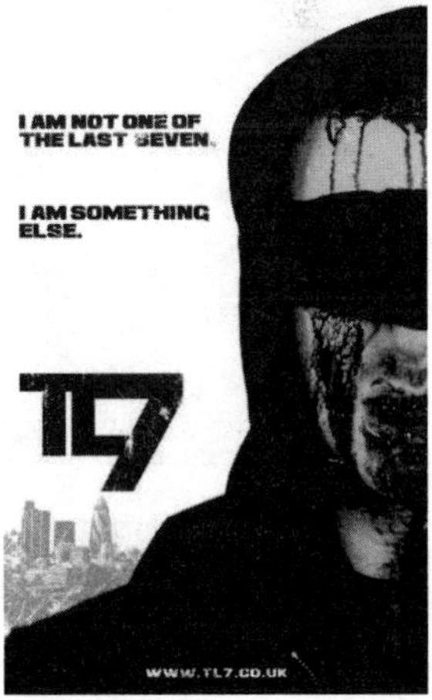

# BASEMENT (2010)

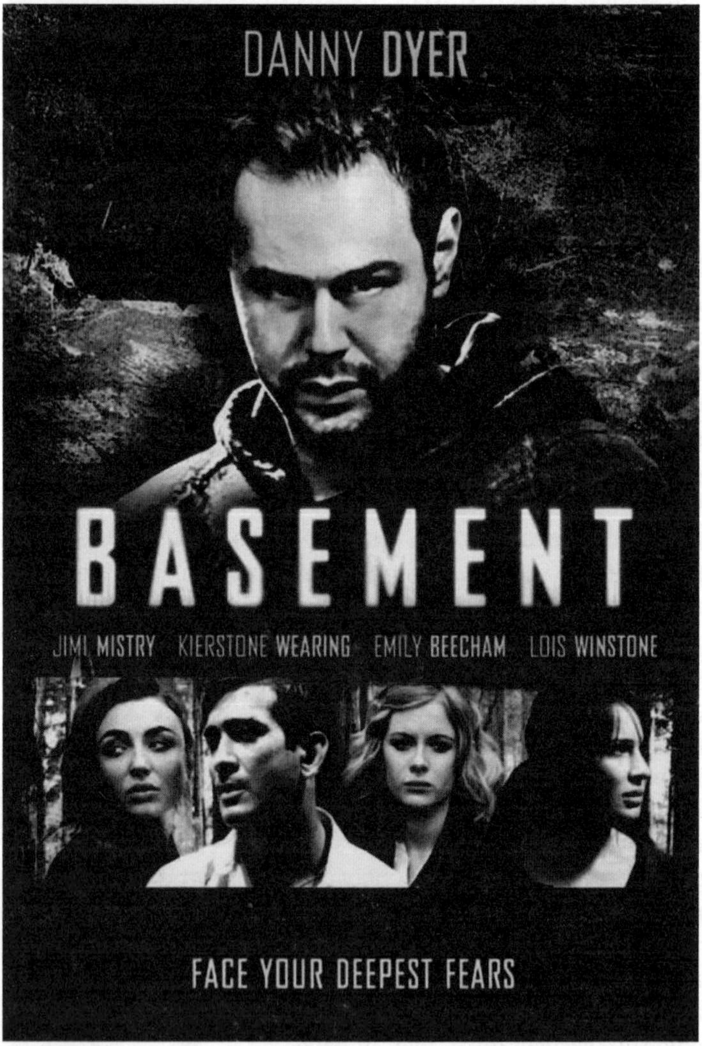


**"The script was constantly changing because we didn't have the money for the prosthetics. It was just a fucking disaster!"**

**Director** Asham Kamboj **Producer** Ish Jalal, Asham Kamboj **Writer** Ewen Glass, Asham Kamboj **Music** Amit Kamboj **Production Designer** Byron Broadbent **Costume Design** Florence Chow **Cinematography** Steel Hudson

**Danny Dyer** Gary **Jimi Mistry** Derek **Kierston Wareing** Sarah **Emily Beecham** Pru **Lois Winstone** Saffron

*After returning from an anti-war demonstration, Gary, Sarah, Saffron, Pru and Derek stop off in the country. Derek and Saffron, separated from the group, discover a metal hatch in the middle of the forest and decide to investigate. Searching for their missing friends, Gary, Pru and Sarah follow Derek and Saffron's footsteps into the hatch. As the door closes behind them, the group realise that they have become victims of a sinister experiment; nobody knows if they will ever escape, let alone survive.*

Filmed at Pinewood Studios, this has an interesting premise and excellent cast (including an uncredited Christopher Ellison), who are unfortunately squandered on a script that fails to understand the notion of suspense. Granted, the tale of a group of people trapped in a bunker is nothing new, but in the right hands this could have been taut, terrifying and thrilling. The miniscule budget is unfortunately apparent at all times, as the lack of a finished script. While the critics were brutal (*Dread Central* called it: "an entertainment black hole. There isn't a single line, performance, camera movement, idea, scene, shot or piece of editing that warrants any kind of praise or attention."), what hurt Dyer the most was letting his fans down.

And the fan comments online speak for themselves:
"I cannot believe how bad this film is.... Quite possibly the worse film I have seen.
I really like Danny Dyer, and thought him and *Severance* were brilliant!
However – this excuse of a horror film had no scares at all.
You will not believe how many times you get a shot of one of

the corridors either in normal shot or green shot. AWFUL!" DompierPapan, Amazon.co.uk

"They said that they couldn't make it without me, so I read it," says Dyer. "I liked the idea of going into horror, as I'd never done proper horror. *Severance* and *Doghouse* were horror comedies, so the idea appealed to me. They let me decide who to cast and I really wanted Kierston Wareing as I've always respected her. We got Jimi Mistry who was a friend of mine and was having a bit of a hard time himself. I feel that he's a much-underrated actor. Since *The Guru*, it all went a bit pear-shaped for him. We'd always spoken about doing something together and this was the perfect opportunity. Unfortunately it was just a fucking disaster from day one. The script was constantly changing because we didn't have the money for the prosthetics. It was just a fucking disaster! The director, who really wanted me, was intimidated by me. He was telling everyone that I was basically fucking the film up. He would sit in his little tent with his monitors and he wouldn't come out and give us notes. He'd send a runner instead. This pissed me off and I had to get it all out in the open because we needed to get the film finished. If I could have walked off any job, it would have been that one. I was thinking, 'This is just horrible!' All the actors were in the same boat, we were all thinking that it just wasn't going to work."

Respected critic Matt Glasby wrote on Totalscifionline.com that: "Very rarely does a film come along with absolutely no redeeming features. *Plan 9 From Outer Space,* for example, was funny. I *Spit On Your Grave* opened debates about the acceptable limits of onscreen sexual cruelty. Even among such unhallowed company, *Basement* is so awful it's almost a non-film, emitting the entertainment equivalent of static or white noise."

The critics were right. But in typical tabloid fashion, *The Sun* ran a story on 19 August 2010 with the headline: "Danny's film is so Dyer". The crux of the piece was that *Basement* is so bad that Dyer didn't even bother turning up to the premiere – going on to report that: "People were even walking out moments after the film started as it was so bad." On the same day, journalist Stuart Heritage ran a comment piece in *The Guardian* asking: "How can Danny save his career?" Despite being occasionally sniffy in the piece, Heritage's main argument was: "Danny Dyer has become the byword for low-budget, no-quality Brit-trash cinema, but beneath the Cockney swagger there's a decent actor struggling to get out."

He went on to say: "*Basement* is different. Squint a bit, and you could even call it a change of direction. It's a psychological thriller from first-time director Asham Kamboj, which means that several well-used Danny Dyer script tropes – bellowed cries of 'fack!' and 'oi!', 'mahg!' and 'mappit' – have been jettisoned in favour of concerned eyebrow-wiggling and scenes of mild peril." Different does not necessarily mean better however. And while Heritage is clearly no fan of Dyer's work with Nick Love (who he blames for ruining Dyer's career), Dyer knew *Basement* would not turn out well. "I knew from day one that it was going to be a disaster," he admits. "I was still getting the backlash from the *Zoo* thing. The tabloids were understandably out to get me for that, so I was thinking, 'This is the last film I need to be doing now. I need to be doing something that's going to be really credible and cool!' But I knew it was terrible and I couldn't wait to just bang it out. I was really, truly hoping that it wouldn't be released. But of course, it was released. No, I didn't go to the premiere. I did eventually sit down and watch it. Well. I tried. I watched twenty minutes of it but couldn't get through to the end..."

His fans agreed. Dyer's presence ensured it sold 5,802 copies in the first week of release. But the word of mouth was not good and soon everyone knew it was a dud so to date it has only sold 20,272 units. A blip on Dyer's career – and arguably, for all of those involved.

# DEAD CERT (2010)

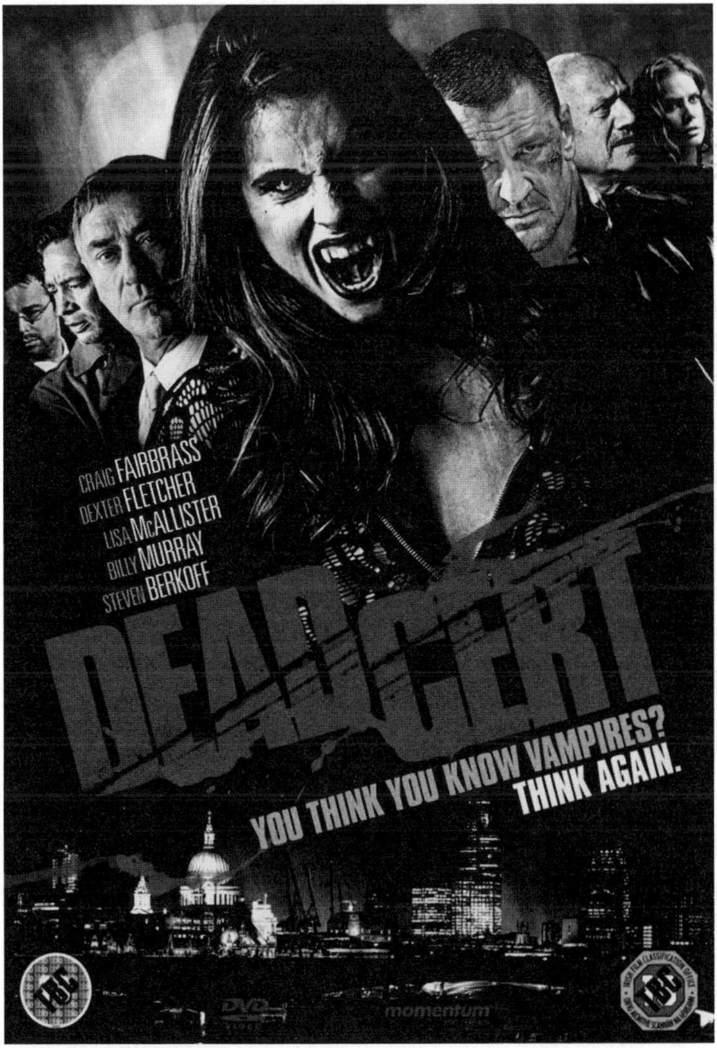


**"I came in for half an hour, did my little bit and I made the cover!"**

**Director** Steve Lawson **Producers** Steve Lawson, Billy Murray, Jonathan Sothcott **Writer** Ben Shillito **Production Designer** Matt Button **Costume Designer** Suzy Peters **Director of Photography** James Friend

**Craig Fairbrass** Freddy Frankham **Janet Montgomery** Giselle **Billy Murray** Dante Livienko **Dexter Fletcher** Eddie Christian **Roland Manookian** Chinnery **Steven Berkoff** Kenneth Mason **Lisa McAllister** Jen Christian **Ciaran Griffiths** Skender **Danny Midwinter** Dennis **Jennifer Matter** Tatiana **Dave Legeno** Yuvesky **Coralie Rose** Charley **Lucinda Rhodes** Katy **Loretta Basey** Steffania **Jason Flemyng** Chelsea Steve **Danny Dyer** Roger Kipling

*Retired villain Freddy Frankham agrees to a bare-knuckle fight between his protégé Dennis Christian and a monstrous member of an Eastern European gang for the rights to his new club, The Paradise. Dennis loses and is killed in the fight, but Freddy soon discovers that his opponent had a supernatural edge – he is a vampire. With vampires now running the club (renamed Inferno), Freddy swears vengeance and the stage is set for a bloody confrontation between bloodsuckers and gangsters.*

Riding high on misplaced self-congratulation after the *Just For The Record* shoot, the same group of film-makers decided to make a more ambitious film on the same model – Steve Lawson's Regency Coins business would bankroll the production, with him directing. The original idea was to film a script by cult horror writer Garry Charles about demons taking over a nightclub. Eventually the script was deemed unsuitable (though Charles received a story credit) and plans for a gangsters vs vampires movie were drawn up, a *From Dusk Till Dagenham* as someone put it, and Lawson enlisted production designer Matthew Button (*Rise Of The Footsoldier, Doghouse*) to turn a huge empty warehouse into a strip club set while Ben Shillito began work on a script. Shillito told journalist MJ

Simpson: "Garry Charles wrote a (very good) screenplay called *Infernal*, in which gangsters from the bare-knuckle boxing world go up against suave demon gangsters who own a fucked-up demon nightclub called Infernal, which the human gangsters must infiltrate to save one of their own after a thrown-fight arrangement goes sour. It was pacy, clever, and had some lovely moments, and it was sent to Steve and me at exactly the point we had begun discussing doing a vampire film, possibly with gangsters in it. Rather than risk ripping off Garry's work, we elected to option the script and repurpose it, changing the demons to vampires, and re-shaping the story. The characters of Frankham, Livienko et al were my work, and were developed over the course of several story conferences between myself, Steve and Nick Onsloe, an actor who is something of an encyclopaedia of bad eighties action and horror films. Between the three of us, we mapped out the shape of the story, then I went to work populating that framework with characters and scenes, working out the beats and scripting. After two quick drafts, we took it to Jonathan Sothcott, who brought his love of Hammer to the table, helping to develop the Livienko character's mythological underpinnings (a strain of Norse mythology from the poetic *Edda*, sadly lost from the finished film) and to construct a Van Helsing character in the form of Steven Berkoff's character."

Initially, the producers hoped to get Sean Pertwee to play Freddy 'Dead Cert' Frankham (the nickname coming from his – ultimately unmentioned – unbroken record as a bare knuckle fighter) and Danny Dyer to play vampire gang boss Dante Livienko. Dyer was unable to commit to the whole shoot and so the tantalising idea of a last-minute cameo raised its head. Meanwhile, as the Freddy Frankham part became more physical through progressive drafts, Craig Fairbrass graduated from the Dennis part in the fantasy casting league to the lead role, while Pertwee moved to the role of vampire hunter Kenneth Mason. A week before production was to begin, Pertwee dropped out altogether, his prior commitment to another film having been called in. Steven Berkoff was a last-minute replacement. Sadly, none of his best scenes (set in the 1987 hurricane as vampires slaughter his brotherhood of monster hunters) made it to the finished film.

The crux of the storyline in the script was the vampire's narcotic, Bliss, supposedly a harmless hallucinogenic but in fact a drug that blurs the lines between reality and fantasy so that people don't realise the undead are on the rise. Like much of the ambitious storyline, this was lost in the translation to film. The Bliss operation is run by faceless businessman Roger Kipling via his vast drug empire. In the proposed sequel (the misplaced self-congratulation very quickly turned to huge optimism) Kipling would be exposed as the real villain of the piece, using the vampires to start a new world order. Danny Dyer agreed to a last minute, unbilled cameo as Kipling as a favour to Jonathan Sothcott.

Filmed on sets built in Dagenham, Essex, and on location in East London in October 2009, *Dead Cert* was plagued by financial and creative problems. Production almost shut down when the money ran out and producer Billy Murray stepped in to plug the shortfall. The usual round of fallings out, accusations and recriminations dogged the project throughout the remainder of filming and into post-production. Ultimately, the script was far too ambitious for the proposed £400,000 budget (which rose to more than twice that as costs spiralled out of control).

Despite the completed film's many shortcomings, a lucrative deal was struck by producer Jonathan Sothcott with Momentum Pictures for the UK. There was no theatrical release of any kind, but the film was selected to play at the prestigious Frightfest horror film festival in August 2010. Attended by most of the key cast, the film was not well received by the genre-savvy audience, and Sothcott and Fairbrass looked suitably embarrassed in the bar afterwards. Dyer, who had graciously allowed his likeness to be used on the art, sensibly stayed at home that night, despite his last-minute on screen appearance prompting the only applause from a disappointed audience.

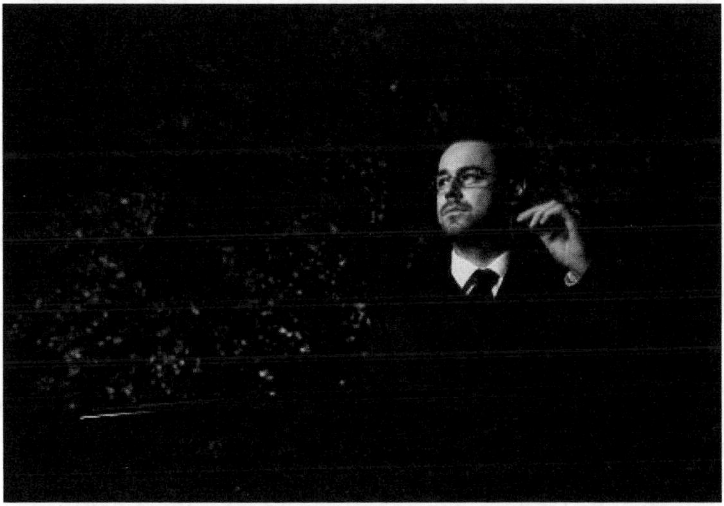

A surprisingly positive review by leading UK trade paper *Screen International* failed to stir up much interest from international buyers – "Clearly the filmmakers have viewed movies like Robert Rodriguez's *From Dusk Till Dawn* before, and make a pretty impressive stab at blending horror and gangster thrills" – and was much kinder than British critics would be upon release.

*Dead Cert* was released on DVD on 27 September 2010 and sold a fairly weak 8,253 in its first week. Momentum did not scrimp on the promotional spend, with solid TV spots and some truly stunning key art which made the film appear to be a far more appealing prospect than it actually was. Word very quickly spread that the movie was a turkey, however. *Total Film* pulled no punches, with Ali Gray opining: "it merely sucks." Writing for *Screenjabber*, Adam Stephen Kelly branded the film "dead forgettable", while James Mudge at *BeyondHollywood* called it "po-faced and unambitious". The public seemed to agree, as by the end of its first month *Dead Cert* had only sold 14,998 units, and to date has yet to break the 30,000 barrier.

Dyer again made the cover of the DVD, as he recalls: "*Dead Cert* was Sothcott again – he asked me to do him a favour. Craig Fairbrass was in it; so I thought, 'Okay, I'll come in on it and I'll do one line.' I never read the script… I didn't feel that I had to. I came in for half an hour, did my little bit and I made the cover!"

*Dead Cert* was received considerably better upon its DVD debut in North America, where the genre press found something to admire in its ambition and enthusiasm for the genre – Barry Keating at *ShockTillYouDrop* called it "a fast-paced, fun 90 minutes" while *HorrorAsylum* praised it as "refreshingly macho". Better critiques didn't help, however, and despite also getting the Blu-ray treatment from American distributor Scream Factory, the film has only sold 7,806 units to date in the USA.

Despite a solid idea and a very strong cast, *Dead Cert* can only be regarded as a mess – the plot is barely coherent, the costumes are appalling, the sound quality is abysmal and the performances are variable, to say the least. Craig Fairbrass is as dependable as ever and there are nice turns by Janet

Montgomery and Ricky Grover, but the vampire gang come across as wooden as the stakes they live in fear of. The big, empty sets feel decidedly cheap and cheerful, and an atmosphere of laziness and disinterest purveys the picture as a whole. Dyer fans won't get any more from watching the film than from looking at the DVD cover, so this one's a dead cert to avoid.

# DEVIL'S PLAYGROUND (2010)

**"It's easier to believe the shit things about yourself than the good things and I realised that I was starting to believe the shit."**

**Director** Mark McQueen **Producers** Jonathan Sothcott, Bart Ruspoli, Freddie Hutton-Mills **Writer** Bart Ruspoli **Production Designer** Sophie Wyatt **Costume Designer** Millie Sloan **Music** James Edward Barker

**Danny Dyer** Joe **Craig Fairbrass** Cole **MyAnna Buring** Angela **Jaime Murray** Lavinia **Shane Taylor** Geoffrey **Lisa McAllister** Kate **Craig Conway** Steve **Colin Salmon** Peter White **Alistair Petrie** Andy Billing **Sean Pertwee** Rob **Bart Ruspoli** Matt Mills

*In the near future, N-Gen Corporation tests RAK295, a performance-enhancing drug, on human subjects, turning them into super-agile, ferocious zombies. The only test subject not affected is Angela Mills, and N-Gen head of security Cole races to find her amid the carnage that is consuming London. Meanwhile Angela is reunited with her ex-cop boyfriend Joe, just released from prison for manslaughter. When Angela realises that she holds the key to a cure, she and her friends (aided by Cole) must try to make their way to a helicopter and escape the city. But the zombies are closing in.*

The origins of *Devil's Playground* go back to a short film called *The Long Night* (2002) produced and written by actor Bart Ruspoli and directed by his drama school friend, actress Isabelle Defaut (who appears, briefly, in *Just For The Record*). A traditional 'group hole up to survive the zombie apocalypse' tale, it features characters who would later appear in *Devil's Playground* – Angela, Joe, Steve, Lavinia and Geoffrey. Recalls Ruspoli: "the initial treatment was written many, many moons ago. At least five years before we even started prepping the film seriously. I'd always been a fan of *Night Of The Living Dead* and just wrote down a synopsis for a film all set in one country house, a bit like the Romero film." Ruspoli extended the story out into a feature length screenplay, which found its way to Jonathan Sothcott. Originally envisioned as a no-stars micro-budget zombie picture with Ruspoli directing, the project grew bigger when Sothcott showed the script to Danny Dyer on the set of the ill-fated *Rapture* project. Ruspoli remembers: "Even back then I always wanted to direct, but I was still too green. Both Jonathan and Freddie were gently trying to talk me out of it... then Danny came on board the budget suddenly quadrupled and it was clear, even to me, that I wasn't the right person for the job."

*Devil's Playground* came to Dyer at an odd time in his career, as he recalls: "I wasn't in the most confident of places and in my mind I had started doubting myself. It's easier to believe the shit things about yourself than the good things and I realised that I was starting to believe the shit. I started to think that I was a bit of a joke to people. I was getting just hate, hate, hate and I wasn't used to it. I think it started to show in some of my performances, certainly in *The Basement. Devil's Playground* was a chance for me to go, 'Right then! Come on, for fuck's sake! It's a nice budget, let's get back to what I do best and what I love doing.' "

With Dyer on board, it seemed an obvious move to draft in Tamer Hassan – at the time the pair were filming *Dead Man Running* and were attached to a number of unrealised projects including *Cockneys Vs Zombies* (in which neither ultimately appeared) – as Steve, who as written, was a hulking Cockney tough guy who made short work of some of the zombies (a far cry from impish Craig Conway's sensitive portrayal). However, it was felt there was a danger of overkill with the Dyer/Hassan team ups and the idea was left there. Bart Ruspoli is at pains to point out just how crucial Dyer's involvement was to the project: "Very simply without his involvement the film would never have been made. He had a very small window of availability and we had to move our shoot days twice to make sure we hit that window. I first met him on our rehearsal day and he immediately struck me as extremely professional. To date one of the most professional actors I've ever worked with." The schedule moves to accommodate Danny's availability were due to weather conditions forcing date changes upon the *Age Of Heroes* production, to which he was already committed.

As the film became bigger and Bart Ruspoli vacated the director's chair, the producers looked to Scott Mann to direct. Mann had impressed with his action film *The Tournament* but was unavailable. Instead he nominated his second unit director from that film, Mark McQueen. McQueen had minimal drama experience but a strong action pedigree and was determined to win the job. Bart Ruspoli remembers: "We were initially sceptical about Mark, due to his lack of feature experience, but he went out and, off his own back, shot a short zombie movie to show us he could do it... it was impressive, to say the least."

Casting took place at Elstree Studios where the production was based and amongst those who auditioned were Hannah Tointon (Angela) and Danny Midwinter (Cole). The standouts of the auditions were MyAnna Buring and Craig Conway who were immediately offered the roles of Angela and Steve. Jaime Murray and Colin Salmon were drafted in by Jonathan Sothcott. So, too, was Sean Pertwee, who graciously waived his fee for his cameo after dropping out of *Dead Cert* at the last minute. The hardest role to fill was Cole – finding an actor with the physicality required but with the chops to pull off the darker scenes was by no means easy. Eventually Jonathan Sothcott hit upon an idea as he recalls: "A friend of mine said 'it's so obvious – Craig Fairbrass! You two are running around together all the time but you haven't seen the wood for the trees!' And of course she was absolutely right – I don't think that anyone other than Craig would have pulled it off quite as well." Fairbrass was excited about the project and passed up reprising his most celebrated role in Essex Boys movie *Bonded By Blood*, which was set to shoot concurrently with *Devil's Playground*. Craig recalls: "I met Jonathan Sothcott at a lunch in Docklands with Billy Murray when we were in pre-production on *Freight*. Me and Jon shared a love of old horror films and immediately hit it off – as well as Jon being a fan of *Rise Of The Footsoldier* and my portrayal of Pat Tate. I knew we would work together – we did on *Just For The Record,* which was a lot of fun by the way! But Jon had bigger plans for me and he quickly developed *Dead Cert* while we were meeting in London over many boozy lunches. He mentioned a script called *Devil's Playground*. I read it and was completely obsessed. I loved the concept and the role of Cole. It was a man's role but was interesting because he was damaged and hunting redemption. Jon gave me the role! I'm still very proud of the film and my work on it."

Dyer welcomed the opportunity to work with such a high-calibre cast: "It was great to go toe to toe with Craig… and MyAnna Buring is a beautiful little actress. Craig Conway was a great actor, and Jaime Murray (who I'd always respected from *Dexter* and stuff like that). So it was a feeling of, 'Come on! You've got to turn this round! Stop fucking feeling sorry for yourself and get back to who you are! Start enjoying it a bit more!' "

To create the zombie-style 'undead', the producers turned to special effects legend Neill Gorton and his Millennium Studios outfit. Gorton recalls: "*Devil's Playground* presented an interesting challenge for the prosthetics. Initially described to me as a 'zombie on steroids' movie, on reading the script I soon realised the term zombie really didn't fit. These weren't people coming back from the dead but people who were very much alive and kicking. Kicking hard in fact. There were a number of practical issues too. The director was going to be using a number of free runners whose acrobatic skills would help cement the idea that these pumped-up, amped-up, infected people were literally running on rocket fuel. The daredevil jumps and balancing acts they would perform required good visibility so we immediately had to ditch the idea of contact lenses as these kind of FX lenses can distort and reduce vision, which would have put our performers at risk. The more traditional zombie look of protruding cheekbones and deathly colours was also out as our characters were far from dead. A further consideration was the fact that production had planned scenes with up to forty or fifty extras. On a restricted budget, putting that number of people into prosthetics is incredibly difficult so we needed to find a signature look that was different from anything seen before and could be easily replicated on a crowd. We eventually hit on the raised vein idea. The infection or change is a progressive effect so we could do earlier stages just with veins airbrushed on to a performer to suggest the infection spreading. As they progressed we would increase the intensity of the veins before taking it further by applying prosthetics that would create raised veins on the skin that looked engorged with blood. We would then amp up the colour intensity of this third prosthetic stage to create our fourth and final stage. This look allowed us to use stencils and free-hand airbrushing techniques that could be easily replicated by a team of make-up artists operating a kind of production line system, and ultimately the prosthetics team, led by Millennium FX producer Karen Spencer, could pump out forty to fifty extras in the space of a couple of hours. The vein prosthetics themselves were applied using a transfer system and after each shoot the moulds were recycled and returned to Millennium FX to be re-cast in silicone and prepared for the next big shoot. Millennium also created a plethora of memorable gore gags and make-up FX that cemented the film's credentials as top popcorn-horror entertainment."

A number of key crew were recruited from previous Dyer/Sothcott films, including production designer Sophie Wyatt (*Just For The Record*), stunt coordinator Dani Biernat (*Dead Cert*) and costume designer Millie Sloan (*The Rapture*). Sloan was delighted to be working with Dyer again, as she recalled: "Danny, well, he is one of these people who has a real presence, he lights up a room with his charisma and charm. He is a dream to work with, unpretentious, really easygoing and considerate; he understood that we may have had only a week to buy and fit 100 costumes and therefore not everything would be perfect. He is unassuming and down to earth. One thing I really respected about him is that he always spoke to the crew. He would sit down and have a chat with members of the crew and ask them questions about themselves and remember their names. By doing little things like that it shows that he definitely has the knack of making people feel good about themselves and making them feel a little bit special for those two minutes he takes to talk to them."

Principal photography commenced in December 2009 in freezing temperatures at Elstree. It wasn't long before heavy snow started falling which, while cinematic was far from conducive to filming. Most of the shoot was in and around Elstree Studios – the N-Gen car park is the studio's own, and sets such as Steve's garage and the long, white N-Gen corridor were built by production designer Sophie Wyatt. The film was plagued with financing problems throughout the shoot and beyond, as financiers consistently failed to deliver on their promises. Despite the sub-zero temperatures, cast and crew were supportive and never lost their enthusiasm. Dyer only filmed for two weeks, his character being absent for all of the N-Gen scenes and many others, but his constant good humour kept spirits high. Bart Ruspoli remembers one particularly funny lunch request from the star: "Shane Taylor, who played Geoffrey in the film, goes up to Danny one day on set –

ST: Danny, we're sending a runner for some McDonalds, you want anything?

DD: Yeah, mate, yeah... a Big Mac... some fries... an apple pie... another Big Mac... a Coke...

ST: OK...

DD: And Shane?

ST: Yeah?
DD: Supersize the cunt for me.

When pick-ups followed early in the spring of 2010, (mostly the climatic zombie showdown with Danny and Craig Fairbrass) there was not a flake of snow to be had. As such, the two actors were showered with polystyrene chips one night in a quarry in the Home Counties. Fairbrass enjoyed working with Dyer, as he recalls: "I was really excited about working with Danny as I was a great admirer of his work. He was always real and believable and came across with an amazing charisma that both men and women found irresistible. I could tell he really cared about the craft and although he had a wild man image, he took it very seriously – he loved being around solid actors who could give him something back – as they say... you are only as good as the person opposite."

Screened at the Cannes Film Festival in 2010, *Devil's Playground* was welcomed by distributors but less so by critics. An early review in top trade paper *Variety* was less than flattering, with Leslie Felperin branding it a "deeply unoriginal but watchable horror pic… Debut helmer Mark McQueen has almost nothing up his ragged, blood-soaked sleeve that hasn't been seen in a slew of recent zombie movies… Risible dialogue and wooden thesping are just the start of the pic's problems, compounded by a disappointing lack of diversity among zombie extras." However, the reviewer was quick to point out Dyer's commercial appeal – "However, presence of regular schlock-horror thesp Danny Dyer (*Severance*) should ensure a few happy rides on the ancillary merry-go-round at least."

And so it was that *Devil's Playground* was bought for the UK by distribution juggernaut eOne early in the summer of 2010. Best known for releasing the *Twilight* franchise in the UK, the company had not released a Danny Dyer film before and clearly didn't anticipate how much effort Revolver were putting into their marketing campaigns to yield their unbroken run of Dyer hits. Dyer's fanbase was huge but if the films weren't promoted (and more importantly promoted *by him*) they wouldn't fly off the shelves. The deal was a good one financially, but failed to guarantee the film that all-important theatrical platform. Fairbrass and Dyer can be heard voicing their dissatisfaction with this state of affairs on the film's lively DVD audio commentary.

*Devil's Playground* had its UK premiere at the (now defunct) Gorezone Horror Film Festival at the Prince Charles Cinema in Leicester Square. Although the screening was well attended, few of the key cast and crew were in attendance and of the lead cast only Craig Fairbrass showed up.

Released in the UK on DVD and Blu-ray on 11 October 2010 with little fanfare, *Devil's Playground* performed reasonably in its first week, shifting 8,856 units, bolstered by a strong TV ad campaign, but soon dropped out of the charts, shifting only a further 6,000 DVDs in the rest of its first month. Twitter promotion was then in its infancy and a weak campaign was run that had 'Angela Mills' (@AngelaM1983) pushing the idea that she was a real person who had taken the RAK295 drug. It soon fizzled out.

Reflecting on the film's reception, Dyer notes: "I really enjoyed *Devil's Playground* but, again, it didn't work out and I didn't know why. I couldn't stop it – it was like a runaway train and I had no control over it. It was a pretty dark time really. It was just a strange period because, like I said, I had no control over it. I felt like the whole world was against me. It's strange how the fame thing can eat you up. This whole world that you're in, it's cut throat! When you're hot, you're *hot* and it's beautiful. When you're not, it's the cruellest and loneliest business to be in."

On 30 October at the inaugural British Horror Film Awards, *Devil's Playground* swept the board, winning Best Producers, Best Film, Best Director and Best Actor (for Danny). It has since gone on to be released in most major territories around the world where it has garnered favorable but rarely spectacular receptions.

So why didn't *Devil's Playground* catch fire? It is a competently made, action-packed in all the right places and well acted by an unusually strong cast. The problem is that it was another zombie film in a seemingly endless procession of them – and it just wasn't different enough to compete with the *28 Days Later* or *Resident Evil* franchises. The parkour/freerunning, done very much on the cheap, just isn't spectacular enough to stand out and certainly doesn't compete with stunt-driven Hollywood action films such as *The Fast & The Furious*.

Danny is effectively the second lead to Craig Fairbrass's *Terminator*-like Cole, but delivers a solid, charismatic performance that gives the film a real emotional core. There is a very convincing chemistry between Danny and the excellent MyAnna Buring and their scenes together are among the best in the film. One thing audiences never see coming is the death of Danny's character under a horde of zombies, and it gives his character an unexpected but ultimately pleasing arc which is quite unusual in these films. Craig Fairbrass comes close to stealing the film, bringing all of the physical intensity he displayed in *Rise Of The Footsoldier*. One real mis-step, however, is the awkward 'comedy' scene of 6' 5" Fairbrass squeezing himself into a tiny car. Thankfully the scene isn't accompanied by a 'wah wah' on the soundtrack. Supporting honours go to Jaime Murray and Shane Taylor as snotty city couple Geoffrey and Lavinia, whose whispered machinations are the film's strongest sub-plot.

Overall, *Devil's Playground* is a slick, watchable action-zombie film with a great cast, but its failure to break out on DVD in the UK didn't help Danny's wavering commercial prospects following the disastrous performances of turkeys *Just For The Record, Jack Said* and *Dead Cert.* And that's a shame, as *Devil's Playground* is a thousand times better than any of them. Perhaps, in time, it will become a cult film.

# 7 LIVES (2011)

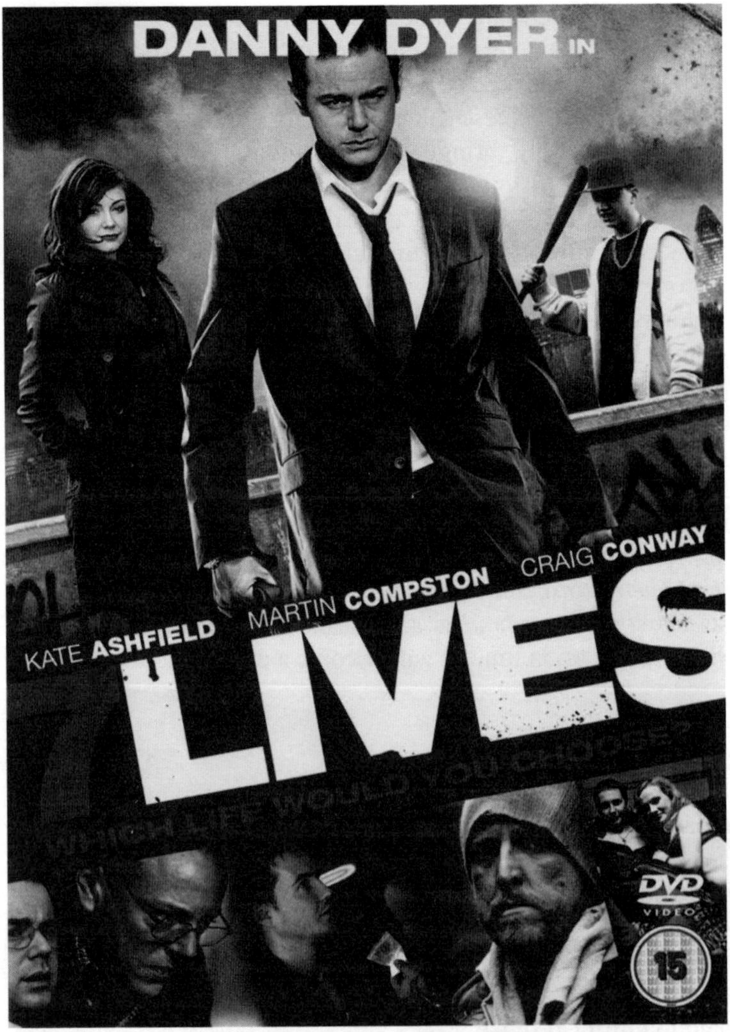


**"I was not in a good place and I didn't believe in myself enough to do it."**

**Director** Paul Wilkins **Producers** Paul Wilkins, Mike Parker **Writer** Paul Wilkins **Production Designer** Libby Uppington **Costume Designer** Hedi Miller **Directors of Photography** James Friend, Nick Gordon Smith

**Danny Dyer** Tom **Kate Ashfield** Cynthia **Nick Brimble** Ted **Craig Conway** Keith **Martin Compston** Rory **Nick Nevern** Detective Echo/Policeman **Helen George** Valerie

*Following a brutal mugging, everyman Tom goes into a coma in which he inhabits the lives of six other men, giving him a taste of how his life might have turned out had he chosen a different path.*

*7 Lives* should have been a tantalising prospect, as for years it was just a promo on YouTube featuring a haunting cover of Kate Bush's *Running Up That Hill*. The footage in the promo had been filmed in 2008 and features Dyer in what appears to be a mixture of *Outlaw* and *Groundhog Day*. Writer/director/producer Paul Wilkins struggled to raise the rest of the finance he needed to make the film, however, and it remained unfinished for some years, looking as though it would join *The Rapture* and *The Battersea Ripper* as 'what ifs' in the Dyer film cannon.

"*7 Lives* was a film that had been around for a long time," recalls Dyer, "I filmed the promo for it. I was going to play all seven characters and that was what was going to make it interesting." Dyer thought long and hard about accepting the offer to complete the film several years later, but eventually felt obliged to finish the job: "The bottom line was that I didn't trust the director. He was a nice guy but it just didn't suit him. I said to him, 'I'll finish it but I'm not playing all the characters.' I wasn't very confident and this was a big ask. When we were first going to do it three years previously I was well up for it. I had to play a hoodie, a homeless character, and a boxer. It was weird because I had to jump into all these different lives. Then it all comes back round full circle and I'm dying on the floor – it's all been a mad dream. But I wasn't confident enough to take it on, so I shied away from it. I can blame the director all I want, but I just felt like I owed him to finish it and to wrap it up. It didn't work because it was just like, 'What the fuck is this film about?' No one gets that they're all meant to be me. In order to get that across, I needed to play every character. I was not in a good place and I didn't believe in myself enough to do it. If there were anything that I could change it would be that. I should have just said, 'Alright, fuck this! I'm just going to completely go for this and put myself out on a limb to see what sort of fucking feedback I get from it.' As an actor, when do you get the opportunity to get seven different roles in a film?"

New producer Mike Parker did a good job of pulling together a decent cast to complete the film, including the ever-dependable Craig Conway and Martin Compston, but it never really stood a chance. Without Dyer playing all of the parts, the film never made sense and it really is a wretched, confusing mess of a movie, second only to *Jack Said* as the worst film in which Dyer has appeared.

Executive producer Jonathan Sothcott, who arranged some additional finance for the film, recalls "I loved the promo, it was really cool, and obviously I wanted to support Danny so getting involved was a bit of a no-brainer. But I had no idea what a disaster it would be, I never went to the set or anything. I remember seeing it at a screening for UK distributors – everyone walked out after ten minutes, all my mates – it was just mortifying. I remember that day someone saying, 'I've heard he's doing a film of *Run For Your Wife* – that must be a joke, right?" So the mood wasn't exactly upbeat."

The only UK distributor interested in picking up the film was, of course, Revolver, but by then the company was struggling and couldn't even afford to run a decent mis-selling campaign. It wisely chose not to screen the film for critics and snuck it out across four screens to qualify for a VOD release, an exercise which earned the film just £59. The distributor ran competitions to win tickets to the film's premiere in a last-ditch effort to give it a profile, but Dyer was noticeable by his absence and wisely didn't do any press for the film.

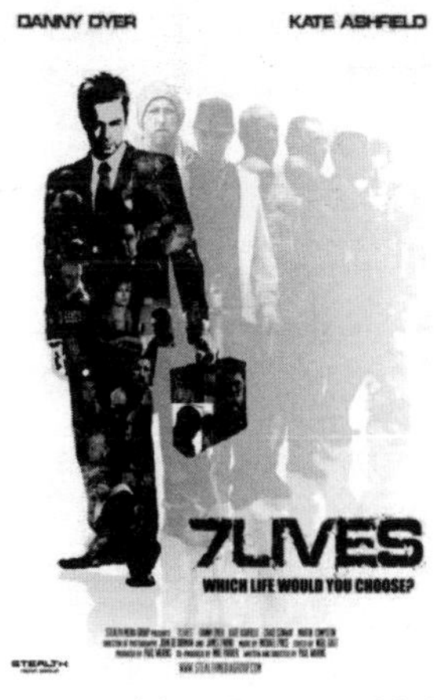


Despite no publicity of any kind and limited availability in stores, *7 Lives* still managed to sell 1,153 units in its first week of release. It was the worst week one number for a legitimate Danny Dyer film since *Greenfingers* and it has only sold some 7,000 copies since. Danny's audience had finally learned the trick with the black, white and red covers and knew that if he wasn't promoting the film then it wasn't worth buying. Revolver would make one more attempt at reviving their flagging fortunes with a Dyer vehicle before that chapter of his career closed forever.

# AGE OF HEROES (2011)

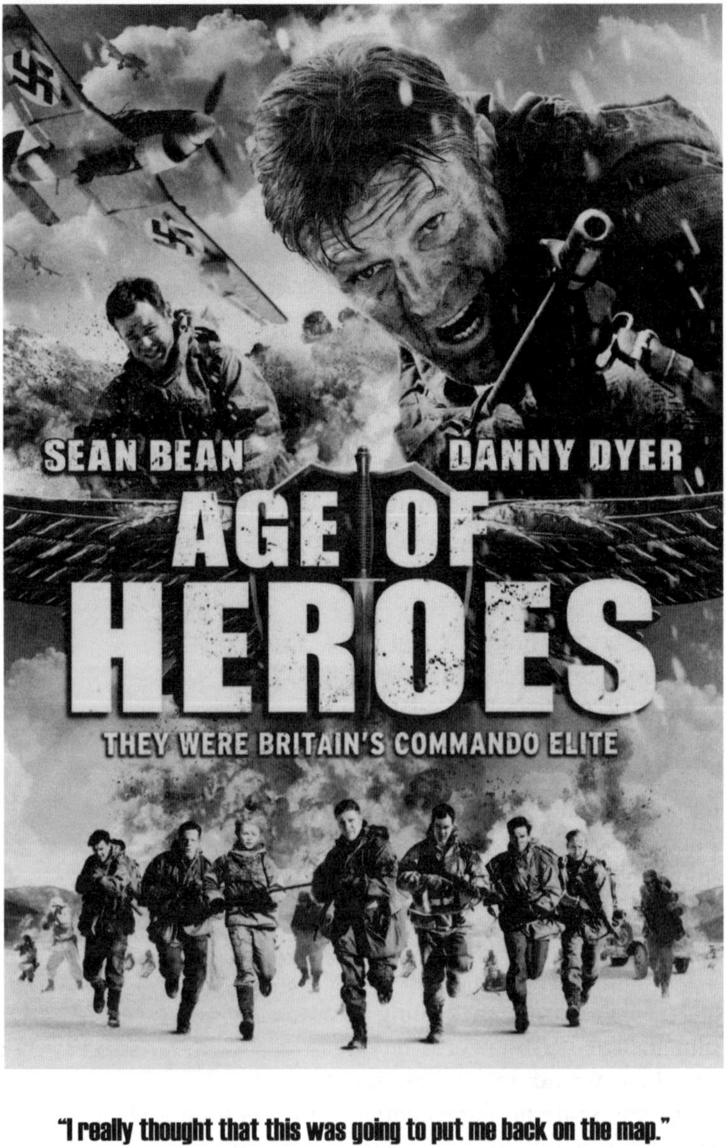


**"I really thought that this was going to put me back on the map."**

**Director** Adrian Vitoria **Producers** Lex Lutzus, James Brown, Nick O'Hagan, James Youngs **Writers** Adrian Vitoria, Ed Scates **Production Designer** Richard Campling **Costume Designer** Elvis Davis **Director of Photography** Mark Hamilton

**Sean Bean** Jack Jones **Danny Dyer** Bob Rains **Aksel Hennie** Mortensen **Izabella Miko** Jensen **James D'Arcy** Ian Fleming **Sebastian Street** Archer **Guy Burnet** Riley **Ewan Ross** Gable **Rosie Fellner** Sophie **Theo Barklem-Biggs** Jimmy **Erik Madsen** Teichman **William Houston** Sgt Mackenzie

*The true story of the formation of Ian Fleming's 30 Commando 'smash and grab' unit in World War Two, a precursor to the elite forces in the UK. Corporal Rains is inducted into the unit and put through intensive training under Major Jones as they prepare for their first mission: to parachute into occupied Norway and capture new radar technology from the Germans that could change the outcome of the war.*

Announced shortly before the Cannes Film Festival in 2010, *Age Of Heroes* appeared to be the tonic that Dyer's career needed. A balls-to-the-wall, boys' own action film in the tradition of *Where Eagles Dare*, it would reunite him with *Outlaw* co-star Sean Bean, whose international pulling power was a match for Dyer's home-grown fanbase.

*Age Of Heroes* was intended to be the first in a planned trilogy of war films from producer Lex Lutzus' Neon Park, in collaboration with Nick O'Hagan's Giant Films and distributor Metrodome. Metrodome executive James Brown joined Lutzus at Neon Park and the pair planned to follow up the film with sequels *Age Of Honour* and *Age Of Glory*. "War seems to be growing as a genre in film," Lutzus told *Screen International*, "with the rising popularity of computer games such as *Call Of Duty* widening the demography of the audience."

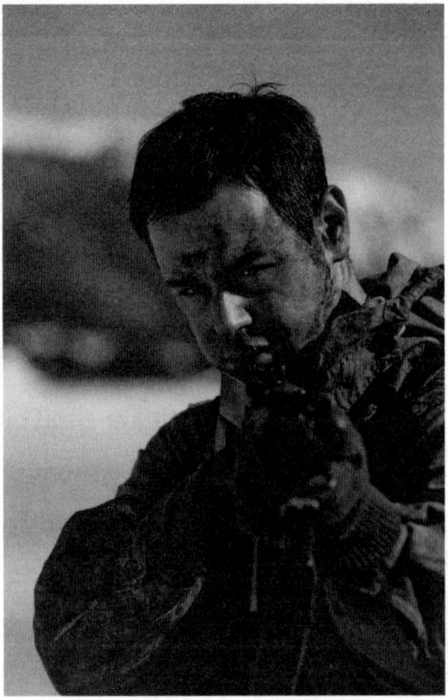

Dyer knew that finally he had a project that he could get his teeth into, and with Bean on board the weight of the film wouldn't solely be on his shoulders: "It was a factual war film about the SAS. Great! A chance to get away from some of the shit I'd been doing, stuff that had been stunting my brain. A chance to say, 'Right! Come on then! Let's go make the fucking movie up in the Norwegian mountains, in the snow!' I loved the character – he was so cool. I was the lead and it was all based around me. It was about my experience of being a good soldier who struggled with discipline and it was based on a true story. It was a fucking good job, man! I loved it and I really behaved myself on that."

Dyer spent some time being drilled by real-life marine instructors: "We had half a day with the Marines and they laugh in the face of adversity. They told us 'Don't be afraid, if you're under fire, to look at each other and have a little bit of a snigger. It's a nervous laugh but it's real, we do that."

*Age Of Heroes* was filmed on location in Norway, in testing conditions for cast and crew, in the spring of 2010. Working with Sean Bean for a second time was an unhappy experience for Dyer: "I worked with him on *Outlaw* and I thought we were friends, but we clearly weren't. He had a bit of a problem with me, I think. Maybe it was the battle of the 'alpha-male'. I wanted it to run smoothly this one. I needed it. I didn't want any distractions or bad press. One night, the producers couldn't get Sean out of the bar. So I got a knock on my door and they said, 'Listen, we can't get Sean out of the bar! Can you help us out?' I was like, 'For fuck's sake! What do you want *me* to do? So I had to get up and go into the fucking bar. I basically said, 'Let's have a booze, come and get out of the bar. I got him out of the bar and I got him up to his room. I was drinking a few cans with him and stuff. Then he went straight off to *Game of Thrones*. I don't know how he managed that. I behaved myself on it and I was such a good boy. I took it, embraced it, and loved every second of it. I'm really happy with what I did; I'm fucking great in it! Sean's my idol and I have to look up to him."

Despite a difficult shoot, the completed film drew early praise from trade paper *Screen International*: "The script aims for simple and accessible genre action, which tends to mean more than few cliché moments. But it is a simply structured film – intended to be the first of a trilogy, with *Age Of Honour* and *Age Of Glory* to come – that ticks the right boxes and delivers some modest wartime adventure thrills."

Metrodome opted to forego a traditional theatrical release for the film, instead putting on special charity previews in aid of ForceSelect at ten Cineworld cinemas in May 2011. The recorded box office was £367 from five screens, but for once the press didn't jump on that story.

Writing for *Total Film*, Neil Smith was distinctly unimpressed: "Whether the real regiment would have recruited an insubordinate lout like Dyer's Corporal Rains is up for debate, but Bean does. Springing him from military lock-up for a Norwegian raid, which has director Adrian Vitoria ransacking *Where Eagles Dare* and *The Guns Of Navarone* for every gung-ho, boy's own cliché available. Two sequels are planned, God help us." The *Express*, however, was more generous, hitting the nail on the head: "Anyone who grew up on manly matinées of *The Heroes Of Telemark* or *Where Eagles Dare* might just take a shine to low-budget Second World War adventure yarn *Age Of Heroes*."

Once more proving that neither box office nor reviews have much impact on mainstream home-entertainment purchases, *Age of Heroes* shifted a phenomenal 23,604 DVDs in its first week of release. It has since gone on to sell a total of over 137,000 units in the UK and been released in virtually every country in the world. The proposed sequels underwent title changes to *Commando Select* and *Commando Elite*, but remain unmade at the time of going to press.

"I really thought that this was going to put me back on the map," reflects Dyer, "Fucking hell! What a great film! I knew that it was a film that my dad would have liked and my granddad would like. It was about the war and a cool SAS soldier – but it didn't do the business it should have done and again I don't know why. It's just the fucking spiral…"

Of course the film *was* a big success, but neither the press nor the film industry wanted to give Dyer any credit for that. Following on the heels of rubbish like *Basement*, *Dead Cert* and *The Last Seven*, it suited people to heap praise on *Age Of Heroes*' other star, Sean Bean. And with Revolver setting up Dyer's final fall from grace, with *Freerunner*, *7 Lives* and *Deviation* looming on the horizon, there was no opportunity for him to get back on a winning streak.

Pitched as '*The Dirty Dozen* and *Where Eagles Dare* meets *Tigerland*, *Age Of Heroes* does exactly what it says on the tin. A fun romp through the Second World War with a strong cast and well-staged action sequences, it is easy to see how it could have become a great franchise for Dyer. Sadly it wasn't to be, and he had to endure two years in the wilderness before the chance arose to play another soldier in *Vendetta*, a film that would finally restore his credibility.

# FREERUNNER (2011)

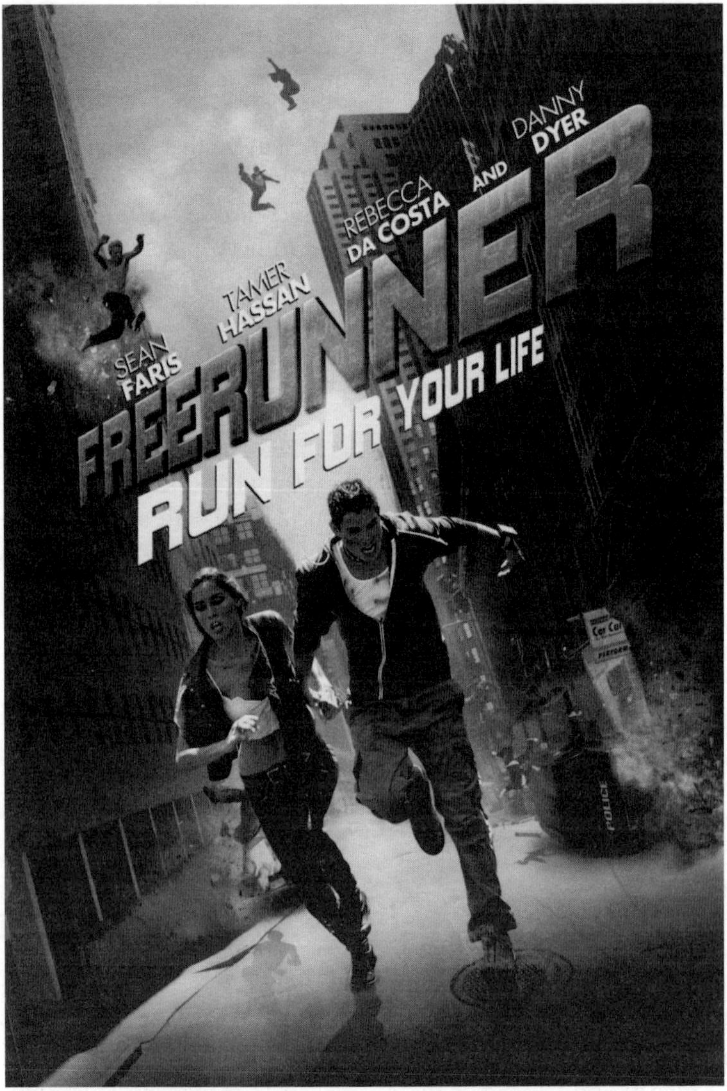


"The part was a bit of a cliché, almost 'Bond villain' role."

**Director** Lawrence Silverstein **Producers** Lawrence Silverstein, Warren Ostergard **Writers** Matthew Chadwick, Raimund Huber, Jeremy Skiar **Production Designer** Jeremy Woolsey **Costume Designer** Caria Shivener **Director of Photography** Claudio Chea

**Danny Dyer** Mr Frank **Tamer Hassan** Reese **Sean Faris** Ryan **Rebecca Da Costa** Chelsea **Seymour Cassel** Gramps **Amanda Fuller** Dolores **Dylan Baker** West

*Ryan and his parkour gang frequently submit themselves to races through the city organised by Reece, a promoter who makes an internet gambling fortune off of them while giving them a pittance in return. With the last race of the season coming up, Ryan decides it's time to secretly break Reece's rule against participants betting on themselves, and he gambles all he has. The stakes are raised against the racers. Reece's boss, Mr Frank, has all along been surreptitiously grooming these athletes for a high-stakes death race for the sadistic entertainment of his billionaire gambling buddies. To guarantee every runner's participation, they're abducted, gassed, and fitted with explosive, remote-controlled collars, forcing them to heed the rules and keep their heads in the race.*

"*Freerunner* was another film that Tamer brought to me," recalls Dyer. "He does bring a few jobs my way, I'll give him that!" The producers of the movie had hoped that by securing Dyer and Hassan they would guarantee a significant release in the UK and achieved a significant presale with eOne in the wake of *City Rats and Dead Man Running*.

For Dyer, the project offered the opportunity to realise a lifelong dream and work in America for the first time – and to play another fun villain after his scene-stealing baddie in *Pimp*: "I read it and I loved the idea. All the sequences in the script looked fucking great! It was being filmed in Cleveland, so it was also an opportunity to work in America. The part was a bit of a cliché, almost 'Bond villain' role. I fucked up really, because when I first went to L.A. after *The Business* they were going mad for me! Everybody was like, 'Who the fuck is this guy? We love him!' But I didn't go back for two years because of my family. If you go out there, you've got to do six months; you can't go out there and do three weeks. You've got to go out there when the buzz is there and stay out there. I couldn't do that to my family – I missed them terribly and struggled with the people. I wanted the work but I couldn't uproot my kids. I just couldn't do that to them. Kevin McKidd is a friend of mine and he did that. He uprooted his fucking wife and kids and went out there. He could have come back with his tail between his legs but he cracked on. I know I could have been a success out there if I had put the time in but I've got children and I couldn't just pack up everything and go. I think the kids were excited by the idea but they were fucking petrified. They wouldn't know anybody! If I did get work, I'd be out for twelve hours of the fucking day while they're stuck

in some house in L.A… It could be worse but my kids were on the verge of taking exams and I had to take that into consideration. I've never been out there since *Freerunner*."

In the wake of *Casino Royale*'s breathtaking pre-credits parkour sequence, freerunning had become a short-lived staple of action movies and this was the second Dyer film over which it cast a shadow, after *Devil's Playground's* wall-climbing zombies. Unfortunately it was also the second Dyer film to suffer in its attempt at executing parkour on screen, due to budgetary restraints. As Dyer recalls: "We started shooting and they didn't have enough freerunners. So they had to cut the sequences down and it all started to get really cheap. I've always loved the idea of working in America on a fucking sexy film with a really cool American crew. That's my fantasy and I'd not been able to do that until then."

Delays in post-production saw the film miss its delivery date with UK distributor eOne, and they invoked a contract clause terminating their obligation to release the film, having been badly burned by their poor return on *Devil's Playground.* As such, Revolver stepped in to pick up the UK rights in another attempt to kickstart a *Borstal Boy/City Rats* sleeper result. The final art really was the final straw for Dyer's fans, featuring the actor's head (badly) photoshopped onto someone else's body, holding what appears to be a pulse rifle from *Aliens*!

Revolver didn't screen the film for the press or release it theatrically but the odd review still surfaced. The *Metro* awarded *Freerunner* one star, lamenting: "If you thought *Freerunner* might be an awe-inspiring documentary on the urban discipline or even a cheesy sports flick in the so-bad-it's-amazing cult category, prepare to be disappointed. The warning here comes in the opening credits 'with Danny Dyer'."

The fact that at this point Dyer was stigmatised as being the hallmark of a bad movie is pretty depressing but also understandable.

Between 2009 and 2011, 12 of his films had been released in the UK – it was no longer 'prolific actor Danny Dyer', it had become 'overkill' – and the public knew it. Dyer didn't promote the release but Tamer Hassan was enticed into a daft stunt racing a freerunner across London on the Tube. It was all a long, long way from the relative sophistication of *Dead Man Running*.

*Freerunner* sold 2,596 units in its first week, a drop of over 20,000 units from what *Age Of Heroes* had achieved. The days of sticking Danny on the cover of a film and hoping for the best were over. The film companies had finally been found out – and not a moment too soon.

# DEVIATION (2012)

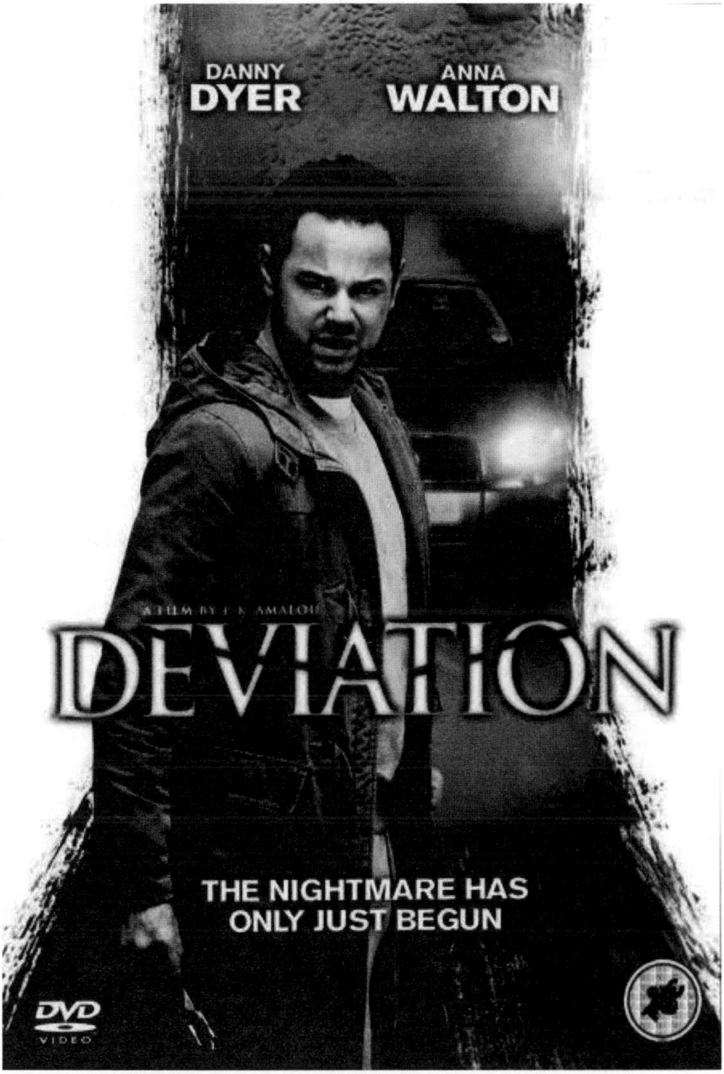


**"I was just thinking that everyone had lost all fucking belief in me, when I met this J.K. guy."**

**Director** JK Amalou **Producers** JK Amalou, Lara Greenway **Writer** JK Amalou **Production Designer** Chloe Brady **Costume Designer** Emma Harding **Director of Photography** Ollie Downey

**Danny Dyer** Frankie **Anna Walton** Amber **James Doherty** Jono **David Fynn** Justin **Alan McKenna** Tough Cop **Roy Smiles** Brian **Ben Wigzell** Bob **Elijah Baker** Hoodie 1 **Miles Hobson** Hoodie 2

*Escaped killer Frankie carjacks and kidnaps nurse Amber and takes her with him on the run across London. Along the way Frankie shows his murderous side repeatedly – but Amber might not be the innocent, helpless victim that she appears to be.*

*Deviation* was the brainchild of filmmaker JK Amalou. A graduate of the London International Film School, Amalou first garnered attention with his debut feature *Hard Men,* which marked the first star turn by Vincent Regan. *Hard Men* took Amalou to Hollywood where he worked with the likes of Martin Scorsese and Ridley Scott but, like many émigré film-makers, he was disillusioned by the frequency of projects collapsing in Tinseltown and was drawn back to the UK to make another independent film. Amalou explains the origins of *Deviation* – "Originally *Deviation* was an American script. Its title was *Captured*. I developed it with my then agency U.T.A. in Los Angeles – a new take on *The Hitcher,* as it was being touted at the time and it did get optioned. However, by that time, I was cooling off on Hollywood and I made a decision to go back. What I really wanted to do after *Hard Men*: make low-budget films without the interference of the studios, producers, etc. Ultimately, the biggest lesson I learned from Los Angeles is you're a gun for hire. The people who dictate what you should be doing are often the marketing department of whatever company you work for, and they pay you good money to toe the line. I loved every minute of it and I would do it again. However, it is not something I wanted to carry on doing at the time. Besides, I missed being behind the camera."

Paring down the story elements of *Captured*, Amalou relocated it to London, a major city, but one better suited to a story set in a single night. As he explains: "First, I have always loved the 'bare bones' of the story: a car, a psycho, a victim. It's very challenging in terms of storytelling and characterisation. Could I keep an audience's attention for 90 minutes with a couple of characters in such a confined space? As a writer-director, I get excited about challenging stuff. I guess, a mathematician would feel the same kind of excitement when presented with a difficult maths problem.

"Furthermore, I wanted to try my hand at a very contained story. Something which I'd never done before. My original American script had car chases, plenty more characters, even rattlesnakes as a major plot point. It was all set against wide vistas as the original 'couple' were travelling from Los Angeles to Arizona. Because of the distances involved, the story took place over several days. So rewriting the whole story for London was all about one thing: compression. Compression of space, characters, timeframe. In fact, the compression I imposed, for example, on the timeframe worked very well. The story of *Deviation* took place over one night. It added fear and more tension as our victim knew that she'd be killed in the morning if she didn't escape. Also, that worked well structurally: set up the conflict early evening, conflict throughout the night, resolution of the conflict at dawn. And compression also meant one thing: micro-budget. I knew I didn't want to hang around forever to make this film. I just wanted to write the script, raise a few quid and hit the road with the car and my two main characters. And this is exactly how it happened. The wonderful, resourceful Lara Greenway to take care of the producing duties whilst I took care of the directing. And off we went. Also, I didn't want to make a micro-budget just because I didn't have enough money. The key here was that the small budget we had would work in favour of the story. The biggest mistake I see is film-makers shooting 'expensive stories' on a micro-budget because they couldn't raise enough money. The results look cheap, clunky, and not very good. On a more personal level, I also wanted to show London after dark. A London very few people encounter or know. London is a fascinating town, a town which never ceases to amaze me. So many dark corners and secrets. In fact, I'd go as far as saying that the most important character in *Deviation* is London."

Amalou, a pragmatic and resourceful film-maker, set his budget at just £70,000, but his decision to shoot on the tiny Canon 5D camera was a creative choice, not a budgetary one: "We shot on Canon 5D. Again, just like the script, it was not a 'budget' choice, it was an artistic choice. I wanted to emulate the style of the French New Wave of the fifties but in a more contemporary way, of course. Those French New Wave films were shot in black and white, handheld, and on 16mm. After numerous talks with Ollie Downey, my DOP, we settled on the Canon 5D. It was the closest we could find to the Bolex camera used by the French New Wave filmmakers. It is a light, nimble, small and unobtrusive camera. *Deviation* is a dark psychological thriller strong on characters, and therefore highly dependent on the actors' performances. I didn't want my actors to feel restricted by the camera: they could go wherever they wanted to go, they could improvise. There was no restriction, as long as it was all done within the parameters of the story I wanted to tell. In that sense, the Canon 5D was perfect. Also, I wanted to shoot *Deviation* from the hip, rock'n'roll style. We stole many shots, we filmed in some locations without permission. The Canon 5D's innocuous appearance and lightness allowed us to do that. I don't remember any real challenges associated with the format. I think it was all in the preparation. Ollie and I knew the limitations before we even shot the film, so we designed *Deviation* within those limitations. As 75% of the film takes place at night, we also chose the locations very carefully in terms of lighting. So we always shot in well-lit areas. I think we did well: I have read quite a few reviews raving about the 'beautiful wide-screen cinematography'. Uh, no. We didn't shoot *Deviation* on 35mm. It was shot digitally on a Canon 5D."

To cast the film the producers selected industry veteran Jeremy Zimmerman, who over the years had worked on such diverse movies as *Legend* (1985), *The Krays* (1990), *Dog Soldiers* (2002), the *Hellboy* series and *Dead Man Running*. Zimmerman suggested Danny Dyer for the role of Frankie. "To be honest, I wasn't too sure at first" recalls Amalou. "Not because I didn't think Danny was a good actor. I wasn't convinced that Danny could play this screwed-up, man-child, nerdy psychopath prone to histrionics." Amalou was intrigued, however, and met up with Dyer to talk about the film: "My first meeting with Danny was memorable. We met in a pub in Kentish Town. My taxi dropped me off and I immediately spotted Danny having a cigarette outside. He glanced at me then swiftly turned his back on me. He probably thought I was a fan about to ask him for an autograph or a photograph. I patiently waited for him to finish his cigarette and introduced myself. Once inside the pub, it all went very smoothly. My first words to him were: 'Look, I am not looking for another brash, loud Cockney for this part. The character of Frankie Norton is basically a dangerous, petulant child in a man's body. So if you're thinking of showing up on the set and doing your 'Cockney' routine, it isn't going to work.' I thought Danny was going to punch me. However, this is how I always operate in this business, which strives on bullshit. Bluntness does save a lot of time sometimes. I didn't want to waste my time or Danny's time. To my surprise, Danny totally agreed with me. He had obviously read the script and understood the character of Frankie Norton. He also surprised me for his honesty about some bad choices he has made in his career, some stuff that was reported in the tabloids and that he regretted doing, etc. To this day, I'll say it again and again: the private Danny Dyer isn't the Danny Dyer that some sections of the press make him out to be. He's an incredibly sensitive man with a huge heart. What clinched the deal really is when Danny said to me:

'Don't go easy on me, mate. Push me, alright? I want to give you the best.' Now as a writer-director, this is precisely my motto too. I strive on working with totally honest, straightforward, tough people. So bluntness not only saves time but it is also the only way to get the best out of people. Now I know Danny very well, I will add something else about him: I love his brutal honesty. What you see is what you get. He tells it like it is. My kind of bloke. So yes, we hit it off very well. Like a house on fire. We were like old mates by the end of our meeting. Complete with the huge hug he gave me before I left (that obviously got me some very dirty looks from the female fans in the pub who kept looking over at us!)"

Dyer recalls: "I was just thinking that everyone had lost all fucking belief in me, when I met this J.K. guy. He was praising me up and saying, 'You know what? This bad press you get is disgusting. You're one of the fucking greatest actors of your generation!' I was thinking, 'Wow! I fucking need this!' I wanted to get back to the acting side of things with someone who really believed in me, someone who was still honoured to be working with me. I hadn't had that in a while. He was a great director and what we achieved for that amount of money in three weeks was pretty fucking amazing really. The movie was made for seventy grand. That's just the catering budget on some of the other jobs I've done! I was playing a child-like serial killer, a fucking freak! It was a two-hander in a car with a fucking actress. Throughout the movie I was driving her to her death. I thought it was brilliant, so I did it for no money. The idea of switching from being this really childlike character to this fucking lunatic and going, 'Oh God, I'm so ill,' really appealed to me. It really turned me on and I loved every second of it."

Amalou was excited to have Dyer on board as he recalls: "I had seen Danny's best films (*The Business, The Football Factory, Human Traffic*), average ones, bad ones. However, as a director, I watched his films, not for the films, but for what I could steal or use from Danny for my film. I studied the actor, not the films. As for the public perception of Danny, well, I was more than aware that he was/is a 'Marmite actor'. You either like him or you don't. It was no mystery to me that he had some rather vicious detractors in the media or among film fans. Some other film-makers warned me: oh, he's difficult, he's a nightmare. However, I had worked with enough big stars in Los Angeles to know that what you read or hear about them is very often untrue. Same goes with the 'business gossip': directors and actors don't always get on for various reasons. So I went into our meeting with a completely open mind. As I said, I thought he was a great and smart bloke. And we got on very well. However, as a director, this was not about whether I liked the guy on a personal level. The bottom line is very simple: is an actor right for the job? As far as I was concerned, Danny was perfect for the part of Frankie Norton."

Finding an actress to hold her own opposite a fired-up and ready-to-go Dyer was no mean feat, but Zimmerman recommended Anna Walton, who he had previously cast in *Hellboy II: The Golden Army*. Amalou notes, "Anna came second. I needed to know who was going to play the psychopath before casting this part. I chose her because I liked her work in *The Vampire Diaries*. She also came highly recommended by my co-producer Michael Riley who'd worked with her before. Most importantly, I didn't want to cast a cute, vulnerable-looking actress in the part. That would've been an obvious, if not lazy, choice. I wanted an actress who could portray a strong, in-charge, tough woman. Oh, and I also wanted the victim to be taller than her kidnapper to emphasise the child-like quality of the psychopath. Anna is over 6' tall. I will always remember Danny's reaction when I first introduced him to Anna. His jaw fell to the floor: 'Blimey! She's taller than me! She's a fucking horse! All I can see is legs!' But both he and Anna understood that I was trying to express this 'woman/petulant child' dynamic on a physical level too."

Dyer and Walton had excellent chemistry on screen and Amalou was thrilled with the dynamic he achieved between his two stars: "Fantastically well. They were inseparable throughout the shoot. And I know they grew very fond of each other. Again, like many other people, Anna reacted the same way towards Danny: 'My God, he is nothing like I thought he'd be. He is so lovely.' This is something I heard again and again throughout the shoot. In regard to the film, I know they spent a lot of time talking about the story, the characters, bouncing off each other. At first, it worried me as I wanted to keep the tension between the two of them going on and off screen. As it turned out, I didn't have to worry because Danny is one of these actors who saves it all for the take. Also, I learned very early on that Danny is an extremely instinctive actor. Just give him the overall 'movements' of what he needs to do, he'll take them and run with them. It was mesmerising to watch sometimes as he'd really surprise me with bits of business that he'd add during a scene. Stuff I hadn't thought about. Danny's way of working was the total opposite of Anna's: she analyses and researches everything. For example, she spent a few days shadowing a real nurse in a hospital before the shoot. Every single line of dialogue or bit of action had to be scrutinised. As a writer, I found this stimulating: she was really confronting me with the material and her character. In the end, I had two polar opposites in terms of actors and it helped the film too. Danny's instinctive acting added a lot to his character: you felt the edginess, that nimble change from sickly sweet, gentle 'kid' to cold killer. Anna's more analytical approach to the part served her character very well: in control and cerebral."

Filming began in the winter of 2011 and adverse weather conditions meant the shoot was a hard one, as Amalou recalls: "Very nice weather conditions. 75% of the shoot in the streets of London at night. Snowstorms for days. Average temperatures of minus 12 degrees centigrade. It was, in fact the coldest winter on record in 100 years. Sure, the weather played havoc with the continuity and brought the whole cast and crew to the edge. But... it was perfect for me." Amalou continues: "Finding locations is never a challenge. The first challenge is

Londoners. They don't give a damn about you making a movie or they certainly don't get starry-eyed. Danny Dyer or no Danny Dyer. And boy, we tried to play the Danny Dyer card to secure locations. 'We've got London's son in our film: Danny Dyer!' , 'You'll get to meet Danny Dyer!' Nobody gave a toss. All we got is 'So what?' blank stares. London for you. So, it all comes down to one thing: money. The amount of money Londoners ask for is unreal. Even the police and the council are in on it. My producing partner Lara asked for permission to shoot in a street near Vauxhall. The police were asking for fees running in the thousands because they felt they had to have police officers present at all times to 'mind the shoot'. But there are always ways around it. We found a couple of streets at the back of Battersea Power Station. Just empty blocks of flats, squats, and plenty of warehouses. A real ghost town after hours. We used those streets free of charge. We also cheated angles and shots to make some of the factories' forecourts look like bona-fide roads (complete with traffic

lights! Check out the hoodies scene in *Deviation*. scene in Deviation. It's all there.) We did the same for the chase scene. Anna runs through many streets in a desperate attempt to escape her kidnapper. In fact, we only used two tiny roads alongside Battersea Power Station. Sometimes, film-making is not about shooting 'reality', it's about creating illusion."

Dyer, however, was on top form throughout the shoot, according to the writer/director: "I am not going to name names but here is the best story about Danny's huge dichotomy between his public and private image. During post-production, Danny had to come in to do a few hours' work. The receptionist at the company was horrified: 'Danny, that horrible, loud, sexist, vulgar boy in my office? No way.' To say that she was totally open about her intense dislike of him would be an understatement. So Danny turns up, sits in the reception area with the receptionist. Unfortunately, we were running late so Danny had to wait an extra hour. I thought, 'Oh God, that receptionist is going to have a nervous breakdown with a man she absolutely loathes in the same room.' However, what people don't know about Danny is that, despite his age, he is very old school around women: polite, courteous and quiet. In fact, this is how he was most of the time around my set. Anyway, I came down to fetch Danny, expecting a bloodbath in the reception area. Guess what? Danny had that receptionist in the palm of his hand. She was totally besotted by him. So Danny went upstairs. Guess what the receptionist said to me? Yes, you've guessed it right. 'Oh, he's not what I thought he'd be. He's lovely!' All of it uttered in a gushing voice."

"On the shoot, Danny certainly regaled us with his trademark quips. Quips which were then repeated *ad nauseam* by members of the cast and crew throughout the shoot. The most memorable one was on a night shoot. After 'dinner' at 1am, we were all readying ourselves to go back on set. The weather outside was horrendous (minus 12 degrees centigrade, heavy snowstorm.) Danny leapt up to his feet and shouted: 'Alright, let's fucking smash the granny out of it!' Whatever that line means, it became the crew's rallying cry throughout the shoot. This is one thing about Danny: he's not that aloof star who only comes out to do his take and retreat back to his trailer. He is a really hard worker. For example, I can recall the scene we shot outside a 24-hour convenience store. It was a seven-page dialogue scene with bits of action thrown in. It was also a scene where he had to change 'personae' within seconds: nice and helpful at first, teary because he felt betrayed, before switching to murderous rage. Three hugely different shades of his character within one scene. Anna also had to do the same: devious when she deceives Danny's character, anxious when her 'scam' gets exposed, and then scared for her life. I was asking for take after take after take, different angles, different deliveries, etc. It was also an exterior scene and, yet again, minus 12 degrees centigrade. Did Danny ever complain once? No. Not a peep from him. He knew I was trying really hard to nail that scene and he trusted me. So he was right in there: into his character, exploring every possibility and variation with me. However, make no mistake. Danny is no fool: if he believes in a film and respects the director, he works hard, and gives all his support. I am not so sure it'd be the case on another film with a director who doesn't know what he or she is talking about. Like a true and good actor, he needs to believe what he is doing. If he doesn't, problems will start. Very often, this is the source of problems between directors and actors. I've got another story to tell you how much he commits to a film he believes in.

On the first day of shoot, he turned up totally ragged. I was confused and worried about his state. He took me aside and admitted that he hadn't slept a wink the night before because he was scared of screwing up the film. Whether this is true or not, I don't care. But I believed him: I could see the fear in his eyes. There's also another Danny moment which has me in stitches to this day. We were on location shooting that scene at a scaffolding place. A muddy, bleak place at the back of Norwood. We used the next door business – a car wash – as a base and green room. To gain access to this 'green room', I befriended the owner of the car wash in a big way in the week before the shoot. In any case, it turned out that the owner knew all about the film business. He had a long career in the porn business in Los Angeles before he came back to London to nurse his cancer-stricken mother (now there must be a film in that...but that's another story). And, of course, the car wash owner was dying to meet Danny. So I went over to Danny and said to him: 'Hey Danny, there's this bloke who wants to meet you. He used to be a porn actor and he made over 4,000 porn flicks in the USA'" Danny's response: 'Yeah, sure but I ain't fucking shaking his hand, mate.' That was not a joke. He was dead serious. The look of disgust on his face was priceless. I was not joking when I said that Danny is old school. For the record, the 4,000 movies? Totally true. For those of you who are into smut, Google 'Dick Nasty' and marvel at his long list of credits as an actor, producer and director. And the titles of his films too."

Once the film was in the can, Amalou's editor St John O'Rorke cut it into a slick, pacy thriller and a screening was arranged for UK distributors. Amalou recalls: "We invited seven distributors to view the film in a screening room in Soho. Within an hour, we had two offers. Twenty-four hours later, five out of the seven distributors had made an offer. The consensus was the same: gritty, scary and so, so, so different from what Danny Dyer had made before. As far as I was concerned, I was happy. We had plenty of offers and I'd achieved what I wanted to do from the very beginning: make a 'Danny Dyer like you've never seen him before' movie."

As luck would have it, however, Amalou and his colleagues were about to make a decision they would come to regret – Revolver were playing their much practised 'Home of Danny Dyer' card and from the outside at least this was appealing. "They were enthusiastic," laments Amalou, "and they'd distributed quite a few of Danny's films so they knew his market intimately. Also, they had that 'urban' feel about them. That kind of London cachet. The marketing people – Jon Sadler and Mike Hewitt – were great: experienced, professional, and very knowledgeable. But that was Revolver before the proverbial poo hit the fan. What we didn't know then is that Revolver was having terrible financial difficulties." As early as 2010 there had been rumours that all was not as it seemed at Revolver and that the distributor was experiencing cash-flow problems after a number of expensive acquisitions – perhaps most notably *The Veteran* – had failed to perform. The departure of Joel Kennedy, an incredibly switched on and unusually honest executive and also one of the architects of Dyer's home entertainment boom across *City Rats*, *Dead Man Running* and *Danny Dyer's Football Foul Ups*, had signified a change in direction for the company as a lack of understanding of the core product set in. Ironically, what had happened at the major studios – the mistaken belief that Dyer on the cover alone was enough to shift 100,000 DVDs – was now happening at Revolver. It was a clear case of chickens coming home to roost.

As more key staff began to leave Revolver in droves, Amalou began to worry: "So Jon Sadler and Mike Hewitt left and they were replaced by guys barely out of college. Even the receptionist suddenly became part of the marketing team. I don't blame these 'college kids' at all. I blame the management for parachuting them in such high positions. To be fair, one of the 'college kids' admitted quite candidly that he and his colleagues were a little out of their depth. From then on, the marketing and distribution of *Deviation* became a kamikaze operation. At first, Lara Greenway and I were very involved with Jon Sadler and Mike Hewitt. We were at the publicity/promotion shoot which was done by top photographer Charles Gray. We had long discussions about promoting the film as 'Danny Dyer as you've never seen him before'. We also agreed on a poster/DVD cover which would reflect the fact that *Deviation* is a psychological thriller. Once Mike Hewitt and Jon Sadler left... Nothing. No contact. We were constantly chasing up the 'college kids' for information. It was obvious that these young guys were lumped with all the releases and they simply couldn't cope. Revolver was not even tweeting about the impending release of the film. In retrospect, it is now obvious that Revolver was too busy keeping their head above water so they didn't have time for anything else."

Perhaps the final nail in *Deviation*'s pre-release coffin was the bizarre, incomprehensible decision to go with cheap lithographic style art, eschewing the glossy dark tones that had served the likes of *City Rats, Dead Man Running* and *Pimp* so well. Amalou recalls, "I hated it. Everything about it. About a year before we made *Deviation*, Danny had been vilified in the press for a very dubious article in *Zoo*. And rightly so. Even Danny apologised profusely – publicly, privately, and in print in his autobiography *Straight Up*. I know personally that, to this day, he hates himself for this tasteless, vile episode. So what did Revolver do? They put Danny on the DVD cover with a knife in his hand terrorising a woman. How insane is that? Some papers quickly picked up on that too. So, that was precisely the moment Revolver's marketing/promotion of *Deviation* turned into a Kamikaze mission. Besides, that was not the artwork we agreed on with the previous marketing team at all. We'd gone from a psychological thriller to a slasher movie DVD cover. Anyway, my first reaction when I saw the front cover was: 'Where are the quotes? Revolver College Kid's answer: 'There are no good quotes we could use.' That was untrue. Revolver was in such a hurry to rush out the film for some quick, needed cash, they simply went ahead with the manufacture of the DVD and the artwork without bothering about the quotes. And it doesn't end there. The back cover read: 'An all-action, adrenaline-fuelled bloodbath that has been compared to *Severance*, *Hostel* and *Saw*..." and "a white-knuckle journey..." and "a murderous rampage through London..." When I saw this, I was so incredulous that I burst out laughing. Revolver College Kid joined in the laughter. He thought I was elated. Well, that was until I told him exactly what I thought of the artwork and the blurbs. I have never seen someone go so pale and so in need of a loo in a matter of seconds. Yes, I was furious. That was two years of hard work fast disappearing down the drain."

On 24 February, Revolver premiered the film in Leicester Square. Nobody of merit turned up besides the *Deviation* team and the result was disastrous. Under the headline 'A Dyer turnout' The *Mail Online* dissected the guest list: "He's been the star of many a successful British film, but Danny Dyer's latest effort will perhaps end up on DVD a lot sooner than planned. That's if the calibre of guests at the premiere of his new movie, *Deviation*, is anything to go by. In fact, there was virtually nobody worth a mention besides a few low-rent glamour models at the screening which took place at the Odeon cinema in London's Covent Garden." An embarrassed JK Amalou recalls the premiere fiasco: "I wasn't the happiest bunny there. I already knew that the release was going to be a disaster. Everything was wrong: the promotion, the marketing, etc. My heart sank when I saw the 'college kids' still putting up posters around the cinema foyer as *the guests were arriving*. The guest list cheapened the whole event because there was no money. I did tell the Revolver guys that if there was going to be no great guests, it'd be better to cancel the premiere as we'd only be humiliated. And I was right. Not even an hour after the premiere, an unflattering article (complete with pictures!) appeared on the *Daily Mail*'s website at around 10 p.m., calling us the 'nobodies premiere'. To be blunt, I felt I was attending the funeral of my movie, not its premiere. Unfortunately I was proven right in the following weeks. I tell you it was damn hard to keep smiling, do the press, and have your investors hovering nearby, knowing fully well that the film was going to be a disaster."

Despite the disastrous premiere, the film gained some begrudgingly positive reviews, often despite Dyer's casting: *Total Film*'s Paul Bradshaw noted "J.K. Amalou's mockney rehash of *The Hitcher* would be duller without him (Dyer)" while The *Evening Standard* opined "No one could call this a notable film, though there is some good location work and a performance from a bearded Dyer that may be a bit over the top but still makes its mark."

Peter Bradshaw in *The Guardian* was less indulgent: "The old Danny Dyer thug schtick makes another appearance in this surprisingly atmospheric thriller," before accusing Dyer of being typecast as "violent psychotic criminal(s)" and dismissing his performance as "bizarrely and excruciatingly acted by Dyer a lot of the time; but actually this film isn't as bad as all that."

Mark Kermode, of course, hated the film, and trotted out his increasingly bizarre Dyer impersonation to his excitable fans. Amalou – like many others – finds Kermode's constant haranguing of Dyer inexcusable: "That is not even funny. That is bullying. Pure and simple. It was even more shocking to see this particular critic's fans egging him on to do his impressions of Danny in the comments section of his Facebook page. This is textbook bullying: people rallying around the bully to pick on someone."

This was nothing, however, compared to a scathing and very personal attack on Dyer by Christopher Tookey in *The Mail*. Under another provocative headline – 'Danny Dyer is a bad actor in a terrible film' – the hysterical journalist launched a vicious, middle class-baiting attack on Dyer:

"This can only be recommended to connoisseurs of terrible acting. Danny Dyer plays a hilariously unconvincing Broadmoor escapee who car-jacks a pretty nurse (Anna Walton). Walton's believable under-playing – even when director JK Amalou's abject script takes preposterous turns – makes Dyer look all the more hopeless. I would leave it there, but the time has surely come to ask why Dyer has been allowed to deliver abysmal performances in many of the most pathetic British films of the past decade. Among his worst are *Outlaw* (*Fight Club* for morons) and *Straightheads* (a rip-off of *Straw Dogs*). The reason Mr Dyer keeps appearing on the big screen is that he has a sizeable, young, male fan base among those who identified with him in his earliest films, especially *The Football Factory* (2004), where he glamorised the thuggery, drunkenness and bone-headed stupidity of football hooligans. His popularity with that demographic is such that he even held down a job as an 'agony uncle' on the lads' mag *Zoo* – until he suggested a reader disfigure his ex-girlfriend. But what's the explanation for Mr Dyer's consistently degrading roles, which serve only to show up his bewildering lack of talent? One clue may come from his 2010 autobiography, in which he confesses to drinking too much, advocates taking drugs and admits using them frequently. He has also boasted to *Attitude* magazine: 'A lot of people want to take drugs with me. I am known as being a f***ing bad boy.' And, I'm afraid, a very bad actor, with zero sense of social responsibility. Mr Dyer is very much a villain for our times. It's an illuminating comment on modern British film that he keeps being cast as a leading man."

This ill-informed, frighteningly opinionated attack pathetically trying to link bad acting with recreational drug use (most of Hollywood watch out) presented Dyer as some kind of bogeyman – 'a villain for our times'. With this kind of rubbish constantly being printed in tabloids and overflowing onto the internet, the public perception of Dyer quickly began to change. His career was in the doldrums, his comeback film, billed as 'a career-defining performance' was on the ropes. His trump card – that his films performed well in the face of critical disdain – was about to face its biggest challenge.

Mercifully, the press didn't pick up on the film's VOD-qualifying theatrical 'release' scraping together just £307 at the box office.

Presumably in panic, Revolver rushed through an intense, but ill-conceived press junket at its West London headquarters. Inviting a rag-tag collection of bloggers, tweeters and online critics, the low point of this last minute 'press campaign' saw Dyer being interviewed (on film of course) by a girl off her head on acid. Predictably, it was the only piece of *Deviation* press to gain any traction.

When the DVD was released, it shifted just 3,840 units in its first week, the worst result for a Danny Dyer film since *The Great Ecstasy Of Robert Carmichael*. The hamfisted, rushed campaign had backfired spectacularly and if Revolver had been banking on another *Dead Man Running* to ease their financial woes, they were in for a disappointment.

Dyer was livid: "It didn't do the business it fucking should have. I was really thinking that this was me just purely acting. Fuck everything else in the bag that comes with 'Danny Dyer', this is me as an actor. Hopefully people can appreciate it. It's just about dialogue – that's the beauty of it. This weird fucking relationship with these two people in this situation. Complete fucking strangers and you just don't know how it's going to pan out. I hate the idea of films spoon-feeding people. People watch films now, obsessed, they know what's going to happen and they can judge the next step. With that film, you never quite knew what would happen. You'd think, 'How the fuck are they going to wrap this up? Either he's going to kill her or she's going to kill him, but how's she going to kill him?' The twist at the end is the genius thing: how she does him with the fucking pills. I had a fucking ball on that film."

When the DVD numbers for the first week came in, there was a palpable euphoria in Soho – the Dyer boom was over, at least for the time being. Distributors who for years now had never managed to understand Dyer's vast appeal, punched the air in excitement at no longer having to brief designers that all they wanted was violent black, white and red covers. With Revolver taking its last gasp and most of its pioneers having long abandoned the sinking ship, it felt as though a sea change in British film was afoot.

"My hope is that, one day, *Deviation* will be rediscovered," notes a philosophical Amalou. "It deserves to be. Not because I wrote it and directed it but for the crew. My producing partner Lara Greenway, our DOP Ollie Downey, production designer Chloe Brady, editor St John O'Rorke and everyone on the crew worked incredibly hard in difficult conditions and they all did a marvellous job. The same goes for the whole cast too. I strongly believe that asking a director to deliver a good film without a good team is like asking a jockey to win the Grand National on a three-legged donkey. Maybe, one day, audiences will properly discover another facet of Danny's talent."

Much like *Pimp*, *Deviation* is a film that has yet to find the audience it deserves. A genuinely tense, gripping thriller with a scope far wider than the 'two people in a car' scenario the critics would have you believe, it is compellingly scripted and stylishly directed and features a bravura performance from Dyer, a complete departure from anything he has done before. Early in the film, his character radically changes his appearance to evade the police and the clean-shaven, slick-haired psychopath who emerges is a chilling, genuinely unsettling characterisation. Anna Walton is solid in the lead and the film really is all about her character, yet still Dyer manages to steal every scene he's in, making the movie very much his own. There's no other Danny Dyer film like *Deviation* and that only adds to its appeal – this one is definitely worth tracking down: it's a film that will stay with you long after the credits roll.

# RUN FOR YOUR WIFE (2012)

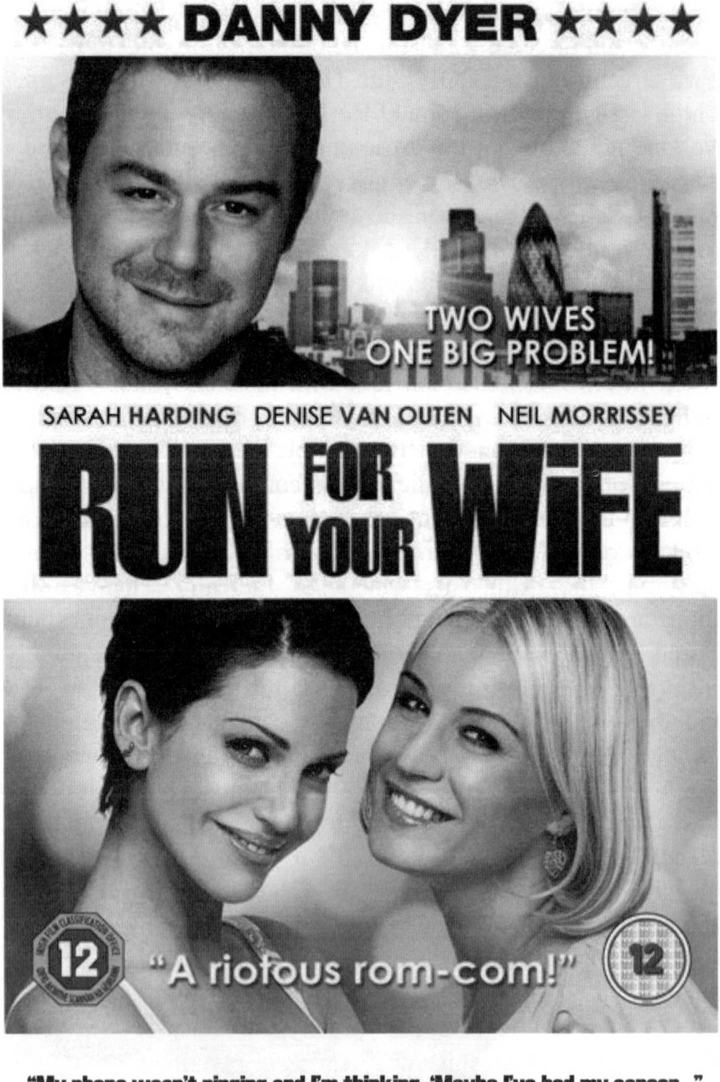


"My phone wasn't ringing and I'm thinking, 'Maybe I've had my career..."

**Directors** Ray Cooney, John Luton **Producer** Graham Fowler, James Simpson **Writer** Ray Cooney **Music** Walter Christian Mair **Production Designer** Fi Russell **Costume Design** Tony Priestley **Cinematography** Graham Fowler

**Danny Dyer** John Smith **Denise van Outen** Michelle Smith **Sarah Harding** Stephanie Smith **Neil Morrissey** Gary Gardner **Ben Cartwright** D S Troughton **Nicholas Le Prevost** D S Porterhouse **Kellie Shirley** Susie Browning **Christopher Biggins** Bobby Franklin **Lionel Blair** Cyril **Jeffrey Holland** Dick Holland **Louise Michelle** Frances

*Taxi driver John Smith (Dyer) rescues a bag lady (Judi Dench) from a mugging and is knocked unconscious. After he is taken to the local hospital, much confusion ensues due to the fact that Smith has two wives (Denise van Outen and Sarah Harding) and the attempts by him and his best mate (Neil Morrissey) become more elaborate and – in theory – hilarious.*

There is not a film in recent (or indeed distant) memory that has received such a bashing from the press. Not the critics, mind. The press. They wanted to get Dyer and they did. Reporting that it had grossed only £602, they claimed it to be the biggest flop of all time. Yet, all of the journalists knew full well how these things work. That it had been released in a handful of cinemas for lunchtime screenings to reach the pensioner market who would be fans of Ray Cooney's stage play and also of the many cameo appearances including June Whitfield, Donald Sinden, Cliff Richard, Su Pollard, Judi Dench and Richard Briers (in his last role before his death). Sure, it's not a blockbuster success, but nor is it the disaster that was reported. But who needs facts when you are out to get someone?

Yet sit and watch this with three generations of family members and you will enjoy the experience. It's a silly, fun film. Nothing offensive, no swearing. It is what it intended to be: a farce. Nowadays we call Judd Apatow films sweet. Have you tried watching these – albeit excellent – filthfests with your grandparents? *Run For Your Wife* is a genuinely silly but undeniably fun romp. Not dissimilar to *'Allo 'Allo* to any children of the eighties, the show in which Vicki Michelle, the producer of this film, made her name.

Prior to receiving the script, Dyer was already in a bad place emotionally. "My phone wasn't ringing and I'm thinking, 'Maybe I've had my career... I've had a fucking good run, I'm blessed.' It wasn't working out for me at that time; it was like I couldn't catch a cold. I was watching these dramas on TV and thinking, 'Why the fuck am I not even auditioning for this? I'm not even getting associated with it, not getting my foot through the fucking door!' I was at a real low point. I couldn't greenlight projects like I could before. I talked to my agent and he's being blunt with me. So it was like nothing, nothing, nothing. My confidence was at a low, *Deviation* failed – and I thought that was going to be the one to put me back on the map. Again, what they did with *Vendetta*, it was a career-defining performance or something like that, which I don't think you should really say before the film has come out. I was just thinking, 'Wow, I can't do nothing right.' It's all about performance and trying to get rid of the baggage and the bullshit, just acting – which is what *Deviation* is – and it fails. It fails because they don't promote it or whatever it is or I'm not cool or whatever. So when I get a letter from Ray Cooney, who is the ambassador of the Shaftesbury Theatre, who wants me. Interestingly he watched *The All Together*, out of all my movies that was the only movie he'd seen, and made his decision on. He saw me as this role, so I read it and thought, 'Wow OK, fucking completely different from *Deviation*. Something I've not got a track record in, playing the fluffy nice *Carry On*-style character.' They threw a shit load of money at me as well, which got me out of a bit of trouble. Ninety grand for four weeks. He didn't know anything about the baggage, he'd never heard of me. It was somebody who recommended me, a producer. I was like, 'Wow, okay.' Slowly the cast became ridiculous. I mean for fuck's sake: Neil Morrissey, Dame Judi Dench, Cliff Richard, Bernard Cribbins, Richard Briers, it was ridiculous. I'm having a ball on set, I'm loving it. I thought that it's a strange film to be making, it's all fluffy and light, every fucking scene there's a gag in it. I'm playing it completely straight, I'm not playing it for the gag. Starring opposite Neil Morrissey and I know he gets a bit of bad press but he's a fucking good comedy actor. I was bought up watching *Men Behaving Badly*, so to be around him was a good fucking experience. I was always questioning it thinking, 'Fucking hell, who's the audience for this?' The film had been translated into two hundred different languages all over the world, it earned a hundred and fifty million worldwide. The backlash for me fed into the movie a little bit."

The press reaction was unprecedented. Dyer believes that it was a mistake to have a premiere when the plan all along was to only put it in a handful of cinemas. "Ray Cooney wanted the Leicester Square premiere, which I think he funded himself," says Dyer. "I think he funded most of the movie himself. You can't give a big premiere and then put it out in four cinemas. A lot of stars turned up – it was a big premiere. They should have just bought it straight out on DVD and done a deal with Sky. It would have done good numbers, it wouldn't have got attacked the way it did. It was the final straw for me, to be honest. Again, I need a hit. My confidence is at a low, I'm in failure after failure, I had a lot fucking riding on it. But for it to be attacked the way it was, I would never have fucking dreamt that it would have been that bad. It was horrible, I knew that that Kermode was sitting there rubbing his hands almost as if he's been proved right. I couldn't bring myself to hear his review of it. I was getting tweeted about it going, 'Have you heard Kermode's thing?' And I couldn't even go there. I was down, depressed and feeling like shit. *The Independent* did that thing on me, *Culture* did that lovely interview on me. And he went on Twitter acting like a child. It was really ugly, he really assassinated me. I was just a bit disappointed that no one stood up for me, no producers came out. I got all the flak for it and that was almost the worst thing for me. It was like, 'Wow, where do I go from here really.' It was a constant Twitter thing as well about how it took seven hundred quid at the box office. What could I say? They believe what they read in the papers, I couldn't really go into the fact that it only came out in four cinemas, and all those four cinemas were rammed. It was one showing at 12 O' clock for the senior citizens, three pound a ticket; really it was quite a success in that respect. It earned about fourteen or fifteen grand over the next couple of weeks. Yeah it's almost like I'm fighting a losing battle. I can't really comment on it and that's why I need other people to talk about it. What can I say? It failed, but that's not because of me, it's because of the idea and the concept and the fact it's a farce and a bit dated. It's for the Caravan Club. It's almost just keeping that fucking belief going, in a way. After that, I did think, 'I'm fucked.' "

Producer Vicki Michelle had been a fan of Dyer's since seeing him in *Human Traffic*. "I was executive producer, so I was raising the money really," she says. "I mean, we had the two producers as well, so they were involved, but Danny I knew from *Human Traffic*. My husband had his own production company, GF films, producing films in town, and the producer of *Human Traffic*, Allan Niblo, rented part of my husband's offices with Fruit Salad. So we knew of Danny from there, before Allan went off to become Vertigo. So my awareness came from *Human Traffic*, which I'd seen, and then I talked to Allan Niblo, and they'd always said how talented Danny was. But I didn't work with him until we did this TV movie called *All In The Game* with Ray Winstone. Ray Winstone played my husband and Danny played my son. That was fantastic. It's amazing, he only lives down the road from me, so I knew he was in the area but we didn't really meet up socially until we were doing the film. But I've always known of him and always heard good things about him to be quite honest. When we were looking for someone from the film, we wanted a cheeky chappy taxi driver, and I'd already worked with Danny – in reality, he is a cheeky chappy. He's very normal, and he's got something that women like, a special charisma that women love. Women love Danny Dyer, that's it. You ask all the young girls, they all love him. It's something that you can't buy: you've either got it or not. So when we were discussing the film, I said I thought he'd be great: he was the right age group, but he was known for gangster films and not comedy. Ray Cooney was directing, and he was like, 'Well let me meet him; he's local.' And Ray only lives nearby, so we got in touch with Danny and asked him to come and meet Ray, and as soon as he walked in the door, Ray said, 'He's perfect.' He is that cheeky chappy, he's got that quality that women like, he's not offensive, and I think that he was perfect for the part and Ray thought so too, but it was a completely different genre for him."

Regardless of the press response, Michelle has good memories of working with Dyer. "He knows his business: he knows the cameras, he knows what's right, and he's very at ease," she states. "I think he's great to work with because you need someone who knows what they're doing. I mean, Ray was directing him, but Danny knows what he's doing. Ray would give him a couple of tips about some comedy stuff or something, but really I think Danny knows comedy comes from staying true to the character – deliver it straight, and you get the comedy out of it. The comedy comes from the lines or the situation. A lot of these new shows don't work because they're trying to play the comedy – well you don't, you play

the comedy for real, and then it comes out from that, though obviously you can have some characters. But with Danny in *Run For Your Wife* – this play has been played all over the world and it's still being played now. It was in the West End for nine years. In fact, he did say that it got slated by the critics when it first came out, and then it ran in the West End for nine years. *'Allo 'Allo!: The Stage Play* got slated by the critics and it ran for years and years and years in the West End and all over the country. I think it's a shame that we don't embrace British comedy. It wasn't rocket science, it was just a laugh. Not violent, not swearing, some great people who did it for Ray, some great names in there, and it should have been received as good old British comedy. But there were different aspects coming in. I think you should have critics. They often want to talk about Chekov or something like that, but to be quite honest, I think critics should talk to the public, and sometimes they don't. I've been with this film all over the country and we've had questions and answers – not one person has said they didn't enjoy the film. I was in Kent at the film festival on Saturday and this guy said he nearly didn't come because he read the reviews online, and he went, 'I'm so pleased I came, it was really fun! I was laughing – I haven't laughed out loud for a long time!' This is laugh-out-loud comedy. You have to laugh about it. I've not had one person – and I've spoken to hundreds with these questions and answers all over the country – not one person has not thought Danny Dyer was great in the role. Not one. And by having a go at Danny, they've also belittled the film as well as British comedy. It's bullying, really. And to the detriment of Ray Cooney, who is a legend. Also, people were on the street were saying – because I spoke to Kate Plantin who was casting director – that this was the most anticipated film, because it was amazing that you were getting Dame Judi Dench and Sir Cliff Richard in this film playing cameos for British comedy. This should have been a really good feel-good film. I don't think it was all down to Danny. Obviously you have critics that don't like that sort of comedy, and I don't think that Danny can take that on his shoulders. It was unfair. Really unfair."

*Run For Your Wife* was finally released on DVD on 16 September. As Dyer points out, it should have begun its journey here because it has an audience at home. But the negative press coverage ruined any chance of that and it limped to 3,000 sales. A genuine shame for a film that, while not perfect, would charm the pants off its intended audience.

DYER
HARDING
VAN OUTEN
MORRISSEY
JOHN LOVED HAVING A WIFE.
SO HE GOT TWO OF THEM.
RUN FOR
YOUR WIFE

# IN A HEARTBEAT (2013)

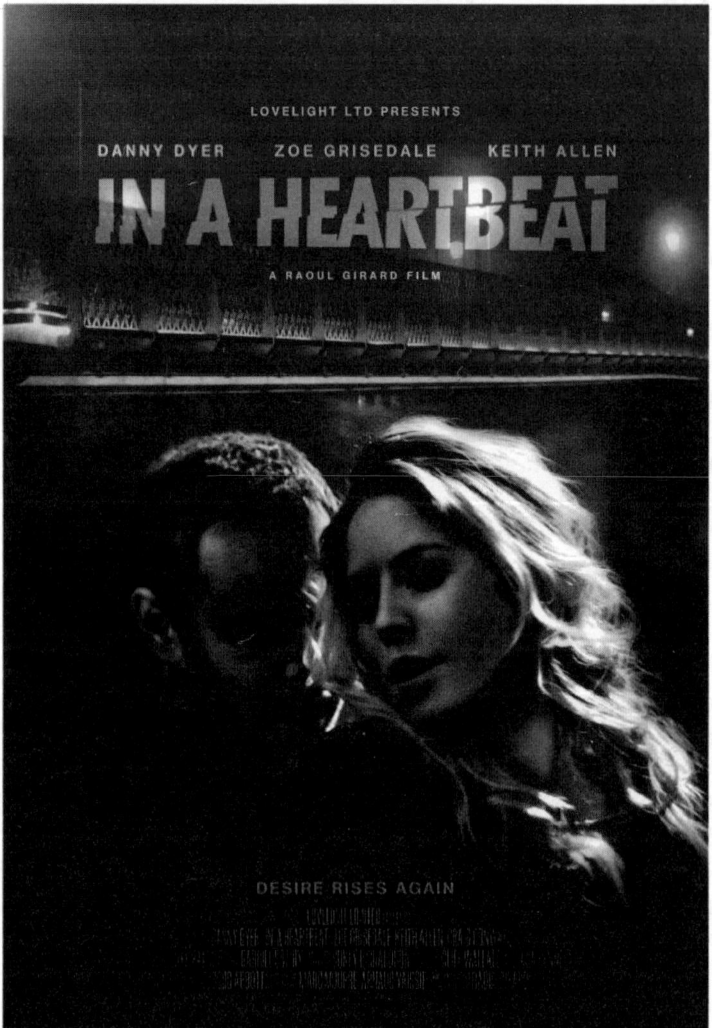


**"Danny was not an immediate choice, though now I think he was a great choice and I'm very happy with it."**

**Director/writer/producer** Raoul Girard **Executive Producer** Doug Abbott **Cinematography** Luke Palmer **Music** Asa Bennett **Editor** Raoul Girard **Sound** Gabriel Sotiry **Special Effects Supervisor** Cliff Wallace

**Danny Dyer** Philip **Zoe Grisedale** Jane **Keith Allen** Peter Smith **Craig Conway** Film Director **Jason Durr** Andrew **Georgina Moffat** Loren **Tom McCall** Shop **Alex Freeborn** Assistant Dave the Techie **Colin Hubbard** Steve the Techie **Stuart Lockwood** Tim the Techie

*If you met somebody in desperate need of help, would you bring them home? This is the dilemma that faces Philip, a London bachelor addicted to horror films. While out jogging one night, he encounters Jane, a dazed and confused model. However this mysterious woman is hiding a shocking secret.*

*In A Heartbeat* is an edgy and unpredictable love story that unfolds like a psychological thriller. It's certainly unlike anything Dyer has done before, and director Raoul Girard admits that he didn't at first think of him for the lead role. "Danny was not an immediate choice, though now I think he was a great choice and I'm very happy with it," says Girard. "At the beginning when I was looking for actors, I wanted to be surprised by some suggestions from agents. So I saw that they'd sent to me Danny, and then I called the agent who said to me, 'Do you know who Danny Dyer is?' Because I am originally from France, she was wondering if I'd heard of him. I said, 'Yes, of course I know who Danny Dyer is – he's doing gangster films.' At that moment, I realised I could use that 'gangster background' in the film and I said to her, 'Well, if he wants to do something different, then you can send him the script.' They sent him the script, and a few days later I got a call from Danny's agent saying that he loved the script and that he wanted to do it. I was quite happy to have a big name – because he is a big name, and he was very enthusiastic about the project. He loved the script, and he loved the character as well. It is basically a love story as well, which is something maybe a little bit unusual for him."

He hadn't met Danny when he had made up his mind that he wanted him for the part. "I knew he would fit the part," says Girard. "But then, of course, you meet the person, and it needs to be confirmed. We had a meeting in Soho at the Groucho Club. That was very nice. I just told him about the character and how I see him, and he was very happy that I like to let my actors act – because there is a lot of dialogue in the film. I myself am a very visual director, but it just so happens that in this film that I wrote there is a lot of dialogue, which was a little bit unusual for me. I was very happy that he understood the part completely. He quite strong and imposing, but at the same time I could feel there was sort of – not frailty, but vulnerability sometimes, which I'm sure was good for the part as well because he could play on different levels and not always be the usual, tough Danny Dyer."

Girard liked the fact that Dyer has been apparently wrongly typecast and feels that this made it all the more interesting because the "real" Danny Dyer is now more like he is in *In A Heartbeat* . "I think there are a lot of people who think of him only as the hard man," he says. "But this is wrong. I think he can be a much more versatile actor, and he's still quite young. His character is a very simple guy, a bachelor, who is out jogging one night, and meets a beautiful woman, who is completely lost and dazed. The big question is, would you take somebody home in order to help them? Somebody who is in desperate need for help – would you take them to your place? And that's what he does. The character of Danny allows that, and allows that people will believe in it, despite his gangster-type image. There is a kind of kindness in his character and he decides to take this woman – this very strange woman – to his place. And then the film begins."

Girard had such confidence in his cast (which also includes Zoe Grisedale and Keith Allen) that he did not feel the need to do numerous takes. "I didn't do many takes," he states. "On average, I made three takes. Sometimes I made eight takes, but it was very rare. I think the most I made was 12. After each take we had to redo some things to achieve technical perfection: because the Steadicam we used needs enough space to move smoothly and follow the actors properly. We used two cameras, and one of them was this Steadicam that we had all the time on set. It's not the usual thing to do that – but I decided to shoot with both cameras all the time. Danny is quite instinctive, and very often he's quite impatient, but this is normal, because he's in the moment. I quickly noticed that he was the best after the second or third take at the maximum, so very often I took the second or the third take for the edit, and that is quite good. I was quite pleased with the result."

Dyer also worked well with the other actors, some of whom were hugely experienced (Allen). Some less so (Grisedale). "Most of the film is a two-hander between Danny and the woman," Girard says. "But at the same time, there are some other characters, actors like Keith Allen, who is a very important character. He plays the psychoanalyst, who is a friend of Danny in the film, and he advises him because Danny is completely disorientated with the behaviour of this strange woman. I was a little worried at the beginning because we had some rehearsals together with Danny at my place in London, and Zoe Grisdale is a newcomer, so it was very tough for her because she was playing in front of Danny who is very much more experienced than her. But he didn't know all his lines, and they were reading, so I was a little bit worried. Just before starting the shooting, is he going to turn up and know his lines? There are a lot of lines in the script – and I was happily surprised. He knew his lines perfectly on the first day, and he was very much in it. He rehearsed with Zoe in the dressing rooms before the takes, but he did say jokes, and he was very nice with the crew and the crew liked him. But I think it's his way to concentrate. He's not always putting his head into his hands and thinking very hard about things. He likes to be relaxed in order to put out the best performance when we say, 'Action!'

Girard echoes the words of many other directors who have worked with Dyer. "He was very easy to work with in the way that he's very experienced, and if he doesn't understand something, he's very honest and asks and is receptive to my answers," says Girard. "As soon as he understands it, he will alter his performance and do something differently, which is satisfying, and which is very good. He is very flexible. This is a very important quality: for him to be flexible despite his experience. I think he helped the newcomer – the actress – because it wasn't easy for her to be intimate with him, or in scenes that were very dramatic with dramatic feelings. It's a love story, so it needed to be moving, because the girl has a deep secret that is going to be revealed during the film, but basically Danny in the film is the point of view of the audience. He's the guy who the audience can relate to. He's the normal guy. And then he's in the position of any guy who discovers and is seduced by an incredible, mysterious new person. He's just met a beautiful girl who is so strange that he doesn't understand her, but she will be revealed to him. And it's worth it."

Despite a relatively modest budget, *In A Heartbeat* has some high production values thanks, in no small part to Girard's bulging contacts book after a long time in the industry. "We shot it with state of the art cameras, and had a wealth of top technicians," he says. "Also, we were very lucky to have Cliff Wallace as a technician. I have known him for a few years, but he's done the special effects and prosthetics for *Hell Boy II,* for lots of films – especially Danny Boyle films like *Trance* and *28 Weeks Later* – so he's a very reliable prosthetic supervisor. He helped this film to become a reality. And I was very happy to go back to Pinewood. The technicians in England are very good, as good as the American ones. This is the reason why so many American films are shot in England. It's an incredible environment for movies. A very good one."

*At the time of going to print, In A Heartbeat has yet to be released*

# VENDETTA (2013)

**"Okay, watch this. This is what I can do."**

**Director** Stephen Reynolds **Producer** Jonathan Sothcott **Writer** Stephen Reynolds **Music** Phil Mountford **Production Designer** Anthony Neale **Costume Design** Lenka Padysakova **Cinematography** Haider Zafar **Make-Up** Fran Hounsom

**Danny Dyer** Jimmy Vickers **Roxanne McKee** Morgan **Vincent Regan** Colonel Leach **Josef Altin** Rob **Bruce Payne** Rooker **Simona Behlikova** Sophia **Alistair Petrie** Spencer Holland **Emma Samms** Sandra Vickers **Christopher Cowlin** Paramedic **Ricci Harnett** Joe Windsor **Nick Nevern** Ronnie **Charlie Bond** Kerry **Lucy Drive** Catherine Hopkins

*Special ops interrogation officer Jimmy Vickers tracks down the gang who slaughtered his parents. With police closing in and his old unit on his trail, he has to evade capture long enough to complete his gruesome crusade.*

This is the one. The one that Dyer was waiting for. A proper action thriller that would please his fans and challenge him as an actor. a dream come true, really. After *Run For Your Wife*, I was in bad state mentally," he admits. "I was wondering if I'd ever get offered another good script or even make another film. And then producer Jonathan Sothcott comes along and gives me a script and I'm like, 'Fucking hell, wow. What a script.' The film I had been waiting for. A proper vigilante thriller that I could get my teeth into and the fans would love. And, of course, we made it for a hundred grand so it wasn't a money thing, it was just a chance for me to go, 'Okay, watch this. This is what I can do.' And I had to do this. I had been feeling really down and low and I think that every cunt's against me and I'm a laughing joke. I can't wait to get a script where I can really fucking go. I'm so pent up in this *Vendetta*, all the fucking hate and the shit I've had, I just completely channel it going, 'I'll fucking show you why I've had the career I've fucking had.' Because I'm passionate about what I do and I'm fucking good at it, and this is me. Every fucking beat in this film *Vendetta* you can see I'm so on it. I'm not missing a fucking trick. I'm just completely living it. It's such a cool role."

The role of Jimmy Vickers is indeed a meaty one, given Dyer is playing a son grieving for his parents, full of rage but SAS-trained to not convey emotion. Unlike most vigilante films where a mild mannered pillar of society turns rogue after the loss of his family, Vickers is a trained killer. So the film poses the terrifying question, what if a man trained in the art of torture went out to clean the streets and rid them from gangs and drug dealers and murderous scum? Dyer knew it was a role he had to think about. "I made this decision of like, 'Right, I'm grieving,'" he says. "That's basically what I'm doing in the film, I'm grieving. I really come alive at these moments when I get them on their own. That's when you really see Jimmy Vickers. He's sad, he's fucking sad, but he does get this little flicker behind the eyes of being a human being. You do like him. He's completely solitary. It's going back to what war can do to people, which I wanted to bring into it. I'm a fucked-up character anyway, but to have this happen to you, and how the fuck would you deal with it?"

This was director Stephen Reynolds's first full-length feature film, not that you would know it to watch it. "I had been writing screenplays for years and shooting my own films for no money," he says. "I made a film called *Snowman* and basically sent it out to the world and Jonathan Sothcott was one of the few producers who displayed any interest. From then we stayed in touch and I wrote a few projects that didn't get made. And then after I wrote *Fall Of The Essex Boys* for him, we decided I was ready to direct and we went full circle cause Jonathan really wanted to make a hard, violent vigilante film in the tradition of *Death Wish*. My *Snowman* screenplay had a lot of the elements but it needed reworking and then *Vendetta* was born."

Reynolds had always dreamed of working with Dyer. "I always thought he was a talented actor, since I saw him first in *Human Traffic* and I was trying to get my film career going all those years ago and saw him and wanted to work with him immediately," he says. "Some filmmakers have a list of actors they want to work with, a kind of Hollywood wish list. Danny was on mine. I finally met Danny about five months before *Vendetta* commenced filming. Danny felt so familiar when we first met because of two reasons: I'd seen a bunch of his movies, but at the same time he's a genuine guy that's very approachable and welcoming and reminded me a lot of friends I've got back home and that I grew up with, so it was very easy to connect with him and he, in turn, made it very easy for me. There's sometimes a real snobbery to new talent in this industry, especially when you are coming in as the leader on a project and especially when you are from out of London, as I am, but Danny was a gent, he trusted me from day one and a lot of why *Vendetta* was such a good shoot – and that comes from the trust he gave me."

For his part, Dyer feels that Reynolds re-lit something within him. "Reynolds was another man who sat me down at this low ebb and said, 'Dan, I can't lie to you, I've always wanted to work with you. I remember watching *Human Traffic,*' going right back to the beginning, and he turned to his missus and said, 'I'm going to work with that man one day.' It choked me because I could tell how sincere he was and he was right. He fucking found me at a point in my life and my career where both fingers were crossed going to move on to the next level. He's given me this great opportunity, and back to *Human Traffic,* he probably thought he couldn't lace my fucking boots. He has now come to the point where has completely given me a lifeline, and a trust and let me run with it so I can fucking make people stand up again and go, 'Fuck you're back'. It has all come full circle, because that was his moment when he said, 'Who is this fucking kid? I've got to work with him, I have to work with him.' We nearly worked together on something and it didn't work out. *Vendetta* comes along, and even then Stephen was like, 'You ain't going to get Danny, I bet you won't get him.' Of course I sat down, read that script and went, 'Sign me the fuck up, I'll pay you to do it.' That is the truth."

One of the biggest misconceptions about Dyer in the media is that he always plays hard men or gangsters. Everyone seems to believe this yet if you look at his films, prior to *Vendetta*, he has never played a proper hard man. He has played boys who wind up involved in things they shouldn't, he has played football hooligans. He has played comedy gangsters. Films like *City Rats* have sold themselves as being gangster films and disappointed fans in the process. But he's never played a proper hard man, until now. Director Stephen Reynolds loves the fact that *Vendetta* is the real deal. "I think finally for the first time he is actually playing a 'hard man'. He gets described as 'hard man Danny Dyer' all the time in the press and lord knows why. Because he presented a show about hard men? Does that make David Attenborough a wild animal? That shows how way off our public view of him is. You look at his catalogue of movies – he's never played a tough guy. But while the media slam Danny all the time, audiences still love him. I think people that liked him originally still like him.I just think a handful of haters have got on his back and that's just escalated. Unfortunately in the British media they love to hate, they love to bully and they are very quick to try not to champion people – and in that way we are very different to the Americans. Danny could've been a massive star in this country but I think the problem is he had the potential to be bigger than the industry itself and we don't have enough top-quality projects out there to house our great actors – that's why we lose them all to the States. Look at Tom Hardy, Gary Oldman, Christian Bale, Idris Elba, Kiera Knightley, they are all in the States and made that move very quickly. Danny became very popular very quickly, he was young and maybe chose some bad movies – it happens. The public are very unforgiving and like to throw shit at our heroes, look at Beckham. We were burning dummies of him in the bloody stands at one point, now he is a national hero. I hated Beckham at one point but I came around. I love him and it would be nice if we as Brits could support our talent a bit more instead of pushing them out, it's a real shame. Danny has said a few things in the press or interviews that have been questionable, but people make mistakes and he really isn't that that gobby, brash geezer some people think he is."

As a result of this, both Reynolds and Sothcott felt enormous pressure to do justice to Dyer and give him the best possible film to come back with. "I didn't put that on myself, and Jonathan is a pretty laidback producer sometimes and very good at putting you at ease, and I wasn't told that that was what I had to do but in my head I wanted to make something special and totally surprise a few people," says Reynolds. "You can only really give it your all where you can. So in any dialogue to production designers, costume designer, make-up, director of photography I was very specific about what I wanted so my vision could seep in everywhere and I knew if I could do that we'd have something a little bit special, but it was my first feature so I really didn't have a clue how it would go down, I just knew I had to work as hard as I could and at least then you can say I did everything I could, I gave it my best shot."

Dyer and producer Jonathan Sothcott had worked before on some less successful films, but their relationship is now cemented, with *Vendetta* and *Assassin* and many more productions over coming years. Sothcott remembers how it all came together. "I had made a picture called *The Rise And Fall Of A White Collar Hooligan* which, though ripped to shreds by critics, had been a minor success on DVD, largely thanks to a strong performance by lead actor Nick Nevern," he says. "Looking for something to do next with Nick, I came up with the idea of a really gritty urban vigilante movie. I talked to a writer I liked, Steve Reynolds, and he started coming up with a story. There was an early idea for a Noel Clarke cameo (he and Nick are friends) which, ironically, is where Ronnie the arms dealer comes from. Steve delivered a solid first draft but it felt small in scale – an ex-soldier killing thugs in East London was very straight to video. So we built him up with the idea that he was a serving SAS soldier gone rogue and that there were huge political implications, shadowy figures in the corridors of power, that kind of thing. It felt bigger, it felt right. Then two things happened – I had a bit of a heart to heart with Danny on the phone about how down he was about his career and I think I was more worried than he was as I knew exactly how *Run For Your Wife* was going to turn out. Obviously he was perfect for the Jimmy part and I really thought it could give him the boost he needed – but I'd lined up Nick Nevern, we even had a rough start date. Then Nick called me and told me his writing/directing/acting/producing baby *The Hooligan Factory* had been greenlit – and there was a date clash. The stars had aligned, I offered Danny the part and he accepted. We were off!"

Dyer has been doing this long enough to know how rare it is to meet someone as honest and loyal as Sothcott. "It's been a weird relationship with Jonathan because obviously there's a lot of snakes and a lot of people that would have told me to stay away from Jonathan, who don't know the films I've done where my face has just been thrown on the cover, I've been in his movies as well. People think it's his fault, it's not his fault, it's the distribution company. It's just jealousy more than anything, it's other producers and people that don't know him like I know him. I've seen the fucking leeches now, I know who they are, they've all scuttled away under their fucking rocks. We were saying with *Vendetta* they all came out again and started sucking at my arse. He's always been there, to be fair. He's always been around. This was a perfect marriage this movie, because the other movies we've done I've just come in for a couple of days, it's been fuck all. He's at a point where he needs to make a fucking decent film as well. *Strippers Versus Werewolves* and all that stuff, he's going to be tarnished with all that. For me, for Stephen, and for Jonathan, this is Stephen's even though he's been writing for a long time, this is really going to take us where I feel we deserve to fucking be. I'm just counting the days down really, I love what I'm doing at the moment to survive, I'm doing *Eight Out Of Ten Cats Does Countdown* shows, I've got to get money in to be fair. I'm coming across well, but it's not what I really want to be doing. Other people have seen the trailer, they're obviously fucking buzzing for it, but they haven't got a clue. The haters that I've got, they fucking relished it. This is what I'm saying, when I have a successful film like *Vendetta* come out what are they going to say? They've always got fucking something to say."

Reynolds was struck not only by Dyer's professionalism on set but also his charm. "Danny's an incredibly focused actor. I have no idea of the level he invests himself on other movies, but he really wanted to embody the character he was playing in *Vendetta* and that made my life very easy because I really wanted to take him to another level with this and he let me. And then on set you can't meet a nicer guy. You know, he's a famous fella and he could be a dick if he wanted but he's got good manners in between takes and he wants to work. He wants to act and that's a director's dream, and when he wanted to he could have me in stitches with the giggles. He's a funny lad. We were standing on the top of this mound overlooking Canary Wharf shooting this scene one night during *Vendetta* and I'm trying to keep the crew warm and geed up 'cause it was cold – and not just cold, the wind was killing us in sound and it was so icy. It's two in the morning and I'm going, 'where would you all rather be, here on a film set with all these people you have come to love making something awesome or at home in one of them cosy beds down there trying to get to sleep dreading the alarm going off in the morning so you go to a shit job you hate?' and they all agreed they wanted to be here, which was cool and then this shadow in the dark jogging to keep warm, wrapped in a warm blanket and a fag in his mouth growls, 'Yeah, where's them fuckin' gas fitters now, eh?' Where's them plumbers, Reynolds? They say an actor never does a hard day's work, they ain't up 'ere in cold with us are they?' and I just howled with laughter it was hilarious, you had to be there, but it was very funny."

Dyer's treatment of other crew is renowned in film circles but – typically – never gets mentioned in the press. "The same with the crew. He treats them with manners and respect and he always makes people feel welcome on set," states Reynolds. "One thing he is great at is helping new actors, but not in that way where it comes from a place of arrogance, it's from a place where he knew what it was like to be an upcoming actor and pushing for a bit more screen time and not being happy with a performance on a certain take, things like that. He notices that in the new kids and really helps them 'cause he understands it but he's great at reading people too. He had some great banter with Roxanne McKee on set, it was warm without you thinking they were going to run off into the next room and shag each other – it was like brother and sister, Roxanne was only on set for three days, and it was the last three days, so it's hard for any actor to come in to a film with a small crew that's really bonded like we had but Danny was the key and he really helped bring the best out of Roxanne. We had some great giggles but they could turn on that intensity and make us believe they were in love when the cameras were rolling. That's Danny all over. A total professional."

Sothcott noticed a big change in Dyer on the set of *Vendetta*. "Although I consider Danny one of my close friends, the actor who came to work on *Vendetta* was different to the one I'd been on set with before," he remembers. "Determined, focused, an obsessive perfectionist. He took it incredibly seriously – and, of course, that shows in his performance. He was still the funniest guy in the world and both cast and crew adore him, but this was a new Danny, a different Danny – the boy had become a man."

Sothcott was aware however that the film had to be geared just right: "There has, of course, been a sharp drop in quality since the days of *Severance* and *The Business*, but I think this is up there with those films," he states. "It's also something of a watershed for Danny, in that it's the first time he's actually played a bona-fide 'hardman' – despite what the press would have you believe. Danny's a gentle soul in real life, so playing such a convincing trained killer was a huge accomplishment but there's no doubt he pulled it off magnificently. A number of other film-makers were very cautious about Danny but since seeing *Vendetta* they all 'get it' and think I am a genius for casting him, even though it was, frankly, blindingly obvious. What surprised me most about Danny though was how much he's matured, not just as an actor but also as a film star – he has educated himself about how the business works, he understands the expectations his fan base have of him (and is very careful not to let them down) and he takes his career very carefully. There was a time when Danny Dyer the character and Danny Dyer the man were almost interchangeable. Those days are long gone."

Sure enough, reviews for *Vendetta* have been positive. *Total Film* raved that it looked "a million dollars" and praised the "gleaming images" by director of photography Haider Zafar. Danny Leigh and Chris Hewitt on BBC One's *Film 2013* were also impressed by the film. Hewitt commented that: "Danny Dyer has become something of a critical punching bag but underneath it all, he's actually an underrated actor and he can deliver when he wants to." Leigh agreed, adding that: "I think Danny Dyer is underrated and the way he is treated by members of the critical fraternity is a little bit repellent. He always brings a lot of commitment to the table. He's a talented actor with a lot of presence. It's a solidly made genre movie. Even Claudia Winkleman stated it was "impressive". It is one of the film's that Dyer is most proud of, so it is wonderful that his hard work has paid off and that critics and fans alike are enjoying it.

# APPENDIX 1 – SHORTS

**Dyer on Andrea Arnold's Oscar-winning Wasp (2003)**

**Writer/director** Andrea Arnold **Producer** Natasha Marsh **Cinematography** Robbie Ryan

**Natalie Press** Zoe **Danny Dyer** Dave **Jodie Mitchell** Kelly **Molly Griffiths** Sinead Kaitlin **Raynor Leanne**

"When I was working with Nathalie Press, I thought she was shit. That's the truth. We wasn't really in sync. But then when watching it back, she was brilliant. I see what she was doing. There's other actors who you work with who you think are brilliant, and then you watch back and go. 'Oh fucking hell, I didn't see that, that's just really over the top.' Andrea Arnold just completely don't believe in action and cut. I remember thinking, 'Just skip my money and fuck off, to be honest with you.' She's a nice girl, Andrea, but the script didn't really jump out at me. I thought it was a bit far-fetched with the sugar and stuff, I thought, 'You know I'm from a broken home, I'm from nothing, but I wasn't fed sugar.' I just thought that was a bit extreme. I just liked Andrea, there's something about her that was just so different and I just met her in a pub and we had a little chat. It hadn't been released yet but I'd just done *Football Factory*, so I was feeling really fucking confident and I knew that it was going to fucking put me on the map. So I was a bit cocky at the time, and I thought, 'Aww, I'll come and do you a favour, you know I'll come and do you a little fucking favour, yeah, it's no problem, I'll come do two days with you up in Crayford,' or wherever the fuck it was.

"It was a tough gig because I'm used to a bit of structure, and there was no structure, and I felt really bad for the kids that were out all night on the night shoot freezing. Their parents were moaning at me going, 'Is it always like this? I swear she's got to go to bed!' And I was like, 'Babe, listen, you've agreed to put your kid in it, this is the process unfortunately.' And it was all very ratty and no one was getting paid again as it was low budget, but you know, fuck me, it won an Oscar. It was really strange when I got the news, and I was actually in Thailand at the time doing a documentary for MTV about the tsunami. I remember it was on and it was maybe 3 o'clock in the afternoon there so I was watching it in a bar. I was on top of the world and I was like, 'fuck'. And they showed our clip at the Oscars. I thought, wow. I was so proud of the way she dealt with it as well, the way she went, 'This is the dog's bollocks.' I thought, 'Go on Angela!' I was just in shock. It was just an amazing feeling to think that I'd been part of something that credible. Like I say, Natalie's gone on to work with her again. I've always been intrigued as to why Angela's never used me again.

"I would have loved to do *Fish Tank.* But Fassbender's obviously fucking Fassbender, so you know I've not really got problems with that, but I could have done it. I think I could have been brilliant in it, I really do, I love the movie and I love what it's about. You know, she got a young Fassbender though, a Fassbender who was hungry, and not where he is now. So fuck me I'd love to work with her again, it's just a strange thing that she has never used me again. I dunno."

**Dyer on Free Speech (2004)**

Short film by the Blaine Brothers, starring Danny Dyer and Jacqueline Oceane.

"I like doing short movies. *Free Speech* is all set in a bath, it was just me and a girl in a bath for the whole thing. Naked obviously, I think that's what swung it for me. She's sitting between my legs and the whole thing is just us talking, and talking about sex and things like that. I just say the wrong thing at the end about her sister, because we're talking about each other's fantasies. There were two brothers who directed it, it was at a period when I wasn't that well known, they were fans of my work. I can't remember being famous or anything at that time. I liked the idea of giving young new directors an opportunity, because there was no money or anything like that. They were at the beginning of their career and they contacted me because they knew who I was. It was a really interesting idea of how you can have these conversations with your missus and it can switch like that. I say the wrong thing at the end, she goes, 'What's your ultimate fantasy?' and I go, 'Well, I've always quite fancied your sister.' Something like that, she just fucking loses it, gets up out of the bath and storms out, and that's the end of the short. It's almost like she's trying to coax it out of me, she keeps prodding me for something, and we're just sitting there stroking. It's only like four minutes, were just stroking in the bath having a lovely time and I just say three speeches and it all goes completely wrong. It was two brothers, I'm hoping they've gone on to other better things. They could be the new Coen brothers or something. They were cool directors; it was a cool script and a good idea."

# APPENDIX 2 – INCOMPLETE FILMS

Unsurprisingly for a star as prolific as Dyer there have been a couple of films that hit production but haven't quite made the finish line.

*Manilla Envelopes* (aka *The Battersea Ripper*)

This comedy mishmash was almost completed but stalled due to the usual 'creative differences' that abound at the bottom of the British film industry pond. Boasting an incredible all-star cast including Dyer, PH Moriarty and Dexter Fletcher, as well as sci-fi refugees Sylvester McCoy and Kenny Baker, the promo for the film can be found online and really does have to be seen to be believed. "It wasn't funded, I remember that," chuckles Dyer, "They just asked me to come in and do a bit and I did it with Sylvester McCoy, I remember that. It had the midget from *Star Wars* who was R2D2, it was the most random fucking thing. I can't remember it really, it was a really strange experience it was. I never saw it or heard from them again. I did a couple of days, the script wasn't finished, they just gave me scenes. It changed because it was called *Ripper of Battersea*, and I remember I was on some sort of mission to find out something but I can't remember what I was, though. It was almost some sort of drunk weird dream that I've had.

**The Rapture**

Conceived as a glossy promo reel to fund (the also unmade) Destiny, Essex's answer to *The Da Vinci Code* (and dubbed The CHAVinci Code by one wag on YouTube), *The Rapture* was filmed immediately after *Dead Man Running*. Tamer Hassan was originally set to star as international smuggler Victor Walker (and he and Dyer had already filmed a short film for the director) but departed the project before filming started. Martin Kemp replaced him, leading a strong cast which included Steven Berkoff, Phil Davis and Colin Salmon. A trailer surfaced on the internet and at one point sales agency Stealth announced that it was selling the film, but it has yet to surface and the material filmed amounts to little more than a choppy short. Dyer recalls: "*Rapture* was a promo, it was meant to be the next *Da Vinci Code*. Again it was the director talking bollocks to me, selling it to me. He gave me the script and I read it and thought, 'Okay.' It's about the spear of destiny, which is this spear which apparently had Jesus' blood on it. Hitler had it for a while and that's what gave him his power and all that. It was quite sci-fi, and I love all that – I'm a bit of a Trekkie. But it was just complete bollocks again, no one knew what they were fucking doing, they didn't have the money to do it. It was this big lavish sci-fi production and they had no fucking money. I'm the head of these free-runners that are trying to get the spear, it was all very confusing. I never had any belief in the fucking project to be honest with you. The guy was called Billy Steel who directed it, the stepson of Sir David Steel, was it? It was an odd fucking job, man."

# APPENDIX 3 – TELEVISION

Dyer's career famously began in 1993 when he was spotted performing at his school by a talent agent who put him forward for an audition. He was soon cast as a rent boy at the tender age of 16 in *Prime Suspect 3* opposite Helen Mirren. Four years previously he had a tiny uncredited part in *Children's Ward* but it was as Martin Fletcher alongside Mirren as well as Peter Capaldi, Tom Bell and David Thewlis that he realised that this is what he wanted to do with the rest of his life. "I was absolutely buzzing during and after *Prime Suspect.* It was an incredible experience working with such great actors at such a young age." Dyer remembers.

His performance was acclaimed and noted by the industry so regular TV work followed, with Dyer appearing in every popular television drama you can think of. *Cadfael*, *A Touch Of Frost* (which pleased Dyer's dad because, "He loves David Jason and there I was in a TV show with fucking Del Boy!"), *Thief Takers, The Ruth Rendall Mysteries, Bramwell, Soldier, Soldier* and, of course, *The Bill.*

The most notable role during this period was in 1995 when he appeared in Peter (*The Full Monty*) Cattaneo's drug drama *Loved Up* alongside Lena Headey and Jason Isaacs. A BBC2 television movie, it was controversial at the time for having the audacity to depict young people having fun on ecstasy. Ultimately, unlike *Human Traffic*, the film bottles it and ends in drug hell for all. Dyer steals the film with a hugely memorable performance as Billy the drug dealer. One of his few lines ("Bag of spikes, bag of dummies, two bags of pure!") is oft quoted in nightclubs almost twenty years on.

That same year he starred alongside Mark Rylance and Georgina Cates in *Loving*. It was a special moment for Dyer. "This was my first time as an adult on a film set," he remembers. "There I was in Dublin filming a love triangle story set during the Second World War. Mark Rylance was amazing and taught me so much about acting. He was unlike, say, David Thewlis in that he didn't need to go all method. He could be messing around, having a laugh before a take and then nail this really serious scene. Mark was a real friend to me and taught me everything I needed to know at that point in my career."

After *Human Traffic*, Dyer concentrated on big-screen work unless jobs came up that were too good to turn down. Namely *Is Harry On The Boat?* for Sky One in 2001. Based on Colin Butts' self published but bestselling memoir of his time as a club rep, the film meant Dyer got to go to Ibiza and party hard and put in a bit of acting. The show was a huge success with young people and is still enjoyable to watch today, which is remarkable because Dyer admits he was "off my nut on MDMA every night".

Throughout his career he returned to television on a number of occasions (*Casualty, Rose and Maloney, Foyle's War, Skins* and now *Hollyoaks Later* and *Eastenders*) but one television movie stands out as being up there with his best work. Playing Ray Winstone's son in 2006's *All In The Game*, Dyer delivers a performance unlike any other. "Ray is a legend so I really wanted to do my best with him," says Dyer. A masterful showcase for the art of understatement, Dyer conveys more with his eyes than many other actors manage with their whole body as a corrupt football agent who seems to be under the wing of his dad, but nothing's that simple. Good thing too as Ray Winstone's on top form as the ranting, spitting, vicious bully who has the dubious honour of spouting more c words than in any other show in television history. Dyer and Winstone go head to head in several scenes and it is a marvel to watch the two Cockney greats con, cheat and lie together before ultimately battling against one another. Running at over 100 minutes, this is a feature-length TV movie and one of Dyer's finest films. Given the dross that makes it to cinema screens, it is a true shame that this didn't get the big-screen treatment.

## Complete list of TV performances

*1989: Children's Ward*
*1993: Prime Suspect 3*
*1994: Mystery!: Cadfael*
*1995: A Touch Of Frost*
*1995: Crown Prosecutor*
*1995: Loved Up*
*1995: Loving*
*1996: Ruth Rendell Mysteries*
*1996: Thief Takers*
*1993-1996: The Bill*
*1997: Bramwell*
*1997: Ain't Misbehavin'*
*1997: Highlander*
*1997: Soldier Soldier*
*2001: Is Harry On The Boat?*
*2002: Dead Casual*
*2002: Foyle's War*
*2003: Serious And Organised*
*2003: Second Generation*
*2004: Family Business*
*2005: M.I.T.: Murder Investigation Team*
*2005: Rose And Maloney*
*2006: All In The Game*
*2007: Hotel Babylon*
*2007: Skins*
*2008: Kiss Of Death*
*2010: Comedy Lab*
*2012: Casualty*
*2013: Plebs*
*2013: Hollyoaks Later*
*2013: Eastenders*

# About the Authors

## James Mullinger

James Mullinger studied english literature and women's studies at Kingston University before embarking on a 14-year career as a journalist. Writing about cinema for *GQ* magazine, he has reviewed hundreds of films and interviewed everyone from Scarlett Johansson and Rachel Weisz to Christopher Guest and Bryan Forbes. He has also written for numerous other publications including *Radio Times, The Guardian, Men's Health, The Erotic Review* and *The Dark Side*. His love of film led to a stint hosting his own movie review show on TV. *Movie Kingdom* featured Mullinger interviewing the likes of Tom Cruise, George Clooney and Daniel Craig, and appearing in sketches with comedians such as Micky Flanagan, Rob Brydon and Jerry Seinfeld. Mullinger's personal highlight, however was when his hero Barry Norman guested on the show. As well as writing and broadcasting, Mullinger is also a critically acclaimed stand-up comedian who performs at comedy clubs all over the world and tours a brand new solo show every year. He is 35 years old and lives in South London with his wife and two young sons. His favourite Danny Dyer film is *Human Traffic*.

Photo credit: Pamela Mullinger

# Jonathan Sothcott

One of the UK's most renowned independent movie producers, with over 25 films to his credit, Jonathan Sothcott is also one of Danny Dyer's most frequent collaborators, having produced half a dozen of his movies, including *Devil's Playground*, *Assassin* and *Vendetta*. He also produced the successful sports special *Danny Dyer's Football Foul Ups* in 2009. Their long friendship gives him a unique insight into Danny and his work. Away from making movies, Jonathan writes a monthly column about them for *Digital FilmMaker* magazine. He is 33 years old and lives in Central London with his partner, actress Charlie Bond. His favourite Danny Dyer film is *The Business*.

Photo credits for this page: Antonio Salgado (Top image) and Matt Crockett (Bottom image)